CLEP-5   COLLEGE-LEVEL EXAMINATION
PROGRAM SERIES

This is your
PASSBOOK for...

Biology

Test Preparation Study Guide
Questions & Answers

COPYRIGHT NOTICE

This book is SOLELY intended for, is sold ONLY to, and its use is RESTRICTED to individual, bona fide applicants or candidates who qualify by virtue of having seriously filed applications for appropriate license, certificate, professional and/or promotional advancement, higher school matriculation, scholarship, or other legitimate requirements of education and/or governmental authorities.

This book is NOT intended for use, class instruction, tutoring, training, duplication, copying, reprinting, excerption, or adaptation, etc., by:

1) Other publishers
2) Proprietors and/or Instructors of "Coaching" and/or Preparatory Courses
3) Personnel and/or Training Divisions of commercial, industrial, and governmental organizations
4) Schools, colleges, or universities and/or their departments and staffs, including teachers and other personnel
5) Testing Agencies or Bureaus
6) Study groups which seek by the purchase of a single volume to copy and/or duplicate and/or adapt this material for use by the group as a whole without having purchased individual volumes for each of the members of the group
7) Et al.

Such persons would be in violation of appropriate Federal and State statutes.

PROVISION OF LICENSING AGREEMENTS – Recognized educational, commercial, industrial, and governmental institutions and organizations, and others legitimately engaged in educational pursuits, including training, testing, and measurement activities, may address request for a licensing agreement to the copyright owners, who will determine whether, and under what conditions, including fees and charges, the materials in this book may be used them. In other words, a licensing facility exists for the legitimate use of the material in this book on other than an individual basis. However, it is asseverated and affirmed here that the material in this book CANNOT be used without the receipt of the express permission of such a licensing agreement from the Publishers. Inquiries re licensing should be addressed to the company, attention rights and permissions department.

All rights reserved, including the right of reproduction in whole or in part, in any form or by any means, electronic or mechanical, including photocopying, recording, or by any information storage and retrieval system, without permission in writing from the Publisher.

Copyright © 2025 by
National Learning Corporation

212 Michael Drive, Syosset, NY 11791
(516) 921-8888 • www.passbooks.com
E-mail: info@passbooks.com

PASSBOOK® SERIES

THE *PASSBOOK® SERIES* has been created to prepare applicants and candidates for the ultimate academic battlefield – the examination room.

At some time in our lives, each and every one of us may be required to take an examination – for validation, matriculation, admission, qualification, registration, certification, or licensure.

Based on the assumption that every applicant or candidate has met the basic formal educational standards, has taken the required number of courses, and read the necessary texts, the *PASSBOOK® SERIES* furnishes the one special preparation which may assure passing with confidence, instead of failing with insecurity. Examination questions – together with answers – are furnished as the basic vehicle for study so that the mysteries of the examination and its compounding difficulties may be eliminated or diminished by a sure method.

This book is meant to help you pass your examination provided that you qualify and are serious in your objective.

The entire field is reviewed through the huge store of content information which is succinctly presented through a provocative and challenging approach – the question-and-answer method.

A climate of success is established by furnishing the correct answers at the end of each test.

You soon learn to recognize types of questions, forms of questions, and patterns of questioning. You may even begin to anticipate expected outcomes.

You perceive that many questions are repeated or adapted so that you can gain acute insights, which may enable you to score many sure points.

You learn how to confront new questions, or types of questions, and to attack them confidently and work out the correct answers.

You note objectives and emphases, and recognize pitfalls and dangers, so that you may make positive educational adjustments.

Moreover, you are kept fully informed in relation to new concepts, methods, practices, and directions in the field.

You discover that you are actually taking the examination all the time: you are preparing for the examination by "taking" an examination, not by reading extraneous and/or supererogatory textbooks.

In short, this PASSBOOK®, used directedly, should be an important factor in helping you to pass your test.

NONTRADITIONAL EDUCATION

Students returning to school as adults bring more varied experience to their studies than do the teenagers who begin college shortly after graduating from high school. As a result, there are numerous programs for students with nontraditional learning curves. Hundreds of colleges and universities grant degrees to people who cannot attend classes at a regular campus or have already learned what the college is supposed to teach.

You can earn nontraditional education credits in many ways:
- Passing standardized exams
- Demonstrating knowledge gained through experience
- Completing campus-based coursework, and
- Taking courses off campus

Some methods of assessing learning for credit are objective, such as standardized tests. Others are more subjective, such as a review of life experiences.

With some help from four hypothetical characters – Alice, Vin, Lynette, and Jorge – this article describes nontraditional ways of earning educational credit. It begins by describing programs in which you can earn a high school diploma without spending 4 years in a classroom. The college picture is more complicated, so it is presented in two parts: one on gaining credit for what you know through course work or experience, and a second on college degree programs. The final section lists resources for locating more information.

Earning High School Credit

People who were prevented from finishing high school as teenagers have several options if they want to do so as adults. Some major cities have back-to-school programs that allow adults to attend high school classes with current students. But the more practical alternatives for most adults are to take the General Educational Development (GED) tests or to earn a high school diploma by demonstrating their skills or taking correspondence classes.

Of course, these options do not match the experience of staying in high school and graduating with one's friends. But they are viable alternatives for adult learners committed to meeting and, often, continuing their educational goals.

GED Program

Alice quit high school her sophomore year and took a job to help support herself, her younger brother, and their newly widowed mother. Now an adult, she wants to earn her high school diploma – and then go on to college. Because her job as head cook and her family responsibilities keep her busy during the day, she plans to get a high school equivalency diploma. She will study for, and take, the GED tests. Every year, about half a million adults earn their high school credentials this way. A GED diploma is accepted in lieu of a high school one by more than 90 percent of employers, colleges, and universities, so it is a good choice for someone like Alice.

The GED testing program is sponsored by the American Council on Education and State and local education departments. It consists of examinations in five subject areas: Writing, science, mathematics, social studies, and literature and the arts. The tests also measure skills such as analytical ability, problem solving, reading comprehension, and ability to understand and apply information. Most of the questions are multiple choice; the writing test includes an essay section on a topic of general interest.

Eligibility rules for taking the exams vary, but some states require that you must be at least 18. Tests are given in English, Spanish, and French. In addition to standard print, versions in large print, Braille, and audiocassette are also available. Total time allotted for the tests is 7 1/2 hours.

The GED tests are not easy. About one-fourth of those who complete the exams every year do not pass. Passing scores are established by administering the tests to a sample of graduating high school seniors. The minimum standard score is set so that about one-third of graduating seniors would not pass the tests if they took them.

Because of the difficulty of the tests, people need to prepare themselves to take them. Often, they start by taking the Official GED Practice Tests, usually available through a local adult education center. Centers are listed in your phone book's blue pages under "Adult Education," "Continuing Education," or "GED." Adult education centers also have information about GED preparation classes and self-study materials. Classes are generally arranged to accommodate adults' work schedules. National Learning Corporation publishes several study guides that aim to thoroughly prepare test-takers for the GED.

School districts, colleges, adult education centers, and community organizations have information about GED testing schedules and practice tests. For more information, contact them, your nearest GED testing center, or:
GED Testing Service
One Dupont Circle, NW, Suite 250
Washington, DC 20036-1163
1(800) 62-MY GED (626-9433)
(202) 939-9490

Skills Demonstration

Adults who have acquired high school level skills through experience might be eligible for the National External Diploma Program. This alternative to the GED does not involve any direct instruction. Instead, adults seeking a high school diploma must demonstrate mastery of 65 competencies in 8 general areas: Communication; computation; occupational preparedness; and self, social, consumer, scientific, and technological awareness.

Mastery is shown through the completion of the tasks. For example, a participant could prove competency in computation by measuring a room for carpeting, figuring out the amount of carpet needed, and computing the cost.

Before being accepted for the program, adults undergo an evaluation. Tests taken at one of the program's offices measure reading, writing, and mathematics abilities. A take-home segment includes a self-assessment of current skills, an individual skill evaluation, and an occupational interest and aptitude test.

Adults accepted for the program have weekly meetings with an assessor. At the meeting, the assessor reviews the participant's work from the previous week. If the task has not been completed properly, the assessor explains the mistake. Participants continue to correct their errors until they master each competency. A high school diploma is awarded upon proven mastery of all 65 competencies.

Fourteen States and the District of Columbia now offer the External Diploma Program. For more information, contact:
>
> External Diploma Program
> One Dupont Circle, NW, Suite 250
> Washington, DC 20036-1193
> (202) 939-9475

Correspondence and Distance Study

Vin dropped out of high school during his junior year because his family's frequent moves made it difficult for him to continue his studies. He promised himself at the time he dropped out that he would someday finish the courses needed for his diploma. For people like Vin, who prefer to earn a traditional diploma in a nontraditional way, there are about a dozen accredited courses of study for earning a high school diploma by correspondence, or distance study. The programs are either privately run, affiliated with a university, or administered by a State education department.

Distance study diploma programs have no residency requirements, allowing students to continue their studies from almost any location. Depending on the course of study, students need not be enrolled full time and usually have more flexible schedules for finishing their work. Selection of courses ranges from vo-tech to college prep, and some programs place different emphasis on the types of diplomas offered. University affiliated schools, for example, allow qualified students to take college courses along with their high school ones. Students can then apply the college credits toward a degree at that university or transfer them to another institution.

Taking courses by distance study is often more challenging and time consuming than attending classes, especially for adults who have other obligations. Success depends on each student's motivation. Students usually do reading assignments on their own. Written exercises, which they complete and send to an instructor for grading, supplement their reading material.

A list of some accredited high schools that offer diplomas by distance study is available free from the Distance Education and Training Council, formerly known as the National Home Study Council. Request the "DETC Directory of Accredited Institutions" from:

> The Distance Education and Training Council
> 1601 18th Street, NW.
> Washington, DC 20009-2529
> (202) 234-5100

Some publications profiling nontraditional college programs include addresses and descriptions of several high school correspondence ones. See the Resources section at the end of this article for more information.

Getting College Credit For What You Know

Adults can receive college credit for prior coursework, by passing examinations, and documenting experiential learning. With help from a college advisor, nontraditional students should assess their skills, establish their educational goals, and determine the number of college credits they might be eligible for.

Even before you meet with a college advisor, you should collect all your school and training records. Then, make a list of all knowledge and abilities acquired through experience, no matter how irrelevant they seem to your chosen field. Next, determine your educational goals: What specific field do you wish to study? What kind of a degree do you want? Finally, determine how your past work fits into the field of study. Later on, you will evaluate educational programs to find one that's right for you.

People who have complex educational or experiential learning histories might want to have their learning evaluated by the Regents Credit Bank. The Credit Bank, operated by Regents College of the University of the State of New York, allows people to consolidate credits earned through college, experience, or other methods. Special assessments are available for Regents College enrollees whose knowledge in a specific field cannot be adequately evaluated by standardized exams. For more information, contact the Regents Credit Bank at:

Regents College
7 Columbia Circle
Albany, NY 12203-5159
(518) 464-8500

Credit For Prior College Coursework

When Lynette was in college during the 1970s, she attended several different schools and took a variety of courses. She did well in some classes and poorly in others. Now that she is a successful business owner and has more focus, Lynette thinks she should forget about her previous coursework and start from scratch. Instead, she should start from where she is.

Lynette should have all her transcripts sent to the colleges or universities of her choice and let an admissions officer determine which classes are applicable toward a degree. A few credits here and there may not seem like much, but they add up. Even if the subjects do not seem relevant to any major, they might be counted as elective credits toward a degree. And comparing the cost of transcripts with the cost of college courses, it makes sense to spend a few dollars per transcript for a chance to save hundreds, and perhaps thousands, of dollars in books and tuition.

Rules for transferring credits apply to all prior coursework at accredited colleges and universities, whether done on campus or off. Courses completed off campus, often called extended learning, include those available to students through independent study and correspondence. Many schools have extended learning programs; Brigham Young University, for example, offers more than 300 courses through its Department of Independent Study. One type of extended learning is distance learning, a form of correspondence study by technological means such as television, video and audio, CD-ROM, electronic mail, and computer tutorials. See the Resources section at the end of this article for more information about publications available from the National University Continuing Education Association.

Any previously earned college credits should be considered for transfer, no matter what the subject or the grade received. Many schools do not accept the transfer of courses graded below a C or ones taken more than a designated number of years ago. Some colleges and universities also have limits on the number of credits that can be transferred and applied toward a degree. But not all do. For example, Thomas Edison State College, New Jersey's State college for adults, accepts the transfer of all 120 hours of credit required for a baccalaureate degree – provided all the credits are transferred from regionally accredited schools, no more than 80 are at the junior college level, and the student's grades overall and in the field of study average out to C.

To assign credit for prior coursework, most schools require original transcripts. This means you must complete a form or send a written, signed request to have your transcripts released directly to a college or university. Once you have chosen the schools you want to apply to, contact the schools you attended before. Find out how much each transcript costs, and ask them to send your transcripts to the ones you are applying to. Write a letter that includes your name (and names used during attendance, if different) and dates of attendance, along with the names and addresses of the schools to which your transcripts should be sent. Include payment and mail to the registrar at the schools you have attended. The registrar's office will process your request and send an official transcript of your coursework to the colleges or universities you have designated.

Credit For Noncollege Courses

Colleges and universities are not the only ones that offer classes. Volunteer organizations and employers often provide formal training worth college credit. The American Council on Education has two programs that assess thousands of specific courses and make recommendations on the amount of college credit they are worth. Colleges and universities accept the recommendations or use them as guidelines.

One program evaluates educational courses sponsored by government agencies, business and industry, labor unions, and professional and voluntary organizations. It is the Program on Noncollegiate Sponsored Instruction (PONSI). Some of the training seminars Alice has participated in covered topics such as food preparation, kitchen safety, and nutrition. Although she has not yet earned her GED, Alice can earn college credit because of her completion of these formal job-training seminars. The number of credits each seminar is worth does not hinge on Alice's current eligibility for college enrollment.

The other program evaluates courses offered by the Army, Navy, Air Force, Marines, Coast Guard, and Department of Defense. It is the Military Evaluations Program. Jorge has never attended college, but the engineering technology classes he completed as part of his military training are worth college credit. And as an Army veteran, Jorge is eligible for a service that takes the evaluations one step further. The Army/American Council on Education Registry Transcript System (AARTS) will provide Jorge with an individualized transcript of American Council on Education credit recommendations for all courses he completed, the military occupational specialties (MOS's) he held, and examinations he passed while in the Army. All Army and National Guard enlisted personnel and veterans who enlisted after October 1981 are eligible for the transcript. Similar services are being considered by the Navy and Marine Corps.

To obtain a free transcript, see your Army Education Center for a 5454R transcript request form. Include your name, Social Security number, basic active service date, and complete address where you want the transcript sent. Mail your request to:
AARTS Operations Center
415 McPherson Ave.
Fort Leavenworth, KS 66027-1373

Recommendations for PONSI are published in *The National Guide to Educational Credit for Training Programs;* military program recommendations are in *The Guide to the Evaluation of Educational Experiences in the Armed Forces.* See the Resources section at the end of this article for more information about these publications.

Former military personnel who took a foreign language course through the Defense Language Institute may request course transcripts by sending their name, Social Security number, course title, duration of the course, and graduation date to:

> Commandant, Defense Language Institute
> Attn: ATFL-DAA-AR
> Transcripts
> Presidio of Monterey
> Monterey, CA 93944-5006

Not all of Jorge's and Alice's courses have been assessed by the American Council on Education. Training courses that have no Council credit recommendation should still be assessed by an advisor at the schools they want to attend. Course descriptions, class notes, test scores, and other documentation may be helpful for comparing training courses to their college equivalents. An oral examination or other demonstration of competency might also be required.

There is no guarantee you will receive all the credits you are seeking – but you certainly won't if you make no attempt.

Credit By Examination

Standardized tests are the best-known method of receiving college credit without taking courses. These exams are often taken by high school students seeking advanced placement for college, but they are also available to adult learners. Testing programs and colleges and universities offer exams in a number of subjects. Two U.S. Government institutes have foreign language exams for employees that also may be worth college credit.

It is important to understand that receiving a passing score on these exams does not mean you get college credit automatically. Each school determines which test results it will accept, minimum scores required, how scores are converted for credit, and the amount of credit, if any, to be assigned. Most colleges and universities accept the American Council on Education credit recommendations, published every other year in the 250-page *Guide to Educational Credit by Examination*. For more information, contact:

> The American Council on Education
> Credit by Examination Program
> One Dupont Circle, Suite 250
> Washington, DC 20036-1193
> (202) 939-9434

Testing programs:

You might know some of the five national testing programs by their acronyms or initials: CLEP, ACT PEP: RCE, DANTES, AP, and NOCTI. (The meanings of these initialisms are explained below.) There is some overlap among programs; for example, four of them have introductory accounting exams. Since you will not be awarded credit more than once for a specific subject, you should carefully evaluate each program for the subject exams you wish to take. And before taking an exam, make sure you will be awarded credit by the college or university you plan to attend.

CLEP (College-Level Examination Program), administered by the College Board, is the most widely accepted of the national testing programs; more than 2,800 accredited schools award credit for passing exam scores. Each test covers material taught in basic undergraduate courses. There are five general exams – English composition, humanities, college mathematics, natural sciences, and social sciences and history – and many subject exams. Most exams are entirely multiple-choice, but English composition exams may include an essay section. For more information, contact:

    CLEP
    P.O. Box 6600
    Princeton, NJ 08541-6600
    (609) 771-7865

ACT PEP: RCE (American College Testing Proficiency Exam Program: Regents College Examinations) tests are given in 38 subjects within arts and sciences, business, education, and nursing. Each exam is recommended for either lower- or upper-level credit. Exams contain either objective or extended response questions, and are graded according to a standard score, letter grade, or pass/fail. Fees vary, depending on the subject and type of exam. For more information or to request free study guides, contact:

    ACT PEP: Regents College Examinations
    P.O. Box 4014
    Iowa City, IA 52243
    (319) 337-1387
    (New York State residents must contact Regents College directly.)

DANTES (Defense Activity for Nontraditional Education Support) standardized tests are developed by the Educational Testing Service for the Department of Defense. Originally administered only to military personnel, the exams have been available to the public since 1983. About 50 subject tests cover business, mathematics, social science, physical science, humanities, foreign languages, and applied technology. Most of the tests consist entirely of multiple-choice questions. Schools determine their own administering fees and testing schedules. For more information or to request free study sheets, contact:

    DANTES Program Office
    Mail Stop 31-X
    Educational Testing Service
    Princeton, NJ 08541
    1(800) 257-9484

The AP (Advanced Placement) Program is a cooperative effort between secondary schools and colleges and universities. AP exams are developed each year by committees of college and high school faculty appointed by the College Board and assisted by consultants from the Educational Testing Service. Subjects include arts and languages, natural sciences, computer science, social sciences, history, and mathematics. Most tests are 2 or 3 hours long and include both multiple-choice and essay questions. AP courses are available to help students prepare for exams, which are offered in the spring. For more information about the Advanced Placement Program, contact:

    Advanced Placement Services
    P.O. Box 6671
    Princeton, NJ 08541-6671
    (609) 771-7300

NOCTI (National Occupational Competency Testing Institute) assessments are designed for people like Alice, who have vocational-technical skills that cannot be evaluated by other tests. NOCTI assesses competency at two levels: Student/job ready and teacher/experienced worker. Standardized evaluations are available for occupations such as auto-body repair, electronics, mechanical drafting, quantity food preparation, and upholstering. The tests consist of multiple-choice questions and a performance component. Other services include workshops, customized assessments, and pre-testing. For more information, contact:

NOCTI
500 N. Bronson Ave.
Ferris State University
Big Rapids, MI 49307
(616) 796-4699

Colleges and universities:

Many colleges and universities have credit-by-exam programs, through which students earn credit by passing a comprehensive exam for a course offered by the institution. Among the most widely recognized are the programs at Ohio University, the University of North Carolina, Thomas Edison State College, and New York University.

Ohio University offers about 150 examinations for credit. In addition, you may sometimes arrange to take special examinations in non-laboratory courses offered at Ohio University. To take a test for credit, you must enroll in the course. If you plan to transfer the credit earned, you also need written permission from an official at your school. Books and study materials are available, for a cost, through the university. Exams must be taken within 6 months of the enrollment date; most last 3 hours. You may arrange to take the exam off campus if you do not live near the university.

Ohio University is on the quarter-hour system; most courses are worth 4 quarter hours, the equivalent of 3 semester hours. For more information, contact:

Independent Study
Tupper Hall 302
Ohio University
Athens, OH 45701-2979
1(800) 444-2910
(614) 593-2910

The University of North Carolina offers a credit-by-examination option for 140 independent study (correspondence) courses in foreign languages, humanities, social sciences, mathematics, business administration, education, electrical and computer engineering, health administration, and natural sciences. To take an exam, you must request and receive approval from both the course instructor and the independent studies department. Exams must be taken within six months of enrollment, and you may register for no more than two at a time. If you are not near the University's Chapel Hill campus, you may take your exam under supervision at an accredited college, university, community college, or technical institute. For more information, contact:

Independent Studies
CB #1020, The Friday Center
UNC-Chapel Hill
Chapel Hill, NC 27599-1020
1(800) 862-5669 / (919) 962-1134

The Thomas Edison College Examination Program offers more than 50 exams in liberal arts, business, and professional areas. Thomas Edison State College administers tests twice a month in Trenton, New Jersey; however, students may arrange to take their tests with a proctor at any accredited American college or university or U.S. military base. Most of the tests are multiple choice; some also include short answer or essay questions. Time limits range from 90 minutes to 4 hours, depending on the exam. For more information, contact:

Thomas Edison State College
TECEP, Office of Testing and Assessment
101 W. State Street
Trenton, NJ 08608-1176
(609) 633-2844

New York University's Foreign Language Program offers proficiency exams in more than 40 languages, from Albanian to Yiddish. Two exams are available in each language: The 12-point test is equivalent to 4 undergraduate semesters, and the 16-point exam may lead to upper level credit. The tests are given at the university's Foreign Language Department throughout the year.

Proof of foreign language proficiency does not guarantee college credit. Some colleges and universities accept transcripts only for languages commonly taught, such as French and Spanish. Nontraditional programs are more likely than traditional ones to grant credit for proficiency in other languages.

For an informational brochure and registration form for NYU's foreign language proficiency exams, contact:

New York University
Foreign Language Department
48 Cooper Square, Room 107
New York, NY 10003
(212) 998-7030

Government institutes:

The Defense Language Institute and Foreign Service Institute administer foreign language proficiency exams for personnel stationed abroad. Usually, the tests are given at the end of intensive language courses or upon completion of service overseas. But some people – like Jorge, who knows Spanish – speak another language fluently and may be allowed to take a proficiency exam in that language before completing their tour of duty. Contact one of the offices listed below to obtain transcripts of those scores. Proof of proficiency does not guarantee college credit, however, as discussed above.

To request score reports from the Defense Language Institute for Defense Language Proficiency Tests, send your name, Social Security number, language for which you were tested, and, most importantly, when and where you took the exam to:

Commandant, Defense Language Institute
Attn: ATFL-ES-T
DLPT Score Report Request
Presidio of Monterey
Monterey, CA 93944-5006

To request transcripts of scores for Foreign Service Institute exams, send your name, Social Security number, language for which you were tested, and dates or year of exams to:

Foreign Service Institute
Arlington Hall
4020 Arlington Boulevard
Rosslyn, VA 22204-1500
Attn: Testing Office (Send your request to the attention of the testing office of the foreign language in which you were tested)

Credit For Experience

Experiential learning credit may be given for knowledge gained through job responsibilities, personal hobbies, volunteer opportunities, homemaking, and other experiences. Colleges and universities base credit awards on the knowledge you have attained, not for the experience alone. In addition, the knowledge must be college level; not just any learning will do. Throwing horseshoes as a hobby is not likely to be worth college credit. But if you've done research on how and where the sport originated, visited blacksmiths, organized tournaments, and written a column for a trade journal – well, that's a horseshoe of a different color.

Adults attempting to get credit for their experience should be forewarned: Having your experience evaluated for college credit is time-consuming, tedious work – not an easy shortcut for people who want quick-fix college credits. And not all experience, no matter how valuable, is the equivalent of college courses.

Requesting college credit for your experiential learning can be tricky. You should get assistance from a credit evaluations officer at the school you plan to attend, but you should also have a general idea of what your knowledge is worth. A common method for converting knowledge into credit is to use a college catalog. Find course titles and descriptions that match what you have learned through experience, and request the number of credits offered for those courses.

Once you know what credit to ask for, you must usually present your case in writing to officials at the college you plan to attend. The most common form of presenting experiential learning for credit is the portfolio. A portfolio is a written record of your knowledge along with a request for equivalent college credit. It includes an identification and description of the knowledge for which you are requesting credit, an explanatory essay of how the knowledge was gained and how it fits into your educational plans, documentation that you have acquired such knowledge, and a request for college credit. Required elements of a portfolio vary by schools but generally follow those guidelines.

In identifying knowledge you have gained, be specific about exactly what you have learned. For example, it is not enough for Lynette to say she runs a business. She must identify the knowledge she has gained from running it, such as personnel management, tax law, marketing strategy, and inventory review. She must also include brief descriptions about her knowledge of each to support her claims of having those skills.

The essay gives you a chance to relay something about who you are. It should address your educational goals, include relevant autobiographical details, and be well organized, neat, and convey confidence. In his essay, Jorge might first state his goal of becoming an engineer. Then he would explain why he joined the Army, where he got hands-on training and experience in developing and servicing electronic equipment.

This, he would say, led to his hobby of creating remote-controlled model cars, of which he has built 20. His conclusion would highlight his accomplishments and tie them to his desire to become an electronic engineer.

Documentation is evidence that you've learned what you claim to have learned. You can show proof of knowledge in a variety of ways, including audio or video recordings, letters from current or former employers describing your specific duties and job performance, blueprints, photographs or artwork, and transcripts of certifying exams for professional licenses and certification – such as Alice's certification from the American Culinary Federation. Although documentation can take many forms, written proof alone is not always enough. If it is impossible to document your knowledge in writing, find out if your experiential learning can be assessed through supplemental oral exams by a faculty expert.

Earning a College Degree

Nontraditional students often have work, family, and financial obligations that prevent them from quitting their jobs to attend school full time. Can they still meet their educational goals? Yes.

More than 150 accredited colleges and universities have nontraditional bachelor's degree programs that require students to spend little or no time on campus; over 300 others have nontraditional campus-based degree programs. Some of those schools, as well as most junior and community colleges, offer associate's degrees nontraditionally. Each school with a nontraditional course of study determines its own rules for awarding credit for prior coursework, exams, or experience, as discussed previously. Most have charges on top of tuition for providing these special services.

Several publications profile nontraditional degree programs; see the Resources section at the end of this article for more information. To determine which school best fits your academic profile and educational goals, first list your criteria. Then, evaluate nontraditional programs based on their accreditation, features, residency requirements, and expenses. Once you have chosen several schools to explore further, write to them for more information. Detailed explanations of school policies should help you decide which ones you want to apply to.

Get beyond the printed word – especially the glowing words each school writes about itself. Check out the schools you are considering with higher education authorities, alumni, employers, family members, and friends. If possible, visit the campus to talk to students and instructors and sit in on a few classes, even if you will be completing most or all of your work off campus. Ask school officials questions about such things as enrollment numbers, graduation rate, faculty qualifications, and confusing details about the application process or academic policies. After you have thoroughly investigated each prospective college or university, you can make an informed decision about which is right for you.

Accreditation

Accreditation is a process colleges and universities submit to voluntarily for getting their credentials. An accredited school has been investigated and visited by teams of observers and has periodic inspections by a private accrediting agency. The initial review can take two years or more.

Regional agencies accredit entire schools, and professional agencies accredit either specialized schools or departments within schools. Although there are no national accrediting standards, not just any accreditation will do. Countless "accreditation associations" have been invented by schools, many of which have no academic programs and sell phony degrees, to accredit themselves. But 6 regional and about 80 professional accrediting associations in the United States are recognized by the U.S. Department of Education or the Commission on Recognition of Postsecondary Accreditation. When checking accreditation, these are the names to look for. For more information about accreditation and accrediting agencies, contact:

> Institutional Participation Oversight Service Accreditation and State Liaison Division
> U.S. Department of Education
> ROB 3, Room 3915
> 600 Independence Ave., SW
> Washington, DC 20202-5244
> (202) 708-7417

Because accreditation is not mandatory, lack of accreditation does not necessarily mean a school or program is bad. Some schools choose not to apply for accreditation, are in the process of applying, or have educational methods too unconventional for an accrediting association's standards. For the nontraditional student, however, earning a degree from a college or university with recognized accreditation is an especially important consideration. Although nontraditional education is becoming more widely accepted, it is not yet mainstream. Employers skeptical of a degree earned in a nontraditional manner are likely to be even less accepting of one from an unaccredited school.

Program Features

Because nontraditional students have diverse educational objectives, nontraditional schools are diverse in what they offer. Some programs are geared toward helping students organize their scattered educational credits to get a degree as quickly as possible. Others cater to those who may have specific credits or experience but need assistance in completing requirements. Whatever your educational profile, you should look for a program that works with you in obtaining your educational goals.

A few nontraditional programs have special admissions policies for adult learners like Alice, who plan to earn their GEDs but want to enroll in college in the meantime. Other features of nontraditional programs include individualized learning agreements, intensive academic counseling, cooperative learning and internship placement, and waiver of some prerequisites or other requirements – as well as college credit for prior coursework, examinations, and experiential learning, all discussed previously.

Lynette, whose primary goal is to finish her degree, wants to earn maximum credits for her business experience. She will look for programs that do not limit the number of credits awarded for equivalency exams and experiential learning. And since well-documented proof of knowledge is essential for earning experiential learning credits, Lynette should make sure the program she chooses provides assistance to students submitting a portfolio.

Jorge, on the other hand, has more credits than he needs in certain areas and is willing to forego some. To become an engineer, he must have a bachelor's degree; but because he is accustomed to hands-on learning, Jorge is interested in getting experience as he gains more technical skills. He will concentrate on finding schools with strong cooperative education, supervised fieldwork, or internship programs.

Residency Requirements

Programs are sometimes deemed nontraditional because of their residency requirements. Many people think of residency for colleges and universities in terms of tuition, with in-state students paying less than out-of-state ones. Residency also may refer to where a student lives, either on or off campus, while attending school.

But in nontraditional education, residency usually refers to how much time students must spend on campus, regardless of whether they attend classes there. In some nontraditional programs, students need not ever step foot on campus. Others require only a very short residency, such as one day or a few weeks. Many schools have standard residency requirements of several semesters but schedule classes for evenings or weekends to accommodate working adults.

Lynette, who previously took courses by independent study, prefers to earn credits by distance study. She will focus on schools that have no residency requirement. Several colleges and universities have nonresident degree completion programs for adults with some college credit. Under the direction of a faculty advisor, students devise a plan for earning their remaining credits. Methods for earning credits include independent study, distance learning, seminars, supervised fieldwork, and group study at arranged sites. Students may have to earn a certain number of credits through the degree-granting institution. But many programs allow students to take courses at accredited schools of their choice for transfer toward their degree.

Alice wants to attend lectures but has an unpredictable schedule. Her best course of action will be to seek out short residency programs that require students to attend seminars once or twice a semester. She can take courses that are televised and videotape them to watch when her schedule permits, with the seminars helping to ensure that she properly completes her coursework. Many colleges and universities with short residency requirements also permit students to earn some credits elsewhere, by whatever means the student chooses.

Some fields of study require classroom instruction. As Jorge will discover, few colleges and universities allow students to earn a bachelor's degree in engineering entirely through independent study. Nontraditional residency programs are designed to accommodate adults' daytime work schedules. Jorge should look for programs offering evening, weekend, summer, and accelerated courses.

Tuition and Other Expenses

The final decisions about which schools Alice, Jorge, and Lynette attend may hinge in large part on a single issue: Cost. And rising tuition is only part of the equation. Beginning with application fees and continuing through graduation fees, college expenses add up.

Traditional and nontraditional students have some expenses in common, such as the cost of books and other materials. Tuition might even be the same for some courses, especially for colleges and universities offering standard ones at unusual times. But for nontraditional programs, students may also pay fees for services such as credit or transcript review, evaluation, advisement, and portfolio assessment.

Students are also responsible for postage and handling or setup expenses for independent study courses, as well as for all examination and transcript fees for transferring credits. Usually, the more nontraditional the program, the more detailed the fees. Some schools charge a yearly enrollment fee rather than tuition for degree completion candidates who want their files to remain active.

Although tuition and fees might seem expensive, most educators tell you not to let money come between you and your educational goals. Talk to someone in the financial aid department of the school you plan to attend or check your library for publications about financial aid sources. The U.S. Department of Education publishes a guide to Federal aid programs such as Pell Grants, student loans, and work-study. To order the free 74-page booklet, *The Student Guide: Financial Aid from the U.S. Department of Education,* contact:

>Federal Student Aid Information Center
>P.O. Box 84
>Washington, DC 20044
>1 (800) 4FED-AID (433-3243)

Resources

Information on how to earn a high school diploma or college degree without following the usual routes is available from several organizations and in numerous publications. Information on nontraditional graduate degree programs, available for master's through doctoral level, though not discussed in this article, can usually be obtained from the same resources that detail bachelor's degree programs.

National Learning Corporation publishes study guides for all of these exams, for both general examinations and tests in specific subject areas. To order study guides, or to browse their catalog featuring more than 5,000 titles, visit NLC online at www.passbooks.com, or contact them by phone at (800) 632-8888.

Organizations

Adult learners should always contact their local school system, community college, or university to learn about programs that are readily available. The following national organizations can also supply information:

>American Council on Education
>One Dupont Circle
>Washington, DC 20036-1193
>(202) 939-9300

Within the American Council on Education, the Center for Adult Learning and Educational Credentials administers the National External Diploma Program, the GED Program, the Program on Noncollegiate Sponsored Instruction, the Credit by Examination Program, and the Military Evaluations Program.

College-Level Examination Program (CLEP)

1. WHAT IS CLEP?

CLEP stands for the College-Level Examination Program, sponsored by the College Board. It is a national program of credit-by-examination that offers you the opportunity to obtain recognition for college-level achievement. No matter when, where, or how you have learned – by means of formal or informal study – you can take CLEP tests. If the results are acceptable to your college, you can receive credit.

You may not realize it, but you probably know more than your academic record reveals. Each day you, like most people, have an opportunity to learn. In private industry and business, as well as at all levels of government, learning opportunities continually occur. If you read widely or intensively in a particular field, think about what you read, discuss it with your family and friends, you are learning. Or you may be learning on a more formal basis by taking a correspondence course, a television or radio course, a course recorded on tape or cassettes, a course assembled into programmed tests, or a course taught in your community adult school or high school.

No matter how, where, or when you gained your knowledge, you may have the opportunity to receive academic credit for your achievement that can be counted toward an undergraduate degree. The College-Level Examination Program (CLEP) enables colleges to evaluate your achievement and give you credit. A wide range of college-level examinations are offered by CLEP to anyone who wishes to take them. Scores on the tests are reported to you and, if you wish, to a college, employer, or individual.

2. WHAT ARE THE PURPOSES OF THE COLLEGE-LEVEL EXAMINATION PROGRAM?

The basic purpose of the College-Level Examination Program is to enable individuals who have acquired their education in nontraditional ways to demonstrate their academic achievement. It is also intended for use by those in higher education, business, industry, government, and other fields who need a reliable method of assessing a person's educational level.

Recognizing that the real issue is not how a person has acquired his education but what education he has, the College Level Examination Program has been designed to serve a variety of purposes. The basic purpose, as listed above, is to enable those who have reached the college level of education in nontraditional ways to assess the level of their achievement and to use the test results in seeking college credit or placement.

In addition, scores on the tests can be used to validate educational experience obtained at a nonaccredited institution or through noncredit college courses.

Some colleges and universities may use the tests to measure the level of educational achievement of their students, and for various institutional research purposes.

Other colleges and universities may wish to use the tests in the admission, placement, and guidance of students who wish to transfer from one institution to another.

Businesses, industries, governmental agencies, and professional groups now accept the results of these tests as a basis for advancement, eligibility for further training, or professional or semi-professional certification.

Many people are interested in the examination simply to assess their own educational progress and attainment.

The college, university, business, industry, or government agency that adopts the tests in the College-Level Examination Program makes its own decision about how it will use and interpret the test scores. The College Board will provide the tests, score them, and report the results either to the individuals who took the tests or the college or agency that administered them. It does NOT, and cannot, award college credit, certify college equivalency, or make recommendations regarding the standards these institutions should establish for the use of the test results.

Therefore, if you are taking the tests to secure credit from an institution, you should FIRST ascertain whether the college or agency involved will accept the scores. Each institution determines which CLEP tests it will accept for credit and the amount of credit it will award. If you want to take tests for college credit, first call, write, or visit the college you wish to attend to inquire about its policy on CLEP scores, as well as its other admission requirements.

The services of the program are also available to people who have been requested to take the tests by an employer, a professional licensing agency, a certifying agency, or by other groups that recognize college equivalency on the basis of satisfactory CLEP scores. You may, of course, take the tests SOLELY for your own information. If you do, your scores will be reported only to you.

While neither CLEP nor the College Board can evaluate previous credentials or award college credit, you will receive, with your scores, basic information to help you interpret your performance on the tests you have taken.

3. WHAT ARE THE COLLEGE-LEVEL EXAMINATIONS?

In order to meet different kinds of curricular organization and testing needs at colleges and universities, the College-Level Examination Program offers 35 different subject tests falling under five separate general categories: Composition and Literature, Foreign Languages, History and Social Sciences, Science and Mathematics, and Business.

4. WHAT ARE THE SUBJECT EXAMINATIONS?

The 35 CLEP tests offered by the College Board are listed below:

COMPOSITION AND LITERATURE:
- American Literature
- Analyzing and Interpreting Literature
- English Composition
- English Composition with Essay
- English Literature
- Freshman College Composition
- Humanities

FOREIGN LANGUAGES
- French
- German
- Spanish

HISTORY AND SOCIAL SCIENCES
- American Government
- Introduction to Educational Psychology
- History of the United States I: Early Colonization to 1877
- History of the United States II: 1865 to the Present
- Human Growth and Development
- Principles of Macroeconomics
- Principles of Microeconomics
- Introductory Psychology
- Social Sciences and History
- Introductory Sociology
- Western Civilization I: Ancient Near East to 1648
- Western Civilization II: 1648 to the Present

SCIENCE AND MATHEMATICS
- College Algebra
- College Algebra-Trigonometry
- Biology
- Calculus
- Chemistry
- College Mathematics
- Natural Sciences
- Trigonometry
- Precalculus

BUSINESS
- Financial Accounting
- Introductory Business Law
- Information Systems and Computer Applications
- Principles of Management
- Principles of Marketing

CLEP Examinations cover material taught in courses that most students take as requirements in the first two years of college. A college usually grants the same amount of credit to students earning satisfactory scores on the CLEP examination as it grants to students successfully completing the equivalent course.

Many examinations are designed to correspond to one-semester courses; some, however, correspond to full-year or two-year courses.

Each exam is 90 minutes long and, except for English Composition with Essay, is made up primarily of multiple-choice questions. Some tests have several other types of questions besides multiple choice. To see a more detailed description of a particular CLEP exam, visit www.collegeboard.com/clep.

The English Composition with Essay exam is the only exam that includes a required essay. This essay is scored by college English faculty designated by CLEP and does not require an additional fee. However, other Composition and Literature tests offer optional essays, which some college and universities require and some do not. These essays are graded by faculty at the individual institutions that require them and require an additional $10 fee. Contact the particular institution to ask about essay requirements, and check with your test center for further details.

All 35 CLEP examinations are administered on computer. If you are unfamiliar with taking a test on a computer, consult the CLEP Sampler online at www.collegeboard.com/clep. The Sampler contains the same tutorials as the actual exams and helps familiarize you with navigation and how to answer different types of questions.

Points are not deducted for wrong or skipped answers – you receive one point for every correct answer. Therefore it is best that an answer is supplied for each exam question, whether it is a guess or not. The number of correct answers is then converted to a formula score. This formula, or "scaled," score is determined by a statistical process called *equating*, which adjusts for slight differences in difficulty between test forms and ensures that your score does not depend on the specific test form you took or how well others did on the same form. The scaled scores range from 20 to 80 – this is the number that will appear on your score report.

To ensure that you complete all questions in the time allotted, you would probably be wise to skip the more difficult or perplexing questions and return to them later. Although the multiple-choice items in these tests are carefully designed so as not to be tricky, misleading, or ambiguous, on the other hand, they are not all direct questions of factual information. They attempt, in their way, to elicit a response that indicates your knowledge or lack of knowledge of the material in question or your ability or inability to use or interpret a fact or idea. Thus, you should concentrate on answering the questions as they appear to be without attempting to out-guess the testmakers.

5. WHAT ARE THE FEES?

The fee for all CLEP examinations is $55. Optional essays required by some institutions are an additional $10.

6. WHEN ARE THE TESTS GIVEN?

CLEP tests are administered year-round. Consult the CLEP website (www.collegeboard.com/clep) and individual test centers for specific information.

7. WHERE ARE THE TESTS GIVEN?

More than 1,300 test centers are located on college and university campuses throughout the country, and additional centers are being established to meet increased needs. Any accredited collegiate institution with an explicit and publicly available policy of credit by examination can become a CLEP test center. To obtain a list of these centers, visit the CLEP website at www.collegeboard.com/clep.

8. HOW DO I REGISTER FOR THE COLLEGE-LEVEL EXAMINATION PROGRAM?

Contact an individual test center for information regarding registration, scheduling and fees. Registration/admission forms can also be obtained on the CLEP website.

9. MAY I REPEAT THE COLLEGE-LEVEL EXAMINATIONS?

You may repeat any examination providing at least six months have passed since you were last administered this test. If you repeat a test within a period of time less than six months, your scores will be cancelled and your fees forfeited. To repeat a test, check the appropriate space on the registration form.

10. WHEN MAY I EXPECT MY SCORE REPORTS?

With the exception of the English Composition with Essay exam, you should receive your score report instantly once the test is complete.

11. HOW SHOULD I PREPARE FOR THE COLLEGE-LEVEL EXAMINATIONS?

This book has been specifically designed to prepare candidates for these examinations. It will help you to consider, study, and review important content, principles, practices, procedures, problems, and techniques in the form of varied and concrete applications.

12. QUESTIONS AND ANSWERS APPEARING IN THIS PUBLICATION

The College-Level Examinations are offered by the College Board. Since copies of past examinations have not been made available, we have used equivalent materials, including questions and answers, which are highly recommended by us as an appropriate means of preparing for these examinations.

If you need additional information about CLEP Examinations, visit www.collegeboard.com/clep.

THE COLLEGE-LEVEL EXAMINATION PROGRAM

How The Program Works

CLEP examinations are administered at many colleges and universities across the country, and most institutions award college credit to those who do well on them. The examinations provide people who have acquired knowledge outside the usual educational settings the opportunity to show that they have learned college-level material without taking certain college courses.

The CLEP examinations cover material that is taught in introductory-level courses at many colleges and universities. Faculties at individual colleges review the tests to ensure that they cover the important material taught in their courses. Colleges differ in the examinations they accept; some colleges accept only two or three of the examinations while others accept nearly all of them.

Although CLEP is sponsored by the College Board and the examinations are scored by Educational Testing Service (ETS), neither of these organizations can award college credit. Only accredited colleges may grant credit toward a degree. When you take a CLEP examination, you may request that a copy of your score report be sent to the college you are attending or plan to attend. After evaluating your scores, the college will decide whether or not to award you credit for a certain course or courses, or to exempt you from them. If the college gives you credit, it will record the number of credits on your permanent record, thereby indicating that you have completed work equivalent to a course in that subject. If the college decides to grant exemption without giving you credit for a course, you will be permitted to omit a course that would normally be required of you and to take a course of your choice instead.

What the Examinations Are Like

The examinations consist mostly of multiple-choice questions to be answered within a 90-minute time limit. Additional information about each CLEP examination is given in the examination guide and on the CLEP website.

Where To Take the Examinations

CLEP examinations are administered throughout the year at the test centers of approximately 1,300 colleges and universities. On the CLEP website, you will find a list of institutions that award credit for satisfactory scores on CLEP examinations. Some colleges administer CLEP examinations to their own students only. Other institutions administer the tests to anyone who registers to take them. If your college does not administer the tests, contact the test centers in your area for information about its testing schedule.

Once you have been tested, your score report will be available instantly. CLEP scores are kept on file at ETS for 20 years; and during this period, for a small fee, you may have your transcript sent to another college or to anyone else you specify. (Your scores will never be sent to anyone without your approval.)

APPROACHING A COLLEGE ABOUT CLEP

The following sections provide a step-by-step approach to learning about the CLEP policy at a particular college or university. The person or office that can best assist students desiring CLEP credit may have a different title at each institution, but the following guidelines will lead you to information about CLEP at any institution.

Adults returning to college often benefit from special assistance when they approach a college. Opportunities for adults to return to formal learning in the classroom are now widespread, and colleges and universities have worked hard to make this a smooth process for older students. Many colleges have established special service offices that are staffed with trained professionals who understand the kinds of problems facing adults returning to college. If you think you might benefit from such assistance, be sure to find out whether these services are available at your college.

How to Apply for College Credit

STEP 1. Obtain the General Information Catalog and a copy of the CLEP policy from the colleges you are considering. If you have not yet applied for admission, ask for an admissions application form too.

Information about admissions and CLEP policies can be obtained by contacting college admissions offices or finding admissions information on the school websites. Tell the admissions officer that you are a prospective student and that you are interested in applying for admission and CLEP credit. Ask for a copy of the publication in which the college's complete CLEP policy is explained. Also get the name and the telephone number of the person to contact in case you have further questions about CLEP.

At this step, you may wish to obtain information from external degree colleges. Many adults find that such colleges suit their needs exceptionally well.

STEP 2. If you have not already been admitted to the college you are considering, look at its admission requirements for undergraduate students to see if you can qualify.

This is an important step because if you can't get into college, you can't get college credit for CLEP. Nearly all colleges require students to be admitted and to enroll in one or more courses before granting the students CLEP credit.

Virtually all public community colleges and a number of four-year state colleges have open admission policies for in-state students. This usually means that they admit anyone who has graduated from high school or has earned a high school equivalency diploma.

If you think you do not meet the admission requirements, contact the admissions office for an interview with a counselor. Colleges do sometimes make exceptions, particularly for adult applicants. State why you want the interview and ask what documents you should bring with you or send in advance. (These materials may include a high school transcript, transcript of previous college work, completed application for admission, etc.) Make an extra effort to have all the information requested in time for the interview.

During the interview, relax and be yourself. Be prepared to state honestly why you think you are ready and able to do college work. If you have already taken CLEP examinations and scored high enough to earn credit, you have shown that you are able to do college work. Mention this achievement to the admissions counselor because it may increase your chances of being accepted. If you have not taken a CLEP examination, you can still improve your chances of being accepted by describing how your job training or independent study has helped prepare you for college-level work. Tell the counselor what you have learned from your work and personal experiences.

STEP 3. Evaluate the college's CLEP policy.

Typically, a college lists all its academic policies, including CLEP policies, in its general catalog. You will probably find the CLEP policy statement under a heading such as Credit-by-Examination, Advanced Standing, Advanced Placement, or External Degree Program. These sections can usually be found in the front of the catalog.

Many colleges publish their credit-by-examination policies in a separate brochure, which is distributed through the campus testing office, counseling center, admissions office, or registrar's office. If you find a very general policy statement in the college catalog, seek clarification from one of these offices.

Review the material in the section of this guide entitled Questions to Ask About a College's CLEP Policy. Use these guidelines to evaluate the college's CLEP policy. If you have not yet taken a CLEP examination, this evaluation will help you decide which examinations to take and whether or not to take the free-response or essay portion. Because individual colleges have different CLEP policies, a review of several policies may help you decide which college to attend.

STEP 4. If you have not yet applied for admission, do so early.

Most colleges expect you to apply for admission several months before you enroll, and it is essential that you meet the published application deadlines. It takes time to process your application for admission; and if you have yet to take a CLEP examination, it will be some time before the college receives and reviews your score report. You will probably want to take some, if not all, of the CLEP examinations you are interested in before you enroll so you know which courses you need not register for. In fact, some colleges require that all CLEP scores be submitted before a student registers.

Complete all forms and include all documents requested with your application(s) for admission. Normally, an admissions decision cannot be reached until all documents have been submitted and evaluated. Unless told to do so, do not send your CLEP scores until you have been officially admitted.

STEP 5. Arrange to take CLEP examination(s) or to submit your CLEP score(s).

You may want to wait to take your CLEP examinations until you know definitely which college you will be attending. Then you can make sure you are taking tests your college will accept for credit. You will also be able to request that your scores be sent to the college, free of charge, when you take the tests.

If you have already taken CLEP examinations, but did not have a copy of your score report sent to your college, you may request the College Board to send an official transcript at any time for a small fee. Use the Transcript Request Form that was sent to you with your score report. If you do not have the form, you may find it online at www.collegeboard.com/clep.

Your CLEP scores will be evaluated, probably by someone in the admissions office, and sent to the registrar's office to be posted on your permanent record once you are enrolled. Procedures vary from college to college, but the process usually begins in the admissions office.

STEP 6. Ask to receive a written notice of the credit you receive for your CLEP score(s).

A written notice may save you problems later, when you submit your degree plan or file for graduation. In the event that there is a question about whether or not you earned CLEP credit, you will have an official record of what credit was awarded. You may also need this verification of course credit if you go for academic counseling before the credit is posted on your permanent record.

STEP 7. Before you register for courses, seek academic counseling.

A discussion with your academic advisor can prevent you from taking unnecessary courses and can tell you specifically what your CLEP credit will mean to you. This step may be accomplished at the time you enroll. Most colleges have orientation sessions for new students prior to each enrollment period. During orientation, students are usually assigned an academic advisor who then gives them individual help in developing long-range plans and a course schedule for the next semester. In conjunction with this counseling, you may be asked to take some additional tests so that you can be placed at the proper course level.

External Degree Programs

If you have acquired a considerable amount of college-level knowledge through job experience, reading, or noncredit courses, if you have accumulated college credits at a variety of colleges over a period of years, or if you prefer studying on your own rather than in a classroom setting, you may want to investigate the possibility of enrolling in an external degree program. Many colleges offer external degree programs that allow you to earn a degree by passing examinations (including CLEP), transferring credit from other colleges, and demonstrating in other ways that you have satisfied the educational requirements. No classroom attendance is required, and the programs are open to out-of-state candidates as well as residents. Thomas A. Edison State College in New Jersey and Charter Oaks College in Connecticut are fully accredited independent state colleges; the New York program is part of the state university system and is also fully accredited. If you are interested in exploring an external degree, you can write for more information to:

Charter Oak College
The Exchange, Suite 171
270 Farmington Avenue
Farmington, CT 06032-1909

Regents External Degree Program
Cultural Education Center
Empire State Plaza
Albany, New York 12230

Thomas A. Edison State College
101 West State Street
Trenton, New Jersey 08608

Many other colleges also have external degree or weekend programs. While they often require that a number of courses be taken on campus, the external degree programs tend to be more flexible in transferring credit, granting credit-by-examination, and allowing independent study than other traditional programs. When applying to a college, you may wish to ask whether it has an external degree or weekend program.

Questions to Ask About a College's CLEP Policy

Before taking CLEP examinations for the purpose of earning college credit, try to find the answers to these questions:

1. Which CLEP examinations are accepted by this college?

A college may accept some CLEP examinations for credit and not others - possibly not the one you are considering. The English faculty may decide to grant college English credit based on the CLEP English Composition examination, but not on the Freshman College Composition examination. Or, the mathematics faculty may decide to grant credit based on the College Mathematics to non-mathematics majors only, requiring majors to take an examination in algebra, trigonometry, or calculus to earn credit. For these reasons, it is important that you know the specific CLEP tests for which you can receive credit.

2. Does the college require the optional free-response (essay) section as well as the objective portion of the CLEP examination you are considering?

Knowing the answer to this question ahead of time will permit you to schedule the optional essay examination when you register to take your CLEP examination.

3. Is credit granted for specific courses? If so, which ones?

You are likely to find that credit will be granted for specific courses and the course titles will be designated in the college's CLEP policy. It is not necessary, however, that credit be granted for a specific course in order for you to benefit from your CLEP credit. For instance, at many liberal arts colleges, all students must take certain types of courses; these courses may be labeled the core curriculum, general education requirements, distribution requirements, or liberal arts requirements. The requirements are often expressed in terms of credit hours. For example, all students may be required to take at least six hours of humanities, six hours of English, three hours of mathematics, six hours of natural science, and six hours of social science, with no particular courses in these disciplines specified. In these instances, CLEP credit may be given as 6 hrs. English credit or 3 hrs. Math credit without specifying for which English or mathematics courses credit has been awarded. In order to avoid possible disappointment, you should know before taking a CLEP examination what type of credit you can receive and whether you will only be exempted from a required course but receive no credit.

4. How much credit is granted for each examination you are considering, and does the college place a limit on the total amount of CLEP credit you can earn toward your degree?

Not all colleges that grant CLEP credit award the same amount for individual tests. Furthermore, some colleges place a limit on the total amount of credit you can earn through CLEP or other examinations. Other colleges may grant you exemption but no credit toward your degree. Knowing several colleges' policies concerning these issues may help you decide which college you will attend. If you think you are capable of passing a number of CLEP examinations, you may want to attend a college that will allow you to earn credit for all or most of them. For example, the state external degree programs grant credit for most CLEP examinations (and other tests as well).

5. What is the required score for earning CLEP credit for each test you are considering?

Most colleges publish the required scores or percentile ranks for earning CLEP credit in their general catalog or in a brochure. The required score may vary from test to test, so find out the required score for each test you are considering.

6. What is the college's policy regarding prior course work in the subject in which you are considering taking a CLEP test?

Some colleges will not grant credit for a CLEP test if the student has already attempted a college-level course closely aligned with that test. For example, if you successfully completed English 101 or a comparable course on another campus, you will probably not be permitted to receive CLEP credit in that subject, too. Some colleges will not permit you to earn CLEP credit for a course that you failed.

7. Does the college make additional stipulations before credit will be granted?

It is common practice for colleges to award CLEP credit only to their enrolled students. There are other stipulations, however, that vary from college to college. For example, does the college require you to formally apply for or accept CLEP credit by completing and signing a form? Or does the college require you to validate your CLEP score by successfully completing a more advanced course in the subject? Answers to these and other questions will help to smooth the process of earning college credit through CLEP.

The above questions and the discussions that follow them indicate some of the ways in which colleges' CLEP policies can vary. Find out as much as possible about the CLEP policies at the colleges you are interested in so you can choose a college with a policy that is compatible with your educational goals. Once you have selected the college you will attend, you can find out which CLEP examinations your college recognizes and the requirements for earning CLEP credit.

DECIDING WHICH EXAMINATIONS TO TAKE

If You're Taking the Examinations for College Credit or Career Advancement:

Most people who take CLEP examinations do so in order to earn credit for college courses. Others take the examinations in order to qualify for job promotions or for professional certification or licensing. It is vital to most candidates who are taking the tests for any of these reasons that they be well prepared for the tests they are taking so that they can advance as rapidly as possible toward their educational or career goals.

It is usually advisable that those who have limited knowledge in the subjects covered by the tests they are considering enroll in the college courses in which that material is taught. Those who are uncertain about whether or not they know enough about a subject to do well on a particular CLEP test will find the following guidelines helpful.

There is no way to predict if you will pass a particular CLEP examination, but answers to the questions under the seven headings below should give you an indication of whether or not you are likely to succeed.

1. Test Descriptions

Read the description of the test provided. Are you familiar with most of the topics and terminology in the outline?

2. Textbooks

Examine the suggested textbooks and other resource materials following the test descriptions in this guide. Have you recently read one or more of these books, or have you read similar college-level books on this subject? If you have not, read through one or more of the textbooks listed, or through the textbook used for this course at your college. Are you familiar with most of the topics and terminology in the book?

3. Sample Questions

The sample questions provided are intended to be typical of the content and difficulty of the questions on the test. Although they are not an exact miniature of the test, the proportion of the sample questions you can answer correctly should be a rough estimate of the proportion of questions you will be able to answer correctly on the test.

Answer as many of the sample questions for this test as you can. Check your answers against the correct answers. Did you answer more than half the questions correctly?

Because of variations in course content at different institutions, and because questions on CLEP tests vary from easy to difficult - with most being of moderate difficulty - the average student who passes a course in a subject can usually answer correctly about half the questions on the corresponding CLEP examination. Most colleges set their passing scores near this level, but some set them higher. If your college has set its required score above the level required by most colleges, you may need to answer a larger proportion of questions on the test correctly.

4. Previous Study

Have you taken noncredit courses in this subject offered by an adult school or a private school, through correspondence, or in connection with your job? Did you do exceptionally well in this subject in high school, or did you take an honors course in this subject?

5. Experience

Have you learned or used the knowledge or skills included in this test in your job or life experience? For example, if you lived in a Spanish-speaking country and spoke the language for a year or more, you might consider taking the Spanish examination. Or, if you have worked at a job in which you used accounting and finance skills, Principles of Accounting would be a likely test for you to take. Or, if you have read a considerable amount of literature and attended many art exhibits, concerts, and plays, you might expect to do well on the Humanities exam.

6. Other Examinations

Have you done well on other standardized tests in subjects related to the one you want to take? For example, did you score well above average on a portion of a college entrance examination covering similar skills, or did you obtain an exceptionally high score on a high school equivalency test or a licensing examination in this subject? Although such tests do not cover exactly the same material as the CLEP examinations and may be easier, persons who do well on these tests often do well on CLEP examinations, too.

7. Advice

Has a college counselor, professor, or some other professional person familiar with your ability advised you to take a CLEP examination?

If your answer was yes to questions under several of the above headings, you probably have a good chance of passing the CLEP examination you are considering. It is unlikely that you would have acquired sufficient background from experience alone. Learning gained through reading and study is essential, and you will probably find some additional study helpful before taking a CLEP examination.

If You're Taking the Examinations to Prepare for College

Many people entering college, particularly adults returning to college after several years away from formal education, are uncertain about their ability to compete with other college students. They wonder whether they have sufficient background for college study, and those who have been away from formal study for some time wonder whether they have forgotten how to study, how to take tests, and how to write papers. Such people may wish to improve their test-taking and study skills prior to enrolling in courses.

One way to assess your ability to perform at the college level and to improve your test-taking and study skills at the same time is to prepare for and take one or more CLEP examinations. You need not be enrolled in a college to take a CLEP examination, and you may have your scores sent only to yourself and later request that a transcript be sent to a college if you then decide to apply for credit. By reviewing the test descriptions and sample questions, you may find one or several subject areas in which you think you have substantial knowledge. Select one examination, or more if you like, and carefully read at least one of the textbooks listed in the bibliography for the test. By doing this, you will get a better idea of how much you know of what is usually taught in a college-level course in that subject. Study as much material as you can, until you think you have a good grasp of the subject matter. Then take the test at a college in your area. It will be several weeks before you receive your results, and you may wish to begin reviewing for another test in the meantime.

To find out if you are eligible for credit for your CLEP score, you must compare your score with the score required by the college you plan to attend. If you are not yet sure which college you will attend, or whether you will enroll in college at all, you should begin to follow the steps outlined. It is best that you do this before taking a CLEP test, but if you are taking the test only for the experience and to familiarize yourself with college-level material and requirements, you might take the test before you approach a college. Even if the college you decide to attend does not accept the test you took, the experience of taking such a test will enable you to meet with greater confidence the requirements of courses you will take.

You will find information about how to interpret your scores in WHAT YOUR SCORES MEAN, which you will receive with your score report, and which can also be found online at the CLEP website. Many colleges follow the recommendations of the American Council on Education (ACE) for setting their required scores, so you can use this information as a guide in determining how well you did. The ACE recommendations are included in the booklet.

If you do not do well enough on the test to earn college credit, don't be discouraged. Usually, it is the best college students who are exempted from courses or receive credit-by-examination. The fact that you cannot get credit for your score means that you should probably enroll in a college course to learn the material. However, if your score was close to the required score, or if you feel you could do better on a second try or after some additional study, you may retake the test after six months. Do not take it sooner or your score will not be reported and your fee will be forfeited.

If you do earn the score required to earn credit, you will have demonstrated that you already have some college-level knowledge. You will also have a better idea whether you should take additional CLEP examinations. And, what is most important, you can enroll in college with confidence, knowing that you do have the ability to succeed.

PREPARING TO TAKE CLEP EXAMINATIONS

Having made the decision to take one or more CLEP examinations, most people then want to know if it is worthwhile to prepare for them - how much, how long, when, and how should they go about it? The precise answers to these questions vary greatly from individual to individual. However, most candidates find that some type of test preparation is helpful.

Most people who take CLEP examinations do so to show that they have already learned the important material that is taught in a college course. Many of them need only a quick review to assure themselves that they have not forgotten some of what they once studied, and to fill in some of the gaps in their knowledge of the subject. Others feel that they need a thorough review and spend several weeks studying for a test. A few wish to take a CLEP examination as a kind of final examination for independent study of a subject instead of the college course. This last group requires significantly more study than those who only need to review, and they may need some guidance from professors of the subjects they are studying.

The key to how you prepare for CLEP examinations often lies in locating those skills and areas of prior learning in which you are strong and deciding where to focus your energies. Some people may know a great deal about a certain subject area, but may not test well. These individuals would probably be just as concerned about strengthening their test-taking skills as they are about studying for a specific test. Many mental and physical skills are used in preparing for a test. It is important not only to review or study for the examinations, but to make certain that you are alert, relatively free of anxiety, and aware of how to approach standardized tests. Suggestions on developing test-taking skills and preparing psychologically and physically for a test are given. The following section suggests ways of assessing your knowledge of the content of a test and then reviewing and studying the material.

Using This Study Guide

Begin by carefully reading the test description and outline of knowledge and skills required for the examination, if given. As you read through the topics listed there, ask yourself how much you know about each one. Also note the terms, names, and symbols that are mentioned, and ask yourself whether you are familiar with them. This will give you a quick overview of how much you know about the subject. If you are familiar with nearly all the material, you will probably need a minimum of review; however, if less than half of it is familiar, you will probably require substantial study to do well on the test.

If, after reviewing the test description, you find that you need extensive review, delay answering the sample question until you have done some reading in the subject. If you complete them before reviewing the material, you will probably look for the answers as you study, and then they will not be a good assessment of your ability at a later date.

If you think you are familiar with most of the test material, try to answer the sample questions.

Apply the test-taking strategies given. Keeping within the time limit suggested will give you a rough idea of how quickly you should work in order to complete the actual test.

Check your answers against the answer key. If you answered nearly all the questions correctly, you probably do not need to study the subject extensively. If you got about half the questions correct, you ought o review at least one textbook or other suggested materials on the subject. If you answered less than half the questions correctly, you will probably benefit from more extensive reading in the subject and thorough study of one or more textbooks. The textbooks listed are used at many colleges but they are not the only good texts. You will find helpful almost any standard text available to you., such as the textbook used at your college, or earlier editions of texts listed. For some examinations, topic outlines and textbooks may not be available. Take the sample tests in this book and check your answers at the end of each test. Check wrong answers.

Suggestions for Studying

The following suggestions have been gathered from people who have prepared for CLEP examinations or other college-level tests.

1. Define your goals and locate study materials

First, determine your study goals. Set aside a block of time to review the material provided in this book, and then decide which test(s) you will take. Using the suggestions, locate suitable resource materials. If a preparation course is offered by an adult school or college in your area, you might find it helpful to enroll.

2. Find a good place to study

To determine what kind of place you need for studying, ask yourself questions such as: Do I need a quiet place? Does the telephone distract me? Do objects I see in this place remind me of things I should do? Is it too warm? Is it well lit? Am I too comfortable here? Do I have space to spread out my materials? You may find the library more conducive to studying than your home. If you decide to study at home, you might prevent interruptions by other household members by putting a sign on the door of your study room to indicate when you will be available.

3. Schedule time to study

To help you determine where studying best fits into your schedule, try this exercise: Make a list of your daily activities (for example, sleeping, working, and eating) and estimate how many hours per day you spend on each activity. Now, rate all the activities on your list in order of their importance and evaluate your use of time. Often people are astonished at how an average day appears from this perspective. They may discover that they were unaware how large portions of time are spent, or they learn their time can be scheduled in alternative ways. For example, they can remove the least important activities from their day and devote that time to studying or another important activity.

4. Establish a study routine and a set of goals

In order to study effectively, you should establish specific goals and a schedule for accomplishing them. Some people find it helpful to write out a weekly schedule and cross out each study period when it is completed. Others maintain their concentration better by writing down the time when they expect to complete a study task. Most people find short periods of intense study more productive than long stretches of time. For example, they may follow a regular schedule of several 20- or 30-minute study periods with short breaks between them. Some people like to allow themselves rewards as they complete each study goal. It is not essential that you accomplish every goal exactly within your schedule; the point is to be committed to your task.

5. Learn how to take an active role in studying.

If you have not done much studying for some time, you may find it difficult to concentrate at first. Try a method of studying, such as the one outlined below, that will help you concentrate on and remember what you read.

    a. First, read the chapter summary and the introduction. Then you will know what to look for in your reading.

    b. Next, convert the section or paragraph headlines into questions. For example, if you are reading a section entitled, The Causes of the American Revolution, ask yourself: *What were the causes of the American Revolution?* Compose the answer as you read the paragraph. Reading and answering questions aloud will help you understand and remember the material.

c. Take notes on key ideas or concepts as you read. Writing will also help you fix concepts more firmly in your mind. Underlining key ideas or writing notes in your book can be helpful and will be useful for review. Underline only important points. If you underline more than a third of each paragraph, you are probably underlining too much.

d. If there are questions or problems at the end of a chapter, answer or solve them on paper as if you were asked to do them for homework. Mathematics textbooks (and some other books) sometimes include answers to some or all of the exercises. If you have such a book, write your answers before looking at the ones given. When problem-solving is involved, work enough problems to master the required methods and concepts. If you have difficulty with problems, review any sample problems or explanations in the chapter.

e. To retain knowledge, most people have to review the material periodically. If you are preparing for a test over an extended period of time, review key concepts and notes each week or so. Do not wait for weeks to review the material or you will need to relearn much of it.

Psychological and Physical Preparation

Most people feel at least some nervousness before taking a test. Adults who are returning to college may not have taken a test in many years or they may have had little experience with standardized tests. Some younger students, as well, are uncomfortable with testing situations. People who received their education in countries outside the United States may find that many tests given in this country are quite different from the ones they are accustomed to taking.

Not only might candidates find the types of tests and the kinds of questions on them unfamiliar, but other aspects of the testing environment may be strange as well. The physical and mental stress that results from meeting this new experience can hinder a candidate's ability to demonstrate his or her true degree of knowledge in the subject area being tested. For this reason, it is important to go to the test center well prepared, both mentally and physically, for taking the test. You may find the following suggestions helpful.

1. Familiarize yourself, as much as possible, with the test and the test situation before the day of the examination. It will be helpful for you to know ahead of time:

a. How much time will be allowed for the test and whether there are timed subsections.

b. What types of questions and directions appear on the examination.

c. How your test score will be computed.

d. How to properly answer the questions on the computer (See the CLEP Sample on the CLEP website)

e. In which building and room the examination will be administered. If you don't know where the building is, locate it or get directions ahead of time.

f. The time of the test administration. You might wish to confirm this information a day or two before the examination and find out what time the building and room will be open so that you can plan to arrive early.

g. Where to park your car or, if you wish to take public transportation, which bus or train to take and the location of the nearest stop.

h. Whether smoking will be permitted during the test.

i. Whether there will be a break between examinations (if you will be taking more than one on the same day), and whether there is a place nearby where you can get something to eat or drink.

2. Go to the test situation relaxed and alert. In order to prepare for the test:

a. Get a good night's sleep. Last minute cramming, particularly late the night before, is usually counterproductive.

b. Eat normally. It is usually not wise to skip breakfast or lunch on the day of the test or to eat a big meal just before the test.

c. Avoid tranquilizers and stimulants. If you follow the other directions in this book, you won't need artificial aids. It's better to be a little tense than to be drowsy, but stimulants such as coffee and cola can make you nervous and interfere with your concentration.

d. Don't drink a lot of liquids before the test. Having to leave the room during the test will disturb your concentration and take valuable time away from the test.

e. If you are inclined to be nervous or tense, learn some relaxation exercises and use them before and perhaps during the test.

3. Arrive for the test early and prepared. Be sure to:

a. Arrive early enough so that you can find a parking place, locate the test center, and get settled comfortably before testing begins. Allow some extra time in case you are delayed unexpectedly.

b. Take the following with you:

- Your completed Registration/Admission Form
- Two forms of identification – one being a government-issued photo ID with signature, such as a driver's license or passport
- Non-mechanical pencil
- A watch so that you can time your progress (digital watches are prohibited)
- Your glasses if you need them for reading or seeing the chalkboard or wall clock

c. Leave all books, papers, and notes outside the test center. You will not be permitted to use your own scratch paper; it will be provided. Also prohibited are calculators, cell phones, beepers, pagers, photo/copy devices, radios, headphones, food, beverages, and several other items.

d. Be prepared for any temperature in the testing room. Wear layers of clothing that can be removed if the room is too hot but will keep you warm if it is too cold.

4. When you enter the test room:

a. Sit in a seat that provides a maximum of comfort and freedom from distraction.

b. Read directions carefully, and listen to all instructions given by the test administrator. If you don't understand the directions, ask for help before test timing begins. If you must ask a question after the test has begun, raise your hand and a proctor will assist you. The proctor can answer certain kinds of questions but cannot help you with the test.

c. Know your rights as a test taker. You can expect to be given the full working time allowed for the test(s) and a reasonably quiet and comfortable place in which to work. If a poor test situation is preventing you from doing your best, ask if the situation can be remedied. If bad test conditions cannot be remedied, ask the person in charge to report the problem in the Irregularity Report that will be sent to ETS with the answer sheets. You may also wish to contact CLEP. Describe the exact circumstances as completely as you can. Be sure to include the test date and name(s) of the test(s) you took. ETS will investigate the problem to make sure it does not happen again, and, if the problem is serious enough, may arrange for you to retake the test without charge.

TAKING THE EXAMINATIONS

A person may know a great deal about the subject being tested, but not do as well as he or she is capable of on the test. Knowing how to approach a test is an important part of the testing process. While a command of test-taking skills cannot substitute for knowledge of the subject matter, it can be a significant factor in successful testing.

Test-taking skills enable a person to use all available information to earn a score that truly reflects his or her ability. There are different strategies for approaching different kinds of test questions. For example, free-response questions require a very different tack than do multiple-choice questions. Other factors, such as how the test will be graded, may also influence your approach to the test and your use of test time. Thus, your preparation for a test should include finding out all you can about the test so that you can use the most effective test-taking strategies.

Before taking a test, you should know approximately how many questions are on the test, how much time you will be allowed, how the test will be scored or graded, what types of questions and directions are on the test, and how you will be required to record your answers.

Taking Multiple-Choice Tests

1. Listen carefully to the instructions given by the test administrator and read carefully all directions before you begin to answer the questions.

2. Note the time that the test administrator starts timing the test. As you proceed, make sure that you are not working too slowly. You should have answered at least half the questions in a section when half the time for that section has passed. If you have not reached that point in the section, speed up your pace on the remaining questions.

3. Before answering a question, read the entire question, including all the answer choices. Don't think that because the first or second answer choice looks good to you, it isn't necessary to read the remaining options. Instructions usually tell you to select the best answer. Sometimes one answer choice is partially correct, but another option is better; therefore, it is usually a good idea to read all the answers before you choose one.

4. Read and consider every question. Questions that look complicated at first glance may not actually be so difficult once you have read them carefully.

5. Do not puzzle too long over any one question. If you don't know the answer after you've considered it briefly, go on to the next question. Make sure you return to the question later.

6. Make sure you record your response properly.

7. In trying to determine the correct answer, you may find it helpful to cross out those options that you know are incorrect, and to make marks next to those you think might be correct. If you decide to skip the question and come back to it later, you will save yourself the time of reconsidering all the options.

8. Watch for the following key words in test questions:

all	generally	never	perhaps
always	however	none	rarely
but	may	not	seldom
except	must	often	sometimes
every	necessary	only	usually

When a question or answer option contains words such as always, every, only, never, and none, there can be no exceptions to the answer you choose. Use of words such as often, rarely, sometimes, and generally indicates that there may be some exceptions to the answer.

9. Do not waste your time looking for clues to right answers based on flaws in question wording or patterns in correct answers. Professionals at the College Board and ETS put

a great deal of effort into developing valid, reliable, fair tests. CLEP test development committees are composed of college faculty who are experts in the subject covered by the test and are appointed by the College Board to write test questions and to scrutinize each question that is included on a CLEP test. Committee members make every effort to ensure that the questions are not ambiguous, that they have only one correct answer, and that they cover college-level topics. These committees do not intentionally include trick questions. If you think a question is flawed, ask the test administrator to report it, or contact CLEP immediately.

Taking Free-Response or Essay Tests

If your college requires the optional free-response or essay portion of a CLEP Composition and Literature exams, you should do some additional preparation for your CLEP test. Taking an essay test is very different from taking a multiple-choice test, so you will need to use some other strategies.

The essay written as part of the English Composition and Essay exam is graded by English professors from a variety of colleges and universities. A process called holistic scoring is used to rate your writing ability.

The optional free-response essays, on the other hand, are graded by the faculty of the college you designate as a score recipient. Guidelines and criteria for grading essays are not specified by the College Board or ETS. You may find it helpful, therefore, to talk with someone at your college to find out what criteria will be used to determine whether you will get credit. If the test requires essay responses, ask how much emphasis will be placed on your writing ability and your ability to organize your thoughts as opposed to your knowledge of subject matter. Find out how much weight will be given to your multiple-choice test score in comparison with your free-response grade in determining whether you will get credit. This will give you an idea where you should expend the greatest effort in preparing for and taking the test.

Here are some strategies you will find useful in taking any essay test:

1. Before you begin to write, read all questions carefully and take a few minutes to jot down some ideas you might include in each answer.

2. If you are given a choice of questions to answer, choose the questions you think you can answer most clearly and knowledgeably.

3. Determine in what order you will answer the questions. Answer those you find the easiest first so that any extra time can be spent on the more difficult questions.

4. When you know which questions you will answer and in what order, determine how much testing time remains and estimate how many minutes you will devote to each question. Unless suggested times are given for the questions or one question appears to require more or less time than the others, allot an equal amount of time to each question.

5. Before answering each question, indicate the number of the question as it is given in the test book. You need not copy the entire question from the question sheet, but it will be helpful to you and to the person grading your test if you indicate briefly the topic you are addressing – particularly if you are not answering the questions in the order in which they appear on the test.

6. Before answering each question, read it again carefully to make sure you are interpreting it correctly. Underline key words, such as those listed below, that often appear in free-response questions. Be sure you know the exact meaning of these words before taking the test.

analyze	demonstrate	enumerate	list
apply	derive	explain	outline
assess	describe	generalize	prove
compare	determine	illustrate	rank
contrast	discuss	interpret	show
define	distinguish	justify	summarize

If a question asks you to outline, define, or summarize, do not write a detailed explanation; if a question asks you to analyze, explain, illustrate, interpret, or show, you must do more than briefly describe the topic.

For a current listing of CLEP Colleges

where you can get credit and be tested, write:

CLEP, P.O. Box 6600, Princeton, NJ 08541-6600

Or e-mail: clep@ets.org, or call: (609) 771-7865

GENERAL BIOLOGY

DESCRIPTION OF THE TEST

The General Biology examination covers material that is usually taught in a one-year biology course at the college level. The subject matter tested covers the broad field of the biological sciences, organized into three major areas: molecular and cellular biology, organismal biology, and populational biology. The examination gives approximately equal weight to these three areas and the questions relating to them are interspersed randomly throughout the test.

The examination consists of approximately 120 multiple-choice questions to be answered in two separately timed 45-minute sections.

KNOWLEDGE AND SKILLS REQUIRED

Questions on the test require candidates to demonstrate one or more of the following abilities:

- Knowledge of facts, principles, and processes of biology
- Understanding of the means by which information is collected, how it is interpreted, how one hypothesizes from available information, how one draws conclusions and makes further predictions
- Understanding that science is a human endeavor with social consequences

The subject matter of the General Biology examination is drawn from the following topics.

<u>Approximate Percent of Examination</u>

33% Molecular and Cellular Biology
- Chemical composition of organisms
    - Elements in organisms
    - Properties of water
    - Chemical structure of carbohydrates, lipids, proteins, organic acids, nucleic acids
- Cells
    - Structure and function of cell organelles
    - Properties of cell membranes
    - Comparison of prokaryotic and eukaryotic cells
- Enzymes
    - Enzyme-substrate complex
    - Role of coenzymes
    - Inorganic cofactors
    - Prosthetic groups
- Energy Transformations
    - Aerobic and anaerobic respiration
    - Photosynthesis

for instructional purposes from the official announcement

- Cell Division
    - Structure of chromosomes
    - Mitosis, meiosis, and cytokinesis in plants and animals
- Chemical Nature of the Gene
    - Watson-Crick model of nucleic acids
    - Self-copying of DNA molecules
    - Mutations
    - Control of protein synthesis
    - Structural and regulatory genes
    - Transformation and transduction
- The Origin of Life
    - Modern theories
    - Experimental evidence

34% Organismal Biology
- Structure and Function in Plants with Emphasis on Angiosperms
    - Root, stem, leaf, flower, seed, fruit
    - Water and mineral absorption and transport
    - Food translocation and storage
- Plant Reproduction and Development
    - Alternation of generations in ferns, pines, and flowering plants
    - Gamete formation and fertilization
    - Growth and development: hormonal control
    - Tropism and photoperiodicity
- Structure and Function in Animals with Emphasis on Vertebrates
    - Major systems
    - Homeostatic mechanisms
    - Hormonal control in homeostasis and reproduction
- Animal Reproduction and Development
    - Gamete formation, fertilization
    - Cleavage, gastrulation, germ layer formation, differentiation of organ systems
    - Experimental analysis of vertebrate development
    - Extraembryonic membranes of vertebrates
    - Formation and function of the mammalian placenta
    - Blood circulation in a human embryo
- Principles of Heredity
    - History of early experiments in heredity
    - Mendelian inheritance (dominance, segregation, independent assortment)
    - Chromosomal basis of inheritance
    - Linkage
    - Sex-linked, sex-influenced, sex-limited inheritance
    - Polygenic inheritance (height, skin color)
    - Multiple alleles (human blood groups)

HOW TO TAKE A TEST

You have studied long, hard and conscientiously.

With your official admission card in hand, and your heart pounding, you have been admitted to the examination room.

You note that there are several hundred other applicants in the examination room waiting to take the same test.

They all appear to be equally well prepared.

You know that nothing but your best effort will suffice. The "moment of truth" is at hand: you now have to demonstrate objectively, in writing, your knowledge of content and your understanding of subject matter.

You are fighting the most important battle of your life—to pass and/or score high on an examination which will determine your career and provide the economic basis for your livelihood.

What extra, special things should you know and should you do in taking the examination?

I. YOU MUST PASS AN EXAMINATION

A. WHAT EVERY CANDIDATE SHOULD KNOW
Examination applicants often ask us for help in preparing for the written test. What can I study in advance? What kinds of questions will be asked? How will the test be given? How will the papers be graded?

B. HOW ARE EXAMS DEVELOPED?
Examinations are carefully written by trained technicians who are specialists in the field known as "psychological measurement," in consultation with recognized authorities in the field of work that the test will cover. These experts recommend the subject matter areas or skills to be tested; only those knowledges or skills important to your success on the job are included. The most reliable books and source materials available are used as references. Together, the experts and technicians judge the difficulty level of the questions.
Test technicians know how to phrase questions so that the problem is clearly stated. Their ethics do not permit "trick" or "catch" questions. Questions may have been tried out on sample groups, or subjected to statistical analysis, to determine their usefulness.
Written tests are often used in combination with performance tests, ratings of training and experience, and oral interviews. All of these measures combine to form the best-known means of finding the right person for the right job.

II. HOW TO PASS THE WRITTEN TEST

A. BASIC STEPS

1) Study the announcement

How, then, can you know what subjects to study? Our best answer is: "Learn as much as possible about the class of positions for which you've applied." The exam will test the knowledge, skills and abilities needed to do the work.

Your most valuable source of information about the position you want is the official exam announcement. This announcement lists the training and experience qualifications. Check these standards and apply only if you come reasonably close to meeting them. Many jurisdictions preview the written test in the exam announcement by including a section called "Knowledge and Abilities Required," "Scope of the Examination," or some similar heading. Here you will find out specifically what fields will be tested.

2) Choose appropriate study materials

If the position for which you are applying is technical or advanced, you will read more advanced, specialized material. If you are already familiar with the basic principles of your field, elementary textbooks would waste your time. Concentrate on advanced textbooks and technical periodicals. Think through the concepts and review difficult problems in your field.

These are all general sources. You can get more ideas on your own initiative, following these leads. For example, training manuals and publications of the government agency which employs workers in your field can be useful, particularly for technical and professional positions. A letter or visit to the government department involved may result in more specific study suggestions, and certainly will provide you with a more definite idea of the exact nature of the position you are seeking.

3) Study this book!

III. KINDS OF TESTS

Tests are used for purposes other than measuring knowledge and ability to perform specified duties. For some positions, it is equally important to test ability to make adjustments to new situations or to profit from training. In others, basic mental abilities not dependent on information are essential. Questions which test these things may not appear as pertinent to the duties of the position as those which test for knowledge and information. Yet they are often highly important parts of a fair examination. For very general questions, it is almost impossible to help you direct your study efforts. What we can do is to point out some of the more common of these general abilities needed in public service positions and describe some typical questions.

1) General information

Broad, general information has been found useful for predicting job success in some kinds of work. This is tested in a variety of ways, from vocabulary lists to questions about current events. Basic background in some field of work, such as sociology or economics, may be sampled in a group of questions. Often these are principles which have become familiar to most persons through exposure rather than through formal training. It is difficult to advise you how to study for these questions; being alert to the world around you is our best suggestion.

2) Verbal ability

An example of an ability needed in many positions is verbal or language ability. Verbal ability is, in brief, the ability to use and understand words. Vocabulary and grammar tests are typical measures of this ability. Reading comprehension or paragraph interpretation questions are common in many kinds of civil service tests. You are given a paragraph of written material and asked to find its central meaning.

IV. KINDS OF QUESTIONS

1. Multiple-choice Questions

Most popular of the short-answer questions is the "multiple choice" or "best answer" question. It can be used, for example, to test for factual knowledge, ability to solve problems or judgment in meeting situations found at work.

A multiple-choice question is normally one of three types:
- It can begin with an incomplete statement followed by several possible endings. You are to find the one ending which best completes the statement, although some of the others may not be entirely wrong.
- It can also be a complete statement in the form of a question which is answered by choosing one of the statements listed.
- It can be in the form of a problem – again you select the best answer.

Here is an example of a multiple-choice question with a discussion which should give you some clues as to the method for choosing the right answer:

When an employee has a complaint about his assignment, the action which will best help him overcome his difficulty is to
- A. discuss his difficulty with his coworkers
- B. take the problem to the head of the organization
- C. take the problem to the person who gave him the assignment
- D. say nothing to anyone about his complaint

In answering this question, you should study each of the choices to find which is best. Consider choice "A" – Certainly an employee may discuss his complaint with fellow employees, but no change or improvement can result, and the complaint remains unresolved. Choice "B" is a poor choice since the head of the organization probably does not know what assignment you have been given, and taking your problem to him is known as "going over the head" of the supervisor. The supervisor, or person who made the assignment, is the person who can clarify it or correct any injustice. Choice "C" is, therefore, correct. To say nothing, as in choice "D," is unwise. Supervisors have and interest in knowing the problems employees are facing, and the employee is seeking a solution to his problem.

2. True/False

3. Matching Questions

Matching an answer from a column of choices within another column.

V. RECORDING YOUR ANSWERS

Computer terminals are used more and more today for many different kinds of exams.

For an examination with very few applicants, you may be told to record your answers in the test booklet itself. Separate answer sheets are much more common. If this separate answer sheet is to be scored by machine – and this is often the case – it is highly important that you mark your answers correctly in order to get credit.

VI. BEFORE THE TEST

YOUR PHYSICAL CONDITION IS IMPORTANT

If you are not well, you can't do your best work on tests. If you are half asleep, you can't do your best either. Here are some tips:

1) Get about the same amount of sleep you usually get. Don't stay up all night before the test, either partying or worrying—DON'T DO IT!
2) If you wear glasses, be sure to wear them when you go to take the test. This goes for hearing aids, too.
3) If you have any physical problems that may keep you from doing your best, be sure to tell the person giving the test. If you are sick or in poor health, you relay cannot do your best on any test. You can always come back and take the test some other time.

Common sense will help you find procedures to follow to get ready for an examination. Too many of us, however, overlook these sensible measures. Indeed, nervousness and fatigue have been found to be the most serious reasons why applicants fail to do their best on civil service tests. Here is a list of reminders:

- Begin your preparation early – Don't wait until the last minute to go scurrying around for books and materials or to find out what the position is all about.
- Prepare continuously – An hour a night for a week is better than an all-night cram session. This has been definitely established. What is more, a night a week for a month will return better dividends than crowding your study into a shorter period of time.
- Locate the place of the exam – You have been sent a notice telling you when and where to report for the examination. If the location is in a different town or otherwise unfamiliar to you, it would be well to inquire the best route and learn something about the building.
- Relax the night before the test – Allow your mind to rest. Do not study at all that night. Plan some mild recreation or diversion; then go to bed early and get a good night's sleep.
- Get up early enough to make a leisurely trip to the place for the test – This way unforeseen events, traffic snarls, unfamiliar buildings, etc. will not upset you.
- Dress comfortably – A written test is not a fashion show. You will be known by number and not by name, so wear something comfortable.
- Leave excess paraphernalia at home – Shopping bags and odd bundles will get in your way. You need bring only the items mentioned in the official notice you received; usually everything you need is provided. Do not bring reference books to the exam. They will only confuse those last minutes and be taken away from you when in the test room.

- Arrive somewhat ahead of time – If because of transportation schedules you must get there very early, bring a newspaper or magazine to take your mind off yourself while waiting.
- Locate the examination room – When you have found the proper room, you will be directed to the seat or part of the room where you will sit. Sometimes you are given a sheet of instructions to read while you are waiting. Do not fill out any forms until you are told to do so; just read them and be prepared.
- Relax and prepare to listen to the instructions
- If you have any physical problem that may keep you from doing your best, be sure to tell the test administrator. If you are sick or in poor health, you really cannot do your best on the exam. You can come back and take the test some other time.

VII. AT THE TEST

The day of the test is here and you have the test booklet in your hand. The temptation to get going is very strong. Caution! There is more to success than knowing the right answers. You must know how to identify your papers and understand variations in the type of short-answer question used in this particular examination. Follow these suggestions for maximum results from your efforts:

1) Cooperate with the monitor

The test administrator has a duty to create a situation in which you can be as much at ease as possible. He will give instructions, tell you when to begin, check to see that you are marking your answer sheet correctly, and so on. He is not there to guard you, although he will see that your competitors do not take unfair advantage. He wants to help you do your best.

2) Listen to all instructions

Don't jump the gun! Wait until you understand all directions. In most civil service tests you get more time than you need to answer the questions. So don't be in a hurry. Read each word of instructions until you clearly understand the meaning. Study the examples, listen to all announcements and follow directions. Ask questions if you do not understand what to do.

3) Identify your papers

Civil service exams are usually identified by number only. You will be assigned a number; you must not put your name on your test papers. Be sure to copy your number correctly. Since more than one exam may be given, copy your exact examination title.

4) Plan your time

Unless you are told that a test is a "speed" or "rate of work" test, speed itself is usually not important. Time enough to answer all the questions will be provided, but this does not mean that you have all day. An overall time limit has been set. Divide the total time (in minutes) by the number of questions to determine the approximate time you have for each question.

5) Do not linger over difficult questions

If you come across a difficult question, mark it with a paper clip (useful to have along) and come back to it when you have been through the booklet. One caution if you do this – be sure to skip a number on your answer sheet as well. Check often to be sure that you have not lost your place and that you are marking in the row numbered the same as the question you are answering.

6) Read the questions
Be sure you know what the question asks! Many capable people are unsuccessful because they failed to read the questions correctly.

7) Answer all questions
Unless you have been instructed that a penalty will be deducted for incorrect answers, it is better to guess than to omit a question.

8) Speed tests
It is often better NOT to guess on speed tests. It has been found that on timed tests people are tempted to spend the last few seconds before time is called in marking answers at random – without even reading them – in the hope of picking up a few extra points. To discourage this practice, the instructions may warn you that your score will be "corrected" for guessing. That is, a penalty will be applied. The incorrect answers will be deducted from the correct ones, or some other penalty formula will be used.

9) Review your answers
If you finish before time is called, go back to the questions you guessed or omitted to give them further thought. Review other answers if you have time.

10) Return your test materials
If you are ready to leave before others have finished or time is called, take ALL your materials to the monitor and leave quietly. Never take any test material with you. The monitor can discover whose papers are not complete, and taking a test booklet may be grounds for disqualification.

VIII. EXAMINATION TECHNIQUES

1) Read the general instructions carefully. These are usually printed on the first page of the exam booklet. As a rule, these instructions refer to the timing of the examination; the fact that you should not start work until the signal and must stop work at a signal, etc. If there are any special instructions, such as a choice of questions to be answered, make sure that you note this instruction carefully.

2) When you are ready to start work on the examination, that is as soon as the signal has been given, read the instructions to each question booklet, underline any key words or phrases, such as least, best, outline, describe and the like. In this way you will tend to answer as requested rather than discover on reviewing your paper that you listed without describing, that you selected the worst choice rather than the best choice, etc.

3) If the examination is of the objective or multiple-choice type – that is, each question will also give a series of possible answers: A, B, C or D, and you are called upon to select the best answer and write the letter next to that answer on your answer paper – it is advisable to start answering each question in turn. There may be anywhere from 50 to 100 such questions in the three or four hours allotted and you can see how much time would be taken if you read through all the questions before beginning to answer any. Furthermore, if you

come across a question or group of questions which you know would be difficult to answer, it would undoubtedly affect your handling of all the other questions.

4) If the examination is of the essay type and contains but a few questions, it is a moot point as to whether you should read all the questions before starting to answer any one. Of course, if you are given a choice – say five out of seven and the like – then it is essential to read all the questions so you can eliminate the two that are most difficult. If, however, you are asked to answer all the questions, there may be danger in trying to answer the easiest one first because you may find that you will spend too much time on it. The best technique is to answer the first question, then proceed to the second, etc.

5) Time your answers. Before the exam begins, write down the time it started, then add the time allowed for the examination and write down the time it must be completed, then divide the time available somewhat as follows:
    - If 3-1/2 hours are allowed, that would be 210 minutes. If you have 80 objective-type questions, that would be an average of 2-1/2 minutes per question. Allow yourself no more than 2 minutes per question, or a total of 160 minutes, which will permit about 50 minutes to review.
    - If for the time allotment of 210 minutes there are 7 essay questions to answer, that would average about 30 minutes a question. Give yourself only 25 minutes per question so that you have about 35 minutes to review.

6) The most important instruction is to read each question and make sure you know what is wanted. The second most important instruction is to time yourself properly so that you answer every question. The third most important instruction is to answer every question. Guess if you have to but include something for each question. Remember that you will receive no credit for a blank and will probably receive some credit if you write something in answer to an essay question. If you guess a letter – say "B" for a multiple-choice question – you may have guessed right. If you leave a blank as an answer to a multiple-choice question, the examiners may respect your feelings but it will not add a point to your score. Some exams may penalize you for wrong answers, so in such cases only, you may not want to guess unless you have some basis for your answer.

7) Suggestions
   a. Objective-type questions
      1. Examine the question booklet for proper sequence of pages and questions
      2. Read all instructions carefully
      3. Skip any question which seems too difficult; return to it after all other questions have been answered
      4. Apportion your time properly; do not spend too much time on any single question or group of questions
      5. Note and underline key words – all, most, fewest, least, best, worst, same, opposite, etc.
      6. Pay particular attention to negatives
      7. Note unusual option, e.g., unduly long, short, complex, different or similar in content to the body of the question
      8. Observe the use of "hedging" words – probably, may, most likely, etc.

9. Make sure that your answer is put next to the same number as the question
10. Do not second-guess unless you have good reason to believe the second answer is definitely more correct
11. Cross out original answer if you decide another answer is more accurate; do not erase until you are ready to hand your paper in
12. Answer all questions; guess unless instructed otherwise
13. Leave time for review

b. Essay questions
1. Read each question carefully
2. Determine exactly what is wanted. Underline key words or phrases.
3. Decide on outline or paragraph answer
4. Include many different points and elements unless asked to develop any one or two points or elements
5. Show impartiality by giving pros and cons unless directed to select one side only
6. Make and write down any assumptions you find necessary to answer the questions
7. Watch your English, grammar, punctuation and choice of words
8. Time your answers; don't crowd material

8) Answering the essay question

Most essay questions can be answered by framing the specific response around several key words or ideas. Here are a few such key words or ideas:

M's: manpower, materials, methods, money, management
P's: purpose, program, policy, plan, procedure, practice, problems, pitfalls, personnel, public relations

a. Six basic steps in handling problems:
1. Preliminary plan and background development
2. Collect information, data and facts
3. Analyze and interpret information, data and facts
4. Analyze and develop solutions as well as make recommendations
5. Prepare report and sell recommendations
6. Install recommendations and follow up effectiveness

b. Pitfalls to avoid
1. Taking things for granted – A statement of the situation does not necessarily imply that each of the elements is necessarily true; for example, a complaint may be invalid and biased so that all that can be taken for granted is that a complaint has been registered
2. Considering only one side of a situation – Wherever possible, indicate several alternatives and then point out the reasons you selected the best one
3. Failing to indicate follow up – Whenever your answer indicates action on your part, make certain that you will take proper follow-up action to see how successful your recommendations, procedures or actions turn out to be
4. Taking too long in answering any single question – Remember to time your answers properly

EXAMINATION SECTION

EXAMINATION SECTION
TEST 1

DIRECTIONS: Each question or incomplete statement is followed by several suggested answers or completions. Select the one that BEST answers the question or completes the statement. *PRINT THE LETTER OF THE CORRECT ANSWER IN THE SPACE AT THE RIGHT.*

1. In the normal human body, an increase in the amount of glucose in the blood stimulates the production of   1.____

    A. cortin B. insulin C. secretin
    D. iodine E. ptyalin

2. Exact similarity between chromosomes of the various cells within the same tissue of a plant or animal is LARGELY due to the mechanism of   2.____

    A. segregation B. meiosis C. mitosis
    D. fertilization E. maturation

3. Marriages of closely related persons are USUALLY inadvisable from a biological standpoint because   3.____

    A. undesirable recessive characters are more likely to appear in following generations
    B. such unions are likely to be sterile
    C. desirable characteristics, even when dominant, are less likely to be transmitted to future generations
    D. such unions generally produce physically weaker children
    E. at least one-fourth of the children are likely to be hemophiles

4. Much of the water entering an amoeba by osmosis is eliminated by the action of the   4.____

    A. contractile vacuole B. gastric vacuole
    C. ectoplasm D. cytoplasmic crystals
    E. pseudopodia

5. The rate of flow (quantity per second) of man's blood is GREATEST in the   5.____

    A. venae cavae B. radial artery
    C. portal vein D. capillaries
    E. aorta

6. MOST of the world's supply of sugar as a commercial product is obtained from _____ and _____.   6.____

    A. leaves; stems B. fruits; stems C. roots; stems
    D. seeds; stems E. seeds; roots

7. The essential cellular component divided and redistributed by the process of mitosis is the   7.____

    A. plasma membrane B. cytoplasm C. plastid
    D. chromatin E. central spindle

8. The discharge of adrenalin into the blood causes

    A. dilation of the blood vessels of the stomach
    B. increased absorption of sugar by the liver
    C. an increase in the speed and force of the heart beat
    D. constriction of the blood vessels of the muscles
    E. a slowing down of respiration

9. Synthesis of glucose from carbon dioxide and water in green plants occurs ONLY in the

    A. epidermis
    B. sieve tubes
    C. cambium
    D. chlorophyll-bearing cells
    E. root hairs

10. Identify the TRUE statement regarding syphilis.

    A. It is transmitted only by sexual contact.
    B. It attacks mainly the reproductive organs.
    C. Its treatment is the same as that for gonorrhea.
    D. Its transmission from one generation to the next follows Mendel's laws.
    E. It is possible to have a latent form of the disease without recognizable symptoms.

11. Similarities in the characteristics of identical twins are caused PRINCIPALLY by

    A. the presence of similar genes in all cells
    B. similar environmental conditions before birth
    C. similar environmental conditions after birth
    D. simultaneous fertilization of an ovum by two similar sperm cells
    E. identical genetic mutation

12. Gametes differ from spores in that gametes

    A. may unite and form zygotes
    B. are produced only by gametophytes
    C. are produced only by animals
    D. are capable of independent motion
    E. are always the larger in size

13. The poisonous effect on the human body of inhaled carbon monoxide is caused by its

    A. chemical action on lung tissue
    B. replacement of the oxygen in oxyhemoglobin
    C. insolubility in blood plasma
    D. forming insoluble precipitates in the blood
    E. paralyzing effect on the respiratory center of the brain

14. Tropisms of leaves are often produced DIRECTLY by

    A. turgor changes in certain cells
    B. contractions of wood fibers
    C. electrical conductivity of sieve tubes
    D. digestion of starch
    E. increase of sugar in the cells

15. A climax community is MOST likely to be found in regions where 15.____

    A. man has greatly modified his surroundings
    B. there are no dominant organisms
    C. conditions have remained relatively constant for a period of many years
    D. distinct changes in climatic conditions have recently occurred
    E. plants are relatively uniform in size

16. An internal secretion of the mucosa of the upper part of the small intestine stimulates the 16.____

    A. flow of ptyalin
    B. flow of pancreatic juices
    C. dilation of the cardiac sphincter
    D. production of thyroxin
    E. absorption of water in the large intestine

17. A hyperthyroid condition is characterized by 17.____

    A. low blood pressure
    B. a tendency toward obesity
    C. low body temperature
    D. increased metabolism
    E. severely retarded mental activity

18. Which of the following types of cells in the human male contains one-half the ordinary number of chromosomes? 18.____

    A. All of the somatic cells
    B. Somatic cell of the reproductive organs only
    C. Spermatozoa
    D. Primary spermatocytes
    E. T-Cells

Questions 19-20.

DIRECTIONS: Questions 19 and 20 are to be answered on the basis of the following information.
S = short-haired (dominant)
s = long-haired (recessive)

19. The parents of a litter of long-haired cats are 19.____

    A. SS+Ss   B. SS +ss   C. Ss+Ss
    D. Ss+ss   E. ss+ss

20. The parents of a litter of short-haired hybrid cats are MOST likely to be 20.____

    A. SS+Ss   B. SS+ss   C. Ss+Ss
    D. Ss+ss   E. SS+SS

Questions 21-23.

DIRECTIONS: Questions 21 through 23 are to be answered on the basis of the following diagram.

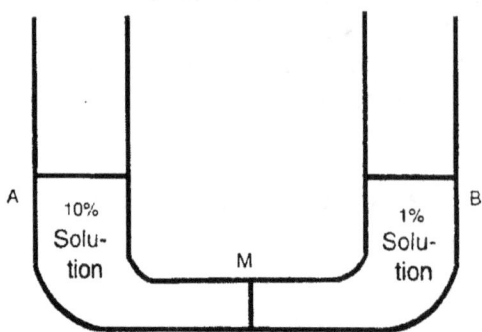

A 10% solution of cane sugar in water (A) is separated from a 1% solution of cane sugar in water (B) by a membrane (M) permeable to water but NOT to cane sugar. The levels of the two liquids are the same.

21. Molecules of water will pass through the membrane   21.___

    A. in one direction only
    B. in both directions at all times
    C. until the total number of molecules is the same on both sides
    D. only until the solution on one side is saturated
    E. only until a final constant difference in level is attained; then their passage will cease

22. When equilibrium between the two solutions is attained,   22.___

    A. the levels of the two solutions will be equal
    B. there will be an equal number of sugar molecules in each solution
    C. there will be an equal number of water molecules in each solution
    D. no molecules will pass through the membrane in either direction
    E. equal numbers of water molecules will be passing through the membrane in each direction

23. If the membrane were equally permeable to water and to sugar,   23.___

    A. the concentration in A and B would remain unchanged, even after a long period of time
    B. the concentration of sugar would ultimately become equal in A and B
    C. no diffusion would take place through the membrane
    D. the level in B would become ten times as high as in A
    E. there would be excessive pressure on the membrane

24. Some insects carry disease germs on their bodies and transmit diseases to man merely 24.___
    by contact. Other insects' bodies act as *culture tubes* in which the disease organisms
    pass a part of their life cycle.
    Which one of these insects is a *culture tube* type of carrier for the disease named after it?

    A. Housefly - tuberculosis   B. Mosquito - malaria
    C. Cockroach - typhoid fever   D. Housefly - common cold
    E. Body louse - typhus fever

25.

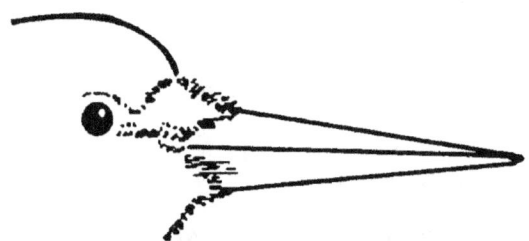

The bird beak shown above is of MOST value to its possessor for

    A. crushing seeds
    B. drilling for and extracting insects
    C. catching fish
    D. tearing flesh from bones
    E. capturing insects in flight

26. One of the MOST important functions of root hairs is to

    A. increase the plant's sensitivity to stimuli
    B. enable roots to penetrate deeper into the soil
    C. increase the root's total absorbing surface
    D. protect the delicate parts of the root from injury
    E. increase the total food storage capacity of the root

27. The presence of certain useless structures in man's body, such as the appendix and the muscles in the outer ears, may be an indication that

    A. man had a remote ancestor who used these organs
    B. man has always been as he is today
    C. man can regenerate organs at will
    D. these structures have helped man to survive
    E. man has undoubtedly descended from the monkey

28. Food is digested in the alimentary tract because

    A. the body needs energy
    B. food is required for building new cells
    C. oxidation would not take place unless the foods were digested
    D. man cannot live unless his nutrition requirements are met
    E. there are enzymes present which change the food into soluble form

29. Which one of the following traits distinguishes all birds from all reptiles?

    A. Birds lay eggs
    B. Birds have internal body skeletons
    C. Birds are warm-blooded
    D. In birds the nerve cord is dorsally located in the body
    E. Birds have legs

30. Each secretes hormones EXCEPT the

    A. pituitary gland
    B. lymph nodes
    C. parathyroid glands
    D. adrenal glands
    E. islets of the pancreas

31. Which is an example of sexual reproduction?

    A. Mature yeast plants develop outgrowths which, when shed, are the young yeast plants.
    B. A mature paramecium divides into two offspring.
    C. A fish hatchery worker pours some salmon milt into a jar of salmon eggs which later hatch into young salmon.
    D. A gardener plants pieces of potatoes containing *eyes* and later harvests a crop of potatoes.
    E. A fern plant produces many brown spores on the undersides of the leaves. These spores give rise to young plants.

32. It is sometimes desirable to mix a small amount of white clover seed with the grass seed when seeding a new lawn because the clover

    A. furnishes shade to the young grass plants when they first come up
    B. tends to crowd out weeds
    C. produces carbon dioxide
    D. protects the young grass plants from injury until the sod is well established
    E. has root structures which harbor nitrogen-fixing bacteria

33. A _____ is *cold-blooded*.

    A. frog
    B. goose
    C. bat
    D. whale
    E. polar bear

34. One of the MOST marked differences between animal cells and plant cells is that

    A. plant cells have chromosomes
    B. animal cells ordinarily have a nucleus
    C. animal cells contain protoplasm
    D. animal cells have a variety of shapes
    E. plant cells usually have thick, rigid walls

35. Blood flowing through the pulmonary veins is distinguished from blood flowing through the large jugular vein in the neck region in that the blood in the pulmonary veins

    A. carries disease-resisting substances known as antibodies
    B. contains nutrient substances, such as sugar, fats, and amino acids
    C. has more white blood cells
    D. carries a fresh supply of oxygen
    E. has a higher concentration of carbon dioxide

36. A group of organisms protected by a *suit of armor* is

    A. sponges
    B. arthropods
    C. amphibians
    D. roundworms
    E. primates

37. All EXCEPT _____ constitute real homes for living things.

    A. the oceans
    B. inland ponds and lakes
    C. the air over the earth
    D. swiftly flowing fresh-water streams
    E. the land mass of the earth

38. Why can a green plant continue to carry on photosynthesis after the oxygen surrounding it has been removed by a chemical absorbing agent?

    A. Green plants do not use oxygen.
    B. Green plants use carbon dioxide in respiration.
    C. Transpiration serves the same function in green plants as respiration does in animals.
    D. Green plants use nitrogen instead of oxygen.
    E. Green plants release free oxygen as a by-product in food manufacturing.

39. Four of the following offer evidence that living things have gone through long ages of gradual development on the earth.
    Which one does NOT offer evidence supporting this theory?

    A. Many fossils of animals and plants show series of changes from simple to complex forms.
    B. The whale has bones, which suggest that its ancestors may have had legs.
    C. A very young human embryo is hardly distinguishable from a very young fish embryo.
    D. The hand and arm of a man are similar, bone for bone, to the forefoot and foreleg of a horse.
    E. There is only one species of mankind living upon the earth at the present time.

40.

    The above skeleton indicates that the animal belonged to the _____ group.

    A. roundworm   B. arthropod   C. echinoderm
    D. chordate   E. mollusk

41. The GREATEST disturbers of the balance of nature have been

    A. the carnivorous animals
    B. the insects
    C. civilized people
    D. volcanoes and earthquakes
    E. bacteria and fungi

42. The Mediterranean fruit fly has eight chromosomes in each of its body cells. The normal number of chromosomes in one of its sperm cells or egg cells would, therefore, be

    A. two
    B. four
    C. eight
    D. sixteen
    E. thirty-two

43. A characteristic of the offspring of asexual reproduction is that they

    A. are apt to resemble each other and the parent more closely than is true of the offspring of sexual reproduction
    B. differ markedly from each other in hereditary traits
    C. are likely to show many mutations
    D. can adapt themselves better to changing environmental conditions than the offspring of sexual reproduction
    E. are very unpredictable as to the physical and genetic traits they will possess

44. Bone tissue is hard because

    A. the body needs a strong, rigid supporting framework
    B. the possession of an internal skeleton distinguishes the chordates from all other phyla of animals
    C. the muscles require places for attachment in order to function properly
    D. it is needed to protect delicate parts of the body from injury
    E. calcium compounds are deposited in the spaces between and around the cells

45. *So we may doubt whether, in cheese and timber, worms are generated or if beetles and wasps in cow dung, or if butterflies, shellfish, eels, and such life be procreated of putrefied matter. To question this is to question reason, sense, and experience. If he doubts this, let him go to Egypt, and there he will find the fields swarming with mice begot of the mud of the Nile, to the great calamity of the inhabitants.*
    In the above paragraph, the theory under question is that of

    A. sexual reproduction
    B. special creation
    C. spontaneous generation
    D. vegetative reproduction
    E. regeneration

46. The wings of India's *dead leaf* butterfly are shaped like a leaf and the undersides are colored like a dead leaf. This butterfly is an example of

    A. symbiosis
    B. protective resemblance
    C. warning coloration
    D. metamorphosis
    E. None of these

47. If you are about the right weight, the BEST way for you to stay that way is to

    A. exercise every day
    B. eat meals that contain enough vitamins and minerals
    C. cut out all desserts and snacks
    D. adjust your calorie intake to your calorie needs
    E. None of the above

48. It has been observed that increasing the amount of x-irradiation increases the number of mutations per thousand irradiated organisms.
Which graph indicates this process?

A.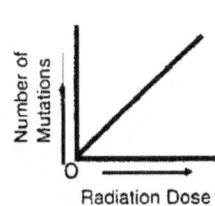

B.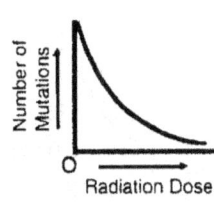

C.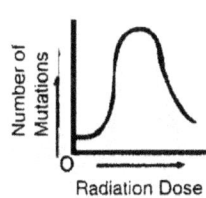

D.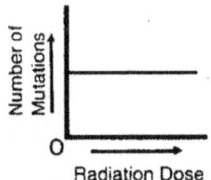

E. None of the above

49. Beans were growing in one garden patch and asparagus was growing in another adjacent patch. Equal amounts of salt were added to the soil in both patches. All of the beans died, and all of the asparagus lived.
Which is the MOST acceptable explanation for these observations?

   A. Asparagus plants can tolerate larger amounts of salt than beans can.
   B. Asparagus plants use the salt to build tissue.
   C. Some substance other than salt killed the beans.
   D. Bean plants do not need as much water as asparagus plants do.
   E. None of the above

50.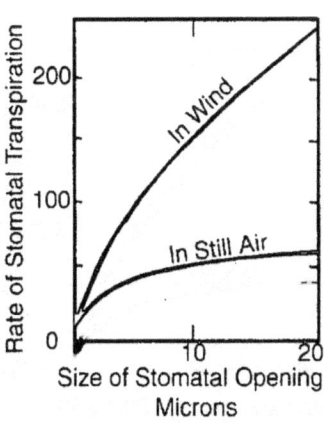

The above graph describes corn plants with equal areas of leaf surface.
A plant in _____ would PROBABLY lose water fastest.

   A. wind, stomatal openings 10 microns
   B. wind, stomatal openings 15 microns
   C. still air, stomatal openings 10 microns
   D. still air, openings 20 microns
   E. None of the above

KEY (CORRECT ANSWERS)

1. B	11. A	21. B	31. C	41. C
2. C	12. A	22. E	32. E	42. B
3. A	13. B	23. B	33. A	43. A
4. A	14. A	24. B	34. E	44. E
5. E	15. C	25. B	35. D	45. C
6. C	16. B	26. C	36. B	46. B
7. D	17. D	27. A	37. C	47. D
8. C	18. C	28. E	38. E	48. A
9. D	19. E	29. C	39. E	49. A
10. E	20. B	30. B	40. D	50. B

TEST 2

DIRECTIONS: Each question or incomplete statement is followed by several suggested answers or completions. Select the one that BEST answers the question or completes the statement. *PRINT THE LETTER OF THE CORRECT ANSWER IN THE SPACE AT THE RIGHT.*

1. Which one of the following statements regarding the endocrine glands is TRUE?   1.____
    A. The removal of any endocrine gland will cause death.
    B. Overactivity of a gland produces effects similar to those produced by underactivity.
    C. Large numbers of different kinds of hormones may be found in the alimentary canal.
    D. Overactivity of a gland may always be corrected by the administration of a synthetic hormone.
    E. The activity of one gland is often affected by the products of others.

2. Differences in genetic composition in similar-appearing individuals may be discovered experimentally by   2.____
    A. the use of x-rays
    B. the use of hormones
    C. a back-cross
    D. crossing-over
    E. regeneration

3. The variety of present day forms of animals and plants may be reasonably explained on the basis that   3.____
    A. each form has been specially created
    B. present forms have resulted from effort on the part of individual organisms to adapt themselves to changing environments
    C. any environmental change always produces structural changes that are hereditary
    D. all new forms are better fitted for survival than their predecessors
    E. all present forms have developed as results of variations that have occurred in previous generations

4. The parathyroid glands in man are important because certain processes in them influence the   4.____
    A. concentration of calcium in the blood
    B. metabolism of carbohydrates
    C. rate of growth
    D. sodium and potassium balance in the blood
    E. oxidative metabolism

5. Enzymes differ from inorganic catalysts in that enzymes   5.____
    A. are more resistant to extremes of temperature
    B. must be present in greater concentration to be effective
    C. are most effective at temperatures of about 212° F
    D. catalyze only specific reactions
    E. cannot be obtained in crystalline form

6. Chemical compounds in dead organisms are transformed into compounds usable by plants CHIEFLY by the action of

   A. inorganic elements in soil
   B. saprophytic bacteria and fungi
   C. parasitic fungi
   D. unicellular animals
   E. pathogenic microorganisms

7. Exchange of material between two homologous chromosomes in synapsis is known as

   A. fertilization
   B. linkage
   C. crossing-over
   D. hybridization
   E. cleavage

8. A person born with an underactive anterior lobe of the pituitary gland is LIKELY to be

   A. a cretin
   B. a giant
   C. a midget
   D. feeble-minded
   E. diabetic

9. The GREATEST amount of heat energy will be furnished to the body by complete oxidation of one gram of

   A. glucose
   B. sucrose
   C. starch
   D. fat
   E. protein

10. Inactivation of the vagus nerve results in

    A. an acceleration of the heart beat
    B. blindness
    C. loss of sensation of pain
    D. an increase in the flow of saliva
    E. impairment of the sense of taste

11. An animal's intelligence is correlated CHIEFLY with

    A. its ability to form conditioned reflexes
    B. the complexity of its pattern of instinctive behavior
    C. the sum of all its simple reflex actions
    D. the usefulness to the animal of its instinctive behavior
    E. the keenness of its sense organs

12. One difference between the nutrition of higher animals and plants is the relatively larger proportion of the animal's food

    A. used in the synthesis of carbohydrates
    B. used in the synthesis of organic components of protoplasm
    C. used in the synthesis of supporting tissue
    D. stored within the organism
    E. oxidized

13. During the development of a fruit from a flower, an ovule becomes the

    A. entire fruit
    B. fleshy part of the fruit
    C. endosperm
    D. embryo
    E. seed

14. The GREATEST degree of precipitation will be obtained when rabbit blood serum which has been immunized against human blood serum is mixed with diluted blood serum of

    A. non-immunized rabbits
    B. squirrels
    C. monkeys
    D. man-like apes
    E. man

15. A disease which might be contracted from some food that an individual has eaten is

    A. typhus fever
    B. anemia
    C. diabetes
    D. trichinosis
    E. ringworm

16. *The evidence seems to show beyond question that our present species of plants have descended...from simpler and fewer species which formerly existed—back, to a single kind which throve in remotest antiquity.*
    On the basis of this statement alone, it might follow that

    A. the number of species of plants is decreasing
    B. generally speaking, plants are becoming simpler
    C. an organism could become so complex that its very complexity would lead to its extinction
    D. the number of species of plants is increasing
    E. ancient plants were more successful than modern plants

17. An example of a flowering plant is a(n)

    A. fern
    B. mushroom
    C. moss
    D. arbor vitae
    E. corn

18. An individual could continue to live a fairly normal life after the removal or destruction of any EXCEPT one

    A. adrenal gland
    B. kidney
    C. lung
    D. cerebral hemisphere
    E. parathyroid gland

19. Two well-watered geranium plants, in sealed pots, were placed under two dry bell jars, X and Y. The leaves of the plant under Jar X were coated with vaseline on both upper and lower surfaces, while those of the plant under Jar Y were not coated. The two bell jars were then placed in bright sunlight for 8 hours.
    At the end of this time, what was the condition of the inside surface of the bell jars?

    A. Jar X showed less moisture than Jar Y.
    B. Jar X showed more moisture than Jar Y.
    C. Each jar was perfectly dry.
    D. Each jar was very moist with no noticeable difference in amount.
    E. Jar X was covered with many fine droplets of vaseline.

20. A man is able to maintain his balance when he sits, stands, or walks PRIMARILY because of the functioning of the

    A. medulla oblongata connecting the brain and the spinal cord
    B. adrenal glands secreting adrenalin into the blood stream
    C. spinal cord
    D. solar plexus or nerve center in the stomach region of the abdomen
    E. semicircular canals in the ears

21. What is the MOST important reason for cutting many branches off a deciduous tree that is to be transplanted? It

    A. prevents too great a water loss until the roots are reestablished
    B. tends to reduce the rate of photosynthesis
    C. increases the rate of water absorption
    D. increases the efficiency of food production
    E. exposes more surface to the atmosphere

22. When a sip of water goes *down the wrong way,* there is improper functioning of the

    A. larynx   B. trachea   C. pharynx
    D. epiglottis E. Eustachian tubes

23. Wheat is planted three years in succession in Field X, while soybeans are planted three years in succession in Field Y.
    The soil nitrogen will PROBABLY

    A. increase in Field X
    B. increase in Field Y
    C. decrease in Field Y
    D. decrease equally in both fields
    E. be unaffected in either field

Questions 24-26.

DIRECTIONS: For each of Questions 24 through 26, select the organism that belongs to a different phylum from the other four.

24. A. Sunfish   B. Starfish   C. Trout
    D. Bass   E. Codfish

25. A. Pine   B. Sunflower   C. Oak
    D. Fern   E. Dandelion

26. A. Ameba   B. Paramecium   C. Euglena
    D. Malarial parasite E. Hydra

27. On the basis of photosynthesis and conditions necessary for this process to occur, it should be possible to produce a marked increase in plant growth in a closed greenhouse room by

    A. slowly releasing a continuous supply of carbon dioxide into the room from a carbon dioxide tank
    B. drying the air in the room with a calcium chloride apparatus
    C. providing electric light during the day in addition to the usual sunlight
    D. uncapping a bottle containing a chlorophyll solution and allowing its vapors to pass into the air in the room
    E. slowly releasing a continuous supply of pure oxygen into the room from an oxygen tank

28. External fertilization in animals is MOST often associated with

    A. a land habitat
    B. small size
    C. parental care of the young
    D. asexual reproduction
    E. living in water

29. Which statement might BEST account for the fact that the trout, which is a very active fish, is most frequently found in the swift, well-churned type of stream?

    A. Swiftly flowing water contains less decaying organic matter.
    B. The trout escapes most of its natural enemies by living in the rapids.
    C. Water in the rapids is more highly oxygenated than relatively still water.
    D. Food is more easily caught in a swiftly flowing stream.
    E. The trout gets considerable satisfaction from skirting danger.

30. When blood passes through the pancreas, the amount of _____ in the blood _____.

    A. digestive enzyme; increases
    B. insulin; increases
    C. sugar; increases
    D. adrenalin; increases
    E. hormone; decreases

31. The scientific name of the leopard frog is *Rana pipiens* and that of the bullfrog is *Rana catesbiana*.
    These scientific names indicate that both frogs belong to the same

    A. genus   B. species   C. class   D. order   E. family

32. Wheat rust can be eliminated BEST by

    A. dusting wheat fields with insect poisons
    B. encouraging ladybird beetles to multiply rapidly
    C. spreading lime on the fields before plowing
    D. getting rid of all common barberry bushes in the vicinity
    E. draining the swamps and wet lands in that region

Questions 33-39.

DIRECTIONS: Questions 33 through 39 are on the MOST effective measures for preventing certain diseases. For each disease named, select from the following KEY the best preventive.

33. Yellow fever

34. Anemia

35. Diphtheria

36. Rabies

37. Rickets

38. Night blindness

39. Undulant fever

KEY
A. Water treatment and milk pasteurization
B. Eradication of insect carriers
C. An addition to or a subtraction from one's diet
D. Immunization, such as vaccination or inoculation
E. Eugenics

Questions 40-43.

DIRECTIONS: For Questions 40 through 43, select from the following KEY the scientific classification which might be applied to each statement.

<u>KEY</u>
A. Generalization
B. Problem
C. Fact by definition
D. Hypothesis
E. Fact by demonstration

40. Would an orchardist who raises cherries for the market consider the robin a harmful or a beneficial bird?   40.___

41. The robin may have developed in antiquity from reptile ancestors.   41.___

42. Why do robins migrate to southern latitudes in the winter?   42.___

43. All members of the thrush family of birds have spotted breasts, either in the young or in the adult stage.   43.___

44. According to current theories, what is the order in which the following plants appeared on Earth, the earliest listed FIRST?   44.___
   I. Ferns
   II. Angiosperms
   III. Algae
   The CORRECT answer is:

   A. I, II, III   B. I, III, II   C. II, I, III
   D. III, I, II   E. II, III, I

45. In a kidney transplant, a person would have the BEST chance for the organ to be accepted by his body if the kidney came from his   45.___

   A. brother   B. fraternal twin   C. mother
   D. identical twin   E. father

46.

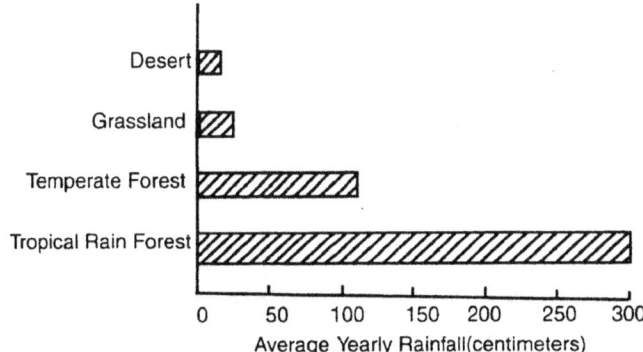

Identify the conclusion MOST closely related to the information presented in the above graph.

A. There is a relationship between temperature and the types of plants existing in an ecosystem.
B. The amount of available water is a factor that determines the types of plants growing in a region.
C. Areas of limited rainfall have the widest variety of plants.
D. There is a relationship between latitude and the types of plants existing in an ecosystem.
E. None of the above

Questions 47-48.

DIRECTIONS: Questions 47 and 48 are to be answered on the basis of the following graph.

BODY TEMPERATURE OF FOUR SPECIES OF ANIMALS
AT VARIOUS EXTERNAL TEMPERATURE

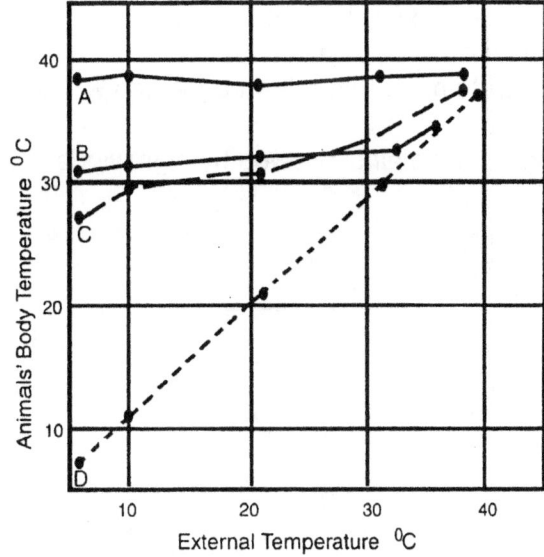

47. Which curve represents a cold-blooded animal?

A. A
B. B
C. C
D. D
E. None of these

48. Which curve represents an animal that is warm-blooded and whose temperature is LEAST affected by changes in external temperature? 48._____

    A. A
    B. B
    C. C
    D. D
    E. None of the above

Questions 49-50.

DIRECTIONS: Questions 49 and 50 are to be answered on the basis of the following illustration.

49. In the scene above, _____ has occurred. 49._____

    A. a dust storm
    B. sheet erosion
    C. gullying
    D. a snowstorm
    E. a flood

50. The MOST probable cause of this occurrence was 50._____

    A. overgrazing range land followed by floods
    B. forest removal followed by heavy rains
    C. a sudden drop in temperature followed by high winds
    D. a forest fire
    E. wheat farming on dry plains followed by high winds

KEY (CORRECT ANSWERS)

1. E	11. A	21. A	31. A	41. D
2. C	12. E	22. D	32. D	42. B
3. E	13. E	23. B	33. B	43. A
4. A	14. E	24. B	34. C	44. D
5. D	15. D	25. D	35. D	45. D
6. B	16. D	26. E	36. D	46. B
7. C	17. E	27. A	37. C	47. D
8. C	18. D	28. E	38. C	48. A
9. D	19. A	29. C	39. A	49. A
10. A	20. E	30. B	40. B	50. E

TEST 3

DIRECTIONS: Each question or incomplete statement is followed by several suggested answers or completions. Select the one that BEST answers the question or completes the statement. *PRINT THE LETTER OF THE CORRECT ANSWER IN THE SPACE AT THE RIGHT.*

1. Three groups of tadpoles of the same age were placed in a bowl containing pond water. The pituitary glands of the tadpoles in Group I were removed; the thyroid glands of the tadpoles in Group II were removed; and the tadpoles of Group II were left intact. In two weeks, only the tadpoles of Group III began to change into frogs.
   These observations are evidence that in frogs, the

   A. thyroid gland controls metamorphosis
   B. pituitary gland controls metamorphosis
   C. pituitary gland controls the thyroid gland
   D. thyroid and pituitary glands are both necessary for metamorphosis
   E. none of the above

   1.____

2. John said that bean seeds sprout faster in the dark than in the light.
   Of the following, the BEST way for him to test this idea would be to moisten the seeds and then place

   A. some of the seeds in a dark refrigerator and the rest in sunlight
   B. all of the seeds in the sunlight for short periods of time and then move them into the dark
   C. some of the seeds in the dark and the rest in the light at the same temperature
   D. some of the seeds in the ground and the rest under a sunlamp
   E. none of the above

   2.____

3. Which of the following would account for a fossil oyster found in your backyard?

   A. The oyster was probably fossilized by a volcanic eruption.
   B. Your backyard was probably once under water for a long time.
   C. The earth in your backyard is acid.
   D. The oyster evolved from a water animal to a land form.
   E. None of the above

   3.____

4. As two students watched two squirrels in a park, the students made specific comments. Which of these comments was an assumption rather than an observation?

   A. The squirrels are getting ready to fight.
   B. One of the squirrels is moving faster than the other.
   C. The squirrels are not the same color.
   D. One of the squirrels dropped his nut.
   E. None of the above

   4.____

5. The usual biological classification of plants and animals is based PRIMARILY on

   A. age   B. structure
   C. geographical distribution   D. size
   E. color

   5.____

20

6. The CHIEF reason it is harder to breathe at high altitudes than at low ones is that at high altitudes

   A. the temperatures are lower
   B. there are fewer plants
   C. there is more CO_2
   D. the air pressure is lower
   E. None of the above

   6._____

7. An animal is surely a bird if it

   A. flies
   C. has feathers
   E. has webbed feet
   B. lays eggs that hatch
   D. is warm-blooded

   7._____

8. The featherlike gills of most species of fish PRIMARILY provide a

   A. large amount of surface area for the exchange of gases
   B. pump for the rapid flow of blood through the gill filaments
   C. filter for obtaining small particles of food from the water
   D. means for breaking down water into hydrogen and oxygen
   E. None of the above

   8._____

Questions 9-26.

DIRECTIONS: In each of the following groups of items, there are Several statements, phrases, or terms, each of which characterizes or suggests one of the five words or phrases listed above the questions. For each question, select that word or phrase from the above list to which it applies, or with which it is MOST significantly associated, and put the letter of your choice in the space at the right.

Questions 9-11.

   A. Conjugation
   B. Hybridization
   C. Maturation
   D. Inbreeding
   E. Dominance

9. The breeding of parents CLOSELY related to each other.

   9._____

10. Crossbreeding of parents differing in one or more hereditary characteristics.

    10._____

11. The appearance of ONLY one of two contrasting characters when the potentialities of both are present in an individual.

    11._____

Questions 12-14.

    A. Ovum
    B. Uterus
    C. Vagina
    D. Ovary
    E. Oviduct

12. An egg; the female reproductive cell which, after fertilization, develops into a new member of the same species. 12.___

13. An organ in which the eggs or young of animals are retained during embryonic development. 13.___

14. An organ in which animal egg cells are produced. 14.___

Questions 15-17.

    A. Dihybrid
    B. Genotype
    C. Mutant
    D. Phenotype
    E. Homozygote

15. An individual described or recognized by its visible characters WITHOUT reference to its hereditary factors. 15.___

16. An individual whose parents differ with respect to two pairs of hereditary characters. 16.___

17. An individual possessing an abrupt and heritable variation differing from any of its ancestors. 17.___

Questions 18-20.

    A. Taxonomy
    B. Paleontology
    C. Cytology
    D. Anatomy
    E. Ecology

18. The scientific study of organisms of past geological periods, based on fossil remains. 18.___

19. The study of the structures and physiology of cells. 19.___

20. The study of the relations of organisms to each other and to their environment. 20.___

Questions 21-23.

    A. Diastole
    B. Peristalsis
    C. Flexion
    D. Tonus
    E. Extension

21. A wave-like series of muscular contractions, progressing along the walls of various tubes of the body, propelling their contents.   21.____

22. A movement that bends one part upon another.   22.____

23. The stage of dilation of the heart or relaxation of the heart muscle.   23.____

Questions 24-26.

    A. Blood
    B. Neurilemma
    C. Biceps
    D. Neuron
    E. Retina of the eye

24. Epithelial tissue   24.____

25. Vascular tissue   25.____

26. Muscular tissue   26.____

27. Identify the TRUE statement regarding the preservation of animal and plant remains.   27.____

    A. The most perfect fossils have been found in metamorphosed rock.
    B. Petrifaction preserves the organism without chemical change.
    C. Most ancient plants and animals ultimately were fossilized.
    D. Complete bodies of large animals have been preserved for thousands of years by low temperatures.
    E. Proterozoic rock is an abundant source of fossils.

28. Injection of pure water into the blood of an animal may indirectly cause its death by   28.____

    A. chemical reaction with hemoglobin
    B. plasmolysis of the corpuscles
    C. increasing external pressure upon the corpuscles
    D. swelling and bursting of the corpuscles
    E. destroying the permeability of the plasma membrane of the corpuscles

29. It is probable that the earliest organisms on the earth were MOST similar to present day   29.____

    A. saprophytic bacteria or fungi
    B. parasitic bacteria
    C. autophytic (autotrophic) bacteria or simple algae
    D. amoeba-like protozoans
    E. lichens

30. Mitotic cell division takes place   30.____

    A. principally in germ cells
    B. more commonly than any other form of cell division in organisms other than the lowest forms
    C. mainly in one-celled organisms
    D. mainly in vertebrates
    E. only under the influence of unfavorable conditions

31. The division of the Class Insecta into orders is made CHIEFLY on the basis of

   A. geographical distribution
   B. complexity of structures
   C. wing structure and mouth parts
   D. size and color
   E. egg-laying habits

32. The diploid number of chromosomes would be found in cells taken from what part of a moss plant?

   A. Archegonium   B. Antheridium   C. Protonema
   D. Calyptra   E. Capsule

33. The existence of cellulose-digesting protozoa in the intestines of termites is an example of

   A. a symbiotic relationship
   B. pathogenic parasitism
   C. saprophytism
   D. ecological succession
   E. a predatory relationship

34. Evidence of man's possible existence in the Pliocene Period is the discovery in sedimentary strata of that period of

   A. crude stone implements or eoliths
   B. crude metallic ornaments
   C. pottery
   D. complete skeletons of man-like creatures
   E. fossil remains of domesticated animals

35. Which one of the following is thought to have borne the GREATEST physical resemblance to man of today?

   A. Pithecanthropus erectus   B. Cro-Magnon man
   C. Neanderthal man   D. Piltdown man
   E. Peking man

36. The evolution of land plants from the Thallophytes to the Spermatophytes has been GENERALLY characterized by a(n)

   A. *decrease* in structural size of the sexual generation
   B. *increase* in the structural size and importance of the sexual generation
   C. *decrease* in the functional importance of the sexual generation
   D. *decreased* dependence on other plants and animals
   E. *decrease* in number of complex structures

37. Colorblindness in man is a recessive sex-linked character. How many of the children of a colorblind mother and a father with normal vision will be colorblind?

   A. All of the children
   B. One-half of the girls and one-half of the boys
   C. All of the girls and none of the boys
   D. All of the boys and none of the girls
   E. None of the children

38. Asphyxiation or suffocation victims are sometimes given a mixture of oxygen and carbon dioxide rather than pure oxygen because the carbon dioxide

    A. stimulates the respiratory center in the medulla
    B. decreases the danger to the victim of a shock resulting from sudden administration of pure oxygen
    C. increases the speed with which gases pass through the lung tissue
    D. decreases the viscosity of the blood
    E. directly stimulates the rib muscles

38.____

39. The organism which is LEAST dependent upon other organisms for the procurement of essential food substances is

    A. an amoeba
    B. an autophytic (autotrophic) bacterium
    C. a mushroom
    D. bread mold
    E. man

39.____

40. Iodide is added to salt to keep people from developing goiters. The reason for using the iodide is MOST similar to the reason for

    A. applying antiseptic to a cut
    B. taking aspirin for a fever
    C. adding chlorine to water to kill bacteria
    D. adding fluoride to drinking water to prevent tooth decay

40.____

41. Which of the following is PROBABLY a drawing of plant cells?

    A.
    B.
    C.
    D.
    E. None of the above

41.____

42. The significance of meiosis for heredity lies in which statement?

    A. The great variety of gene combinations that it makes possible
    B. The doubling of the chromosome number in the sex cells of the offspring
    C. The production of offspring identical with the parents
    D. The potential for many offspring
    E. None of the above

42.____

43. An experimenter wants to know whether a mouse is more likely to turn left or right in a maze. 43.____
Which experimental design is BEST for this purpose?

A.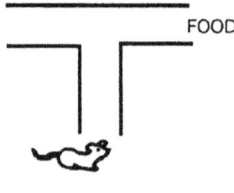

B.

C.

D.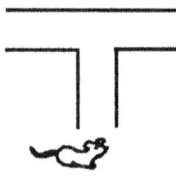

E. None of the above

44. Two plants with pink flowers were crossed, and the following results were obtained: 27 red, 31 white, and 63 pink-flowered plants. 44.____
These data indicate that the color of the pink flowers is due to

   A. sex-linked recessiveness
   B. sex-linked dominance
   C. incomplete dominance
   D. translocation
   E. chromotropsin

45. What is the BEST reason why only consumer organisms and very few producer organisms are found at great ocean depths? 45.____

   A. In deep water, consumer organisms ingest any producer organisms at a rate that prevents reproduction of the producers.
   B. Photosynthesis requires the presence of light.
   C. Increased pressure favors the survival of heterotrophs and not of autotrophs.
   D. Autotrophs are independent of heterotrophs in deep water.
   E. The enormous pressure inhibits growth.

Questions 46-47.

DIRECTIONS: Questions 46 and 47 are to be answered on the basis of the following diagram of the food web.

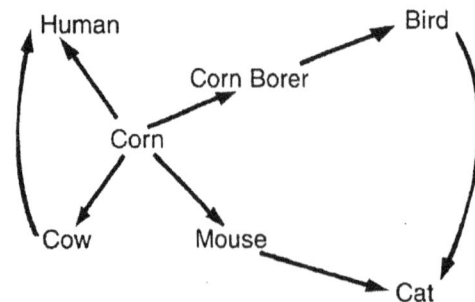

46. Which of these is a PRIMARY producer in this food web? 46._____

   A. Bird   B. Cat   C. Corn   D. Human   E. Mouse

47. The food web above includes _____ primary (first-order) consumers? 47._____

   A. One   B. Two   C. Three   D. Four   E. Five

Questions 48-50.

DIRECTIONS: Questions 48 through 50 are to be answered on the basis of the following table.

POPULATION RECORDS FOR 9 SPECIES OF BIRDS THAT APPEARED TO BE MOST SERIOUSLY AFFECTED BY APPLICATION OF DDT DUST ON A 40-ACRE PLOT

SPECIES	NO. OF BIRDS COUNTED BEFORE DUSTING	NUMBER OF BIRDS COUNTED DURING FIRST 6 DAYS AFTER DUSTING					
		1st Day	2nd Day	3rd Day	4th Day	5th Day	6th Day
Texas wren	3	2	2	1	0	0	0
Carolina wren	5	1	0	0	0	0	0
Kentucky warbler	1	0	0	0	0	0	0
Yellow-breasted chat	3	0	0	0	0	0	0
Cardinal	10	8	6	5	2	1	1
Blue grosbeak	2	0	0	0	0	0	0
Painted bunting	4	4	3	2	2	0	0
Lark sparrow	8	2	2	2	2	1	1
Field sparrow	5	4	4	4	3	3	1
Total	41	21	17	14	9	5	3

Study the above table and read each question carefully. Then, in the space at the right, mark the letter of your answer according to the KEY below.

KEY
   A. The table tends to support the statement.
   B. The table tends to contradict the statement.
   C. The table furnishes no conclusive evidence, either supporting or contradicting the statement.

48. Within two days after application of DDT to the 40-acre plot, a decrease in numbers was noted in all nine species of birds listed. 48._____

49. Ground-nesting birds were MOST seriously affected by the spreading of DDT over the plot. 49._____

50. DDT MUST be used with extreme caution in areas occupied by birds. 50._____

KEY (CORRECT ANSWERS)

1. D	11. E	21. B	31. C	41. D
2. C	12. A	22. C	32. E	42. A
3. B	13. B	23. A	33. A	43. D
4. A	14. D	24. E	34. A	44. C
5. B	15. D	25. A	35. B	45. B
6. D	16. A	26. C	36. A	46. C
7. C	17. C	27. D	37. D	47. D
8. A	18. B	28. D	38. A	48. A
9. D	19. C	29. C	39. B	49. C
10. B	20. E	30. B	40. D	50. A

EXAMINATION SECTION
TEST 1

DIRECTIONS: Each question or incomplete statement is followed by several suggested answers or completions. Select the one that BEST answers the question or completes the statement. *PRINT THE LETTER OF THE CORRECT ANSWER IN THE SPACE AT THE RIGHT.*

1. A certain bacterium has the ability to make Substance D from Substance A through a series of steps:

    A → B → C → D

    Each step is dependent on the presence of an enzyme:
    Enzyme 1 Enzyme 2 Enzyme 3

    A → B → C → D

    A mutant form of the bacterium can make D ONLY if B is provided by the experimenter even though the mutant bacterium is found to contain adequate amounts of A. This result is explained by the fact that the mutant bacterium lacks

    A. Enzyme 1 *only*
    B. Enzyme 2 *only*
    C. Enzyme 3
    D. both Enzymes 1 and 2
    E. Enzyme 1, 2 and 3

    1.____

2. _____ act as the PRINCIPAL site of protein synthesis in cells.

    A. Vacuoles
    B. Spindle fibers
    C. Centrosomes
    D. Ribosomes
    E. Mitochondria

    2.____

3. For every human birth, the chance that the child will be a girl is one in two or 50 percent. The basic fact supporting this prediction is that

    A. the child's mother has two X chromosomes
    B. during meiosis, the chromosome number is reduced by half
    C. the child's father has one X chromosome and one Y chromosome
    D. during fertilization, the chromosome number is restored to the full value of 46
    E. None of the above

    3.____

4. A student does an experiment to determine the effects of different concentrations of fertilizer on plant growth. She starts with five groups of plants all of the same species and of nearly equal size.
    The experimental treatment is as follows
    Group I: 50 ml/day of a 5% fertilizer solution
    Group II: 50 ml/day of a 10% fertilizer solution
    Group III: 50 ml/day of a 15% fertilizer solution
    Group IV: 50 ml/day of a 20% fertilizer solution
    Group V serves as a control
    What treatment should Group V receive?

    A. 50 ml of full-strength fertilizer not diluted in solution
    B. 50 ml of fertilizer solution, the concentration the average of that of the other four solutions

    4.____

C. 50 ml of water and no fertilizer
D. Neither water nor fertilizer
E. 50 ml of water and 50 ml of fertilizer

5. In human beings, energy is used for all of the following EXCEPT the

   A. contraction of muscles
   B. maintenance of breathing
   C. maintenance of body temperature on cold days
   D. manufacture of food from CO_2 and H_2O
   E. exchange of blood gases

6. Insects introduced into a new environment may become serious pests PRINCIPALLY because

   A. the insects can make efficient use of the food in the new environment
   B. the insects and birds that usually prey on them are missing
   C. change leads to adaptations and survival of the fittest
   D. waste products of the insects have not yet reached a significant level of concentration in the new environment
   E. None of the above

7. The two hosts necessary for the completion of the life cycle of the sheep liver fluke are the sheep and a

   A. human being   B. pig
   C. rabbit   D. mosquito
   E. fresh-water snail

8. _____ in insects are physiologically comparable to the kidneys in man.

   A. Trachese   B. Malpighian tubules
   C. Nephridia   D. Ovipositors
   E. Green glands

9. The MOST practical control of wheat rust (Puccinia graminis) so far discovered is

   A. the destruction of one of its hosts
   B. the introduction and propagation of its natural enemies
   C. chemical treatment of the seed before planting
   D. control of insects that might spread spores of the fungus
   E. the spraying of infected fields

10. _____ is an event in the formation and discharge of the human egg which precedes the other four.

    A. Discharge of the egg from the ovary
    B. Rupture of the Graafian follicle
    C. Formation of the corpus luteum
    D. Formation of the follicular hormone (estrone)
    E. Formation of progestin (progesterone)

11. The FALSE statement about both aerobic and anaerobic respiration is that they   11._____

    A. produce ATP
    B. can use glucose as a substrate
    C. produce CO_2
    D. require oxygen
    E. All of the above

Questions 12-26.

DIRECTIONS: In Questions 12 through 26, each letter refers to the structure labeled with the same letter in the diagram below. For each item, select one of the five lettered words or phrases that appears above each set of questions which applies to the structure, and put the letter of your choice in the space at the right.

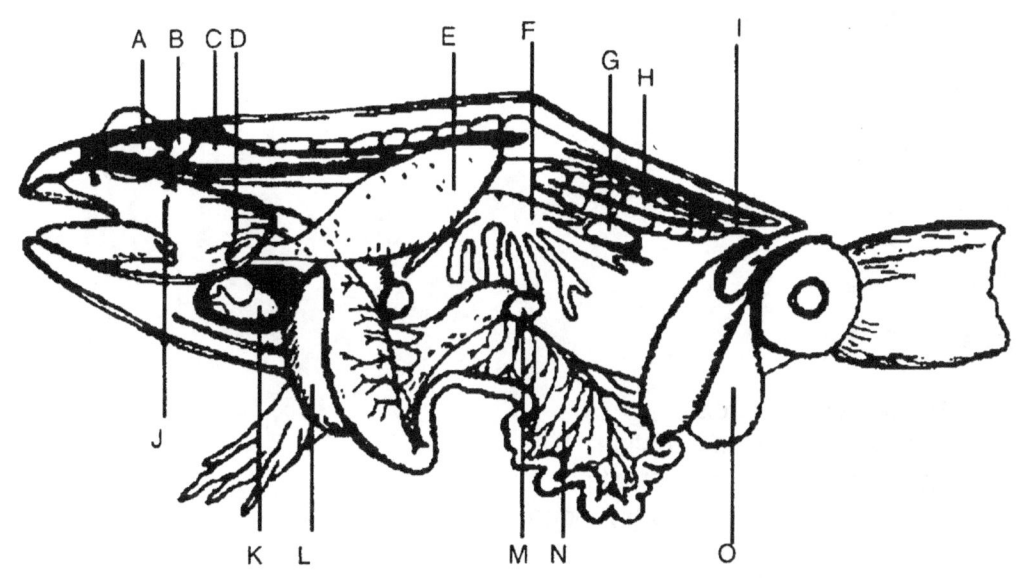

DISSECTION OF MALE FROG

Questions 12-14.

    A. Cerebrum
    B. Cerebellum
    C. Medulla
    D. Optic lobe
    E. Olfactory lobe

12. The structure at A is the   12._____

13. The structure at B is the   13._____

14. The structure at C is the   14._____

Questions 15-17.

    A. Spleen
    B. Testis
    C. Gall bladder
    D. Cloaca
    E. Kidney

15. The structure at G is the

16. The structure at H is the

17. The structure at M is the

Questions 18-20.

    A. Admits air to the mouth from the nostrils
    B. Admits food to the esophagus
    C. Admits air to the lungs
    D. Equalizes pressure on the two sides of the tympanum
    E. Aerates the blood

18. The structure at D

19. The structure at E

20. The structure at J

Questions 21-23.

    A. Produces spermatozoa
    B. Carries blood to the intestine
    C. Stores food in the form of fats
    D. Stores carbohydrates as glycogen
    E. Carries urine and sperm

21. The structure at F

22. The structure at L

23. The structure at I

Questions 24-26.

    A. Forces blood through the arteries
    B. Supports the digestive system
    C. Furnishes oxygen to the blood
    D. Stores liquid wastes
    E. Extracts digested food by osmosis

24. The structure at K

25. The structure at N

26. The structure at O

Questions 27-32.

DIRECTIONS: Questions 27 through 32 are to be answered on the basis of the following diagram. For each question, select one of the five lettered words or phrases that appears above each set of questions which applies to the question, and put the letter of your choice in the space at the right.

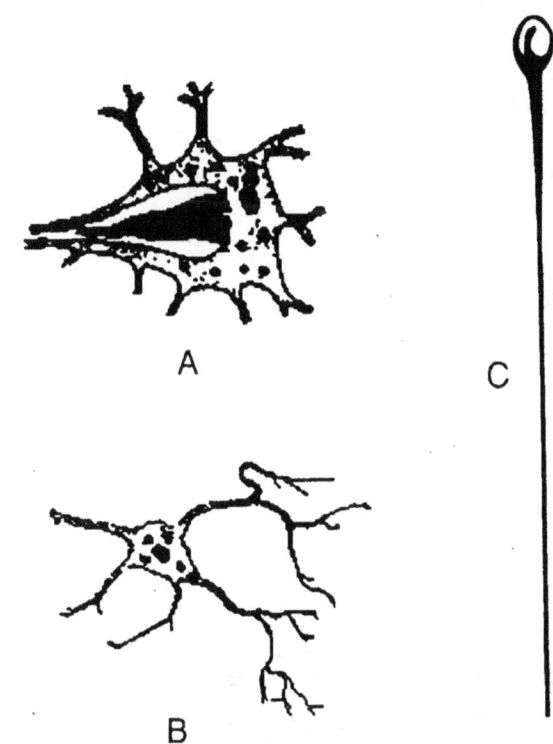

Questions 27-29.

    A. A flame cell
    B. An interstitial cell
    C. A nerve cell
    D. A sperm cell
    E. A phagocyte

27. Diagram A represents   27.____

28. Diagram B represents   28.____

29. Diagram C represents   29.____

Questions 30-32.

    A. Transmits paternal factors
    B. Paralyzes enemies of the hydra
    C. Transmits nerve impulses
    D. Digests foreign organisms in blood
    E. Excretes wastes in flatworms

30. The structure in Diagram A   30.___

31. The structure in Diagram B   31.___

32. The structure in Diagram C   32.___

Questions 33-35.

DIRECTIONS: Questions 33 through 35 are to be answered on the basis of the following diagrams. For each question, select one of the five lettered words or phrases that appears above the questions which applies to the question, and put the letter of your choice in the space at the right.

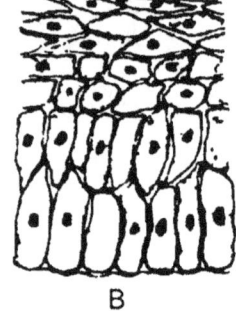
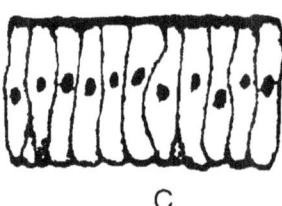

A   B   C

    A. Mammalian erythrocytes
    B. Amphibian erythrocytes
    C. Squamous epithelium
    D. Columnar epithelium
    E. Stratified epithelium

33. Diagram A represents   33.___

34. Diagram B represents   34.___

35. Diagram C represents   35.___

Questions 36-41.

DIRECTIONS: Questions 36 through 41 are to be answered on the basis of the following diagrams. For each question, select one of the five lettered words or phrases that appears above each set of the questions which applies to the question, and put the letter of your choice in the space at the right.

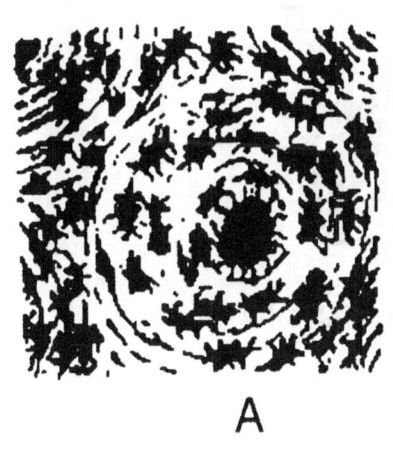
A

B

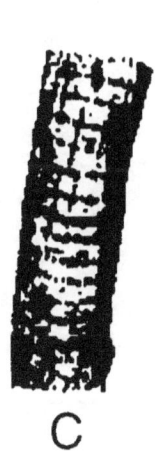
C

Questions 36-38.

    A. Striated muscle
    B. A smooth muscle cell
    C. Cartilage
    D. Bone
    E. Fibrous connective tissue

36. Diagram A represents   36._____

37. Diagram B represents   37._____

38. Diagram C represents   38._____

Questions 39-41.

    A. Absorbs shocks by its resiliency
    B. Produces movement of the limbs
    C. Produces peristaltic movement
    D. Connects striated muscle with bone
    E. Gives rigidity to the vertebrate

39. The structure in Diagram A   39._____

40. The structure in Diagram B   40._____

41. The structure in Diagram C   41._____

Questions 42-50.

DIRECTIONS: In Questions 42 through 50, each letter refers to the structure labeled with the same letter in the diagram below. For each item, select one of the five lettered words or phrases that appears above each set of questions which applies to the structure, and put the letter of your choice in the space at the right.

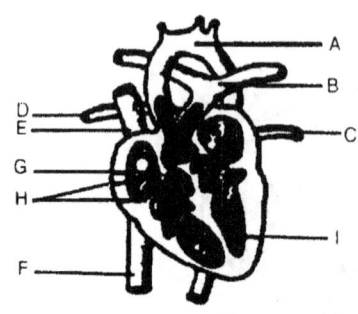

MAMMALIAN HEART

Questions 42-44.

42. A represents
43. B represents
44. C represents

A. Superior vena cava
B. Sinus venosus
C. Aorta
D. Pulmonary vein
E. Pulmonary artery

42.___
43.___
44.___

Questions 45-47.

45. The structure at D
46. The structure at E
47. The structure at F

A. Carries venous blood from the upper part of the body
B. Carries venous blood from the lower part of the body
C. Carries blood under the highest pressure in the body
D. Carries oxygenated blood from the right lung
E. Carries oxygenated blood to the right side of the body

45.___
46.___
47.___

Questions 48-50.

48. The structure at G
49. The structure at H
50. The structure at I

A. Receives oxygenated blood from the lungs
B. Prevents flow of blood from ventricle to auricle
C. Changes pulsating to smoothly flowing blood
D. Receives blood with high carbon dioxide content
E. Pumps arterial blood

48.___
49.___
50.___

KEY (CORRECT ANSWERS)

1.	A	11.	D	21.	C	31.	C	41.	B
2.	D	12.	A	22.	D	32.	A	42.	C
3.	C	13.	D	23.	E	33.	A	43.	E
4.	C	14.	C	24.	A	34.	E	44.	D
5.	D	15.	B	25.	B	35.	D	45.	D
6.	B	16.	E	26.	D	36.	D	46.	A
7.	E	17.	A	27.	A	37.	B	47.	B
8.	B	18.	C	28.	C	38.	A	48.	D
9.	A	19.	E	29.	D	39.	E	49.	B
10.	D	20.	D	30.	E	40.	C	50.	E

TEST 2

DIRECTIONS: Each question or incomplete statement is followed by several suggested answers or completions. Select the one that BEST answers the question or completes the statement. *PRINT THE LETTER OF THE CORRECT ANSWER IN THE SPACE AT THE RIGHT.*

1. A characteristic of the close of the Mesozoic Era was the

   A. formation of coal deposits
   B. dominance of cycads
   C. extinction of dinosaurs
   D. origin of primates
   E. origin of man

   1.____

2. Starvation in animals leads to the consumption of the reserves of the organic materials in the organs and organic materials in the organs and body cells.
The LIKELY order for consuming these substances is

   A. fats, proteins, and carbohydrates
   B. fats, carbohydrates, and proteins
   C. carbohydrates, proteins, and fats
   D. carbohydrates, fats, and proteins
   E. proteins, fats, and carbohydrates

   2.____

3. The effectiveness of a septic tank made for the disposal of sewage depends PRINCIPALLY on the action of

   A. filtrable viruses   B. bacteriophage
   C. aerobic bacteria   D. anaerobic bacteria
   E. nitrifying bacteria

   3.____

4. In man, lymph is returned to the bloodstream in the

   A. skin capillaries   B. glomeruli
   C. alveoli   D. inferior vena cava
   E. subclavian vein

   4.____

5. A HIGHLY branched digestive tract that transports digested food directly to the tissues, and the virtual absence of a circulatory system are characteristic of

   A. earthworms   B. flatworms   C. mollusks
   D. crustaceans   E. spiders

   5.____

6. In a growing root tip, root hairs FIRST appear

   A. at the root cap
   B. in the mature region
   C. in the region of differentiation
   D. in the region of elongation
   E. at the growing point

   6.____

7. The _____ develops from the embryonic endoderm in man.

   A. nervous system
   B. inner epithelium of the lungs

   7.____

C. muscles
D. bones
E. circulatory system

8. The Y-chromosome in man USUALLY differs from the X-chromosome in that the Y-chromosome

    A. contains fewer genes
    B. contains more genes
    C. is present only in germ cells
    D. is produced by reduction division
    E. is present in all gametes produced in the male body

9. The MOST reliable method of estimating the age of the oldest rocks in the earth is by determination of

    A. their chemical composition
    B. the number and kind of fossils they contain
    C. the rates of disintegration of radioactive substances
    D. their proximity to the surface of the earth
    E. the rates of evolutionary change

10. One characteristic of MOST dicotyledonous plants is the presence of

    A. flowers with parts in multiples of three
    B. vascular bundles scattered irregularly throughout the stem
    C. a continuous ring of cambium layer in the stem
    D. leaves with parallel veining
    E. seeds with several seed leaves

11. The _____ in the human ear transforms physical vibration into nerve impulses.

    A. tympanic membrane   B. auditory nerve
    C. vestibulum   D. organ of Corti
    E. utriculus

12. Bending of a young plant toward light is indirectly related to the presence in its growing parts of an unequal distribution of

    A. auxins   B. diastase   C. catalase
    D. chromatin   E. plastids

13. The life cycle of the moss DIFFERS from that in flowering plants in that the sporophyte

    A. produces spores
    B. is in the form of a protonema
    C. is independent of the gametophyte
    D. is dependent on the gametophyte
    E. bears archegonia and antheridia

14. The structures in the human eye upon which the perception of color is MOST dependent are the

    A. peripheral cone cells
    B. peripheral rod cells

C. cone cells in the region of the fovea centralis
D. rod cells in the region of the fovea centralis
E. rods and cones at the point where the optic nerve passes through the retina

15. The existence today of a(n) _____ would be MOST improbable.	15._____

   A. parasitic plant containing chlorophyll
   B. living seed containing no embryo
   C. cell without a cell wall
   D. egg-laying mammal
   E. flowering fern

Questions 16-40.

DIRECTIONS: In answering Questions 16 through 40, select the word or phrase from the list appearing above each set of questions which applies to each question.

Questions 16-18.

   A. Lipase
   B. Trypsin
   C. Zymase
   D. Ptyalin
   E. Maltase

16. Accelerates the hydrolysis of starch to maltose	16._____

17. Accelerates the hydrolysis of proteoses and peptones to amino acids in an alkaline medium	17._____

18. Accelerates the hydrolysis of fats to fatty acids and glycerol	18._____

Questions 19-21.

   A. Maltase
   B. Rennin
   C. Lipase
   D. Erepsin
   E. Pepsin

19. Catalyzes the hydrolysis of proteins in an acid medium	19._____

20. Aids in changing maltose sugar to glucose by its action in the small intestine	20._____

21. In association with trypsin in the small intestine, completes the digestion of proteins	21._____

Questions 22-24.

   A. Sucrose
   B. Fat
   C. Glucose

D. Cellulose
E. Starch

22. Is a carbohydrate insoluble in cold water and unaffected by man's digestive juices   22.____

23. Is a carbohydrate that can be used directly by the human body without digestion   23.____

24. Is NOT a carbohydrate, although it contains the same chemical elements   24.____

Questions 25-27.

A. Tendon
B. Ligament
C. Smooth muscle
D. Striated muscle
E. Cardiac muscle

25. Fibrous tissue connecting the ends of bones   25.____

26. Contractile tissue producing alimentary peristalsis   26.____

27. Connective tissue connecting muscles with the skeleton   27.____

Questions 28-30.

A. Paramecium
B. Spirogyra
C. Field mushroom
D. Corn smut
E. Frog

28. Autophytic   28.____

29. Saprophytic   29.____

30. Parasitic   30.____

Questions 31-33.

A. Trapezius
B. Ciliary
C. Gastrocnemius
D. Biceps
E. Triceps

31. Extends the foot at the ankle joint   31.____

32. Straightens the arm at the elbow   32.____

33. Varies the curvature of the lens in the eye   33.____

Questions 34-40.

   A. True of crayfishes only
   B. True of grasshoppers only
   C. True of spiders only
   D. True of two of the above, but not all three
   E. True of all three of the above

34. The adults have compound eyes only   34.___

35. The adults have no antennae   35.___

36. The adults have head and thorax fused into one   36.___

37. The food of the adult consists principally of plant materials   37.___

38. The main part of the nervous system is a ventral nerve chain of ganglia 38.___

39. The adults breathe by means of book lungs   39.___

40. Lost legs and eyes of adults may regenerate   40.___

Questions 41-43.

   DIRECTIONS: Questions 41 through 43 are to be answered on the basis of the following concepts.
   A. Life came from simple molecules.
   B. The acquired traits of an individual can be transmitted to her offspring.
   C. The fitness of an organism will determine its survival.
   D. Living organisms are necessary to produce other living organisms.

   For each question, select the concept that is appropriate. A concept may be the answer to one question, more than one question, or no question.

41. Maggots emerge when meat is exposed to flies; they do NOT emerge if the flies are prevented from laying eggs on the meat.   41.___

42. This principle would be illustrated if a cow were to lose one leg and her calves were then born with three legs each.   42.___

43. Amino acids have been prepared from methane, water, ammonia, and hydrogen after an electric spark was passed through them.   43.___

44. If a freshwater fish is placed in salt water, which of the following BEST summarizes the result?   44.___

   A. The fish loses water from its tissues.
   B. The fish swells and becomes turgid.
   C. Salt diffuses out of the cells into the surrounding salt water.
   D. The fish absorbs salt until the salt concentration in its tissues equals that of the salt water.
   E. None of these

45. Large numbers of certain species of ladybird beetles are liberated in the orange groves of California PRIMARILY because the ladybird beetles 45._____

   A. attract birds
   B. are the best pollinating insects known
   C. controls rusts and smuts
   D. secrete a substance beneficial to the trees
   E. feed upon scale insects

46. The number of bacteria present in a tube of liquid medium can be measured indirectly by the amount of light that passes through the tube. The greater the number of bacteria, the less the light that is transmitted through the tube. 46._____
    Which graph BEST represents this relationship?

    A.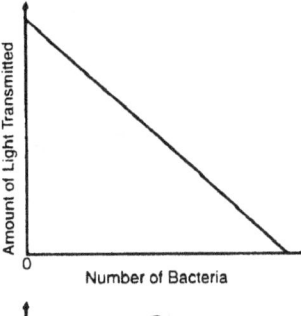
    B.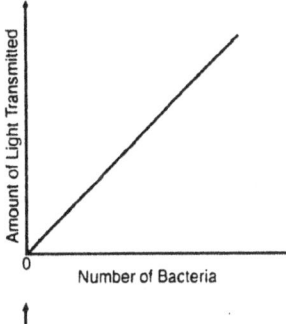
    C.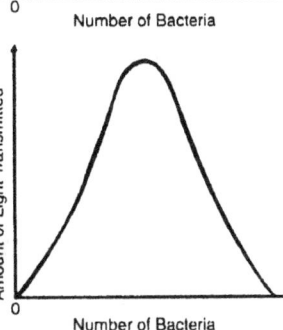
    D.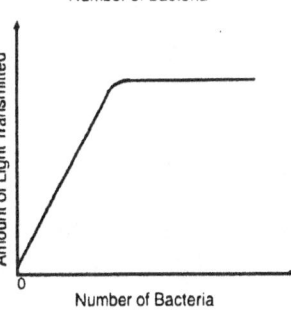

    E. None of these

47. During the fifteenth century, a few European rabbits were introduced into the Madeira Islands off the west coast of Africa. Today, the island rabbits are smaller and darker than their ancestors and can no longer be mated with present day European rabbits. These observations BEST illustrate which point? 47._____

   A. A species change resulting from geographic isolation
   B. Separation of alleles that act as independent units
   C. The appearance of recessive traits that were formerly concealed by dominant traits
   D. Environmental changes resulting in phenotypic changes only
   E. None of these

Questions 48-49.

DIRECTIONS: Questions 48 and 49 are to be answered on the basis of the following table.

	Gestation Period (in days)	Earliest Breeding Age of Females
White Rat	21-22	4 months
Mouse	20-22	60 days
Guinea Pig	62-64	9 months
Golden Hamster	16-19	70 days
Rabbit	30-32	10 months

48. According to the above table, the _____ has the LONGEST period of development before birth.

   A. Mouse B. Guinea Pig C. Golden hamster
   D. Rabbit E. White Rat

49. According to the above table, which animal is the OLDEST when it is FIRST able to breed?

   A. White Rat B. Guinea Pig C. Golden hamster
   D. Rabbit E. Mouse

50. Each of these is a procedure for determining the effectiveness of a bird disease vaccine. Which would be considered MOST satisfactory from a scientific viewpoint?
Vaccinate

   A. 100 birds and expose all 100 to the disease
   B. 100 birds and expose *only* 50 of them to the disease
   C. 50 birds, do NOT vaccinate 50 other birds, and expose all 100 to the disease
   D. 50 birds, do NOT vaccinate 50 other birds, and expose *only* the vaccinated birds to the disease
   E. All of the above

KEY (CORRECT ANSWERS)

1. C	11. D	21. D	31. C	41. D
2. D	12. A	22. D	32. E	42. B
3. D	13. D	23. C	33. B	43. A
4. E	14. C	24. B	34. A	44. A
5. B	15. E	25. B	35. C	45. E
6. C	16. D	26. C	36. D	46. A
7. B	17. B	27. A	37. B	47. A
8. A	18. A	28. B	38. E	48. B
9. C	19. E	29. C	39. C	49. D
10. C	20. A	30. D	40. A	50. C

TEST 3

DIRECTIONS: Each question or incomplete statement is followed by several suggested answers or completions. Select the one that BEST answers the question or completes the statement. *PRINT THE LETTER OF THE CORRECT ANSWER IN THE SPACE AT THE RIGHT.*

1. Below are four possible body shapes for one-celled animals.
   If all have the same volume, which form can exchange materials with its surroundings MOST quickly?

   A. (elongated oval)   B. (wavy ribbon)

   C. (circle)   D. (curved shape)

   E. One cannot determine from the information given

2. A certain nontoxic chemical compound in solution is red at a pH of 7 and blue at a pH of 5; that is, the compound changes to blue as the solution becomes acid. The red solution may be used to impart a red color to yeast cells. After paramecia ingest red yeast cells, the cells can be seen concentrated within food vacuoles.
   If in time the cells turn blue, a logical interpretation of the color change would be that

   A. the cytoplasm of the paramecium has a pH below 7
   B. paramecia prefer foods that have an acid reaction
   C. within food vacuoles, a chemical reaction such as digestion is taking place
   D. if yeast cells are ingested quickly by paramecia, the cells change color
   E. None of these

3. Complications associated with antibody formation sometimes affect newborn babies if the mother is _____ and the father is _____.

   A. AB; A   B. A; O   C. Rh⁻; Rh⁻
   D. Rh⁻; Rh⁺   E. O; A

4. _____ is NOT a function of blood.

   A. Protection of the body against disease
   B. Transport of oxygen to cells
   C. Transport of digestive enzymes to cells
   D. Transport of metabolic wastes from cells
   E. None of these

5. Photosynthesis and respiration are ALIKE in that both

   A. are energy-releasing processes
   B. are performed by all plants and animals
   C. convert stored chemical energy to useful heat energy
   D. involve energy conversions
   E. require oxygen

6. A student believes that male roaches are attracted to female roaches by certain chemical gases released by the females and that it is NOT necessary for the males to see the females. The best way to test this hypothesis is to have male roaches that are free and to place the females in a cage.
   This experimental cage should have which of these qualities?
   I. One-way entrances
   II. Porous walls
   III. Transparent walls
   The CORRECT answer is:

   A. I and II   B. I and III   C. II and III
   D. I, II, III   E.

Questions 7-8

DIRECTIONS: Questions 7 and 8 are to be answered on the basis of the table below, which lists a few enzymes, the substance that each digests (substrate), and the acidity at which each functions most effectively (optimal pH). The acidity is reported by use of the pH scale; a pH of 1 is highly acid, a pH of 7 is neutral, and a pH of 14 is highly alkaline.

Enzyme	Substrate	Optimal pH
Amylase (pancreas)	Starch	6.7-7.0
Lactase	Lacrose	5.7
Pepsin	Protein	1.5-1.6
Lipase (pancreas)	Fat	8.0
Trypsin	Protein	7.8-8.7
Maltase	Maltose	6.1-6.8

7. Which series CORRECTLY lists the enzymes according to optimal pH, from most acid to least acid?

   A. Pepsin, lactase, maltase, lipase
   B. Pepsin, amylase, trypsin, maltase
   C. Trypsin, lipase, amylase, pepsin
   D. Lipase, amylase, lactase, pepsin
   E. Lipase, lactose, pepsin, amylase

8. From the data in the table, identify the CORRECT conclusion concerning the enzymes which digest proteins.

   A. Enzymes that digest proteins function best in acid media.
   B. Enzymes that digest proteins function best in alkaline media.
   C. Enzymes that digest proteins function best in neutral media.
   D. Pepsin functions best in acid media; trypsin functions best in alkaline media.
   E. None of these

Questions 9-16.

DIRECTIONS: Questions 9 through 16 are to be answered on the basis of the following data on the inheritance of dominant and recessive traits.

In summer squashes, the gene for white is dominant over the gene for yellow, and the gene for disc shape is dominant over the gene for sphere shape.

Two white disc squash plants were crossed and produced offspring as follows:

9 white disc

3 yellow disc

3 white sphere

1 yellow sphere

Let: W represent the gene for white color

w represent the gene for yellow color

D represent the gene for disc shape

d represent the gene for sphere shape

The KEY below lists five possible crosses involving the traits: white (W), yellow (w), disc (D), and sphere (d). For each question, determine which cross given in the KEY applies. Mark the letter of the CORRECT answer in the space at the right.

KEY–Crosses
A. WwDd x WwDd
B. WWDD x WWDD
C. WWdd x wwDD
D. wwdd x wwdd
E. WwDd x wwdd

9. Which cross would yield ONLY pure dominant offspring for both traits? 9._____

10. Which cross should a truck gardener use if he wanted to raise only pure yellow sphere squashes? 10._____

11. If a truck gardener desired to raise white disc squashes ONLY, season after season, which cross should he select as the source of seed? 11._____

12. Which cross would produce squashes all of which would breed true for the recessive traits? 12._____

13. The two squashes that were crossed to produce the four kinds of offspring given above are represented by which one of the crosses? 13._____

14. Which cross represents a mating between the yellow sphere offspring and a squash like one of its parents? 14._____

15. The parents of the two squashes that were crossed are represented by which one of the crosses? 15._____

16. Which cross would yield only hybrid offspring? 16._____

Questions 17-20.

DIRECTIONS: Questions 17 through 20 are concerned with the functions of certain endocrine glands. For each question, select from the sketch below the gland whose secretion is involved.

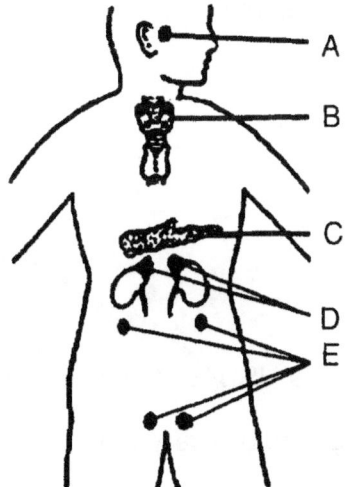

17. A hormone from this(these) gland(s) is associated with the changes of the *awkward age* through which many young people pass in their transition from childhood to young adulthood 17._____

18. This hormone regulates the body's utilization of carbohydrate foods. The gland(s) whose islets secrete it also discharge(s) enzymes capable of digesting proteins, starches, and fats. 18._____

19. The life of a patient lying on the operating table seems to be ebbing away. The doctor administers a substance which causes the heart to beat faster, the arteries to contract, the hair to bristle, and the breathing rate to increase.
Such a substance is manufactured by which gland(s)?

19.____

20. A basal metabolism test reveals that a young lady is consuming more than the normal amount of oxygen for her height, weight, and age. She is the author of several novels which have been bestsellers. She seems to thrive on long hours of work and little sleep.

20.____

Questions 21-35.

DIRECTIONS: Match the statements or words in Questions 21 through 35 with the items listed above each set of questions. Write the CORRECT letter for each question in the space at the right.

Questions 21-23.

    A. Riboflavin
    B. Ethylene
    C. Thiamin
    D. Carotene
    E. Colchicine

21. Used as a means of increasing the number of chromosomes in cells of plants.

21.____

22. Used to hasten the ripening of fruits.

22.____

23. Is a precursor of vitamin A in the animal body.

23.____

Questions 24-26.

    A. Thallophytes
    B. Bryophytes
    C. Pteridophytes
    D. Gymnosperms
    E. Angiosperms

24. Leafy sporphyte, both generations USUALLY independent, no seeds develop.

24.____

25. Seed plants, ovule NOT surrounded by ovary wall.

25.____

26. Relatively little cell differentiation, may be single-celled, colonial, or multicellular.

26.____

Questions 27-29.

    A. Coelenterata
    B. Annelida
    C. Nemathelminthes
    D. Platyhelminthes
    E. Echinodermata

27. Bilaterally symmetrical, triploblastic, contain a single gastrovascular cavity, no anus, flame cells. 27.____

28. Radially symmetrical, triploblastic, contain a well-developed coelom, anus usually present. 28.____

29. Radially symmetrical, diploblastic, contain a single gastrovascular cavity, no anus. 29.____

Questions 30-32.

    A. Chaetopoda
    B. Nematoda
    C. Mastigophora
    D. Reptilia
    E. Arachnida

30. The class to which the earthworm belongs. 30.____

31. The class to which the scorpion belongs. 31.____

32. The class to which Euglena belongs. 32.____

Questions 33-35.

    A. Mushrooms
    B. Yeasts
    C. Ferns
    D. Mosses
    E. Flowering plants

33. Gills 33.____

34. Prothallium 34.____

35. Embryo sac 35.____

Questions 36-44.

DIRECTIONS: Questions 36 through 44 are to be answered on the basis of the following diagram. Match the statements or words in these questions with the items listed above each set of questions. Write the CORRECT letter for each question in the space at the right.

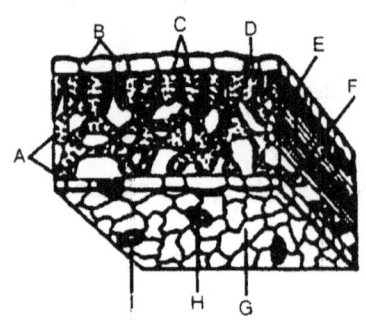

CROSS-SECTION OF LEAF

Questions 36-38.

    A. Transpiration is most actively taking place from these cells
    B. Photosynthesis is most active here
    C. Conducts sap to the root
    D. Protects the leaf, transmits light
    E. No respiration takes place in these cells

36. The structure at A

37. The structure at B

38. The structure at C

Questions 39-41.

    A. Regulates leaf temperature
    B. Utilizes solar energy in the synthesis of glucose
    C. Conducts water coming from the root
    D. Protects the leaf from mechanical injury
    E. Conducts organic food from the leaf

39. The structure at D

40. The structure at E

41. The structure at F

Questions 42-44.

    A. Sieve cell
    B. Guard cell
    C. Mesophyll
    D. Lower epidermis
    E. Stoma

42. G represents   42._____

43. H represents   43._____

44. I represents   44._____

Questions 45-47.

DIRECTIONS: Questions 45 through 47 are to be answered on the basis of the following chart.

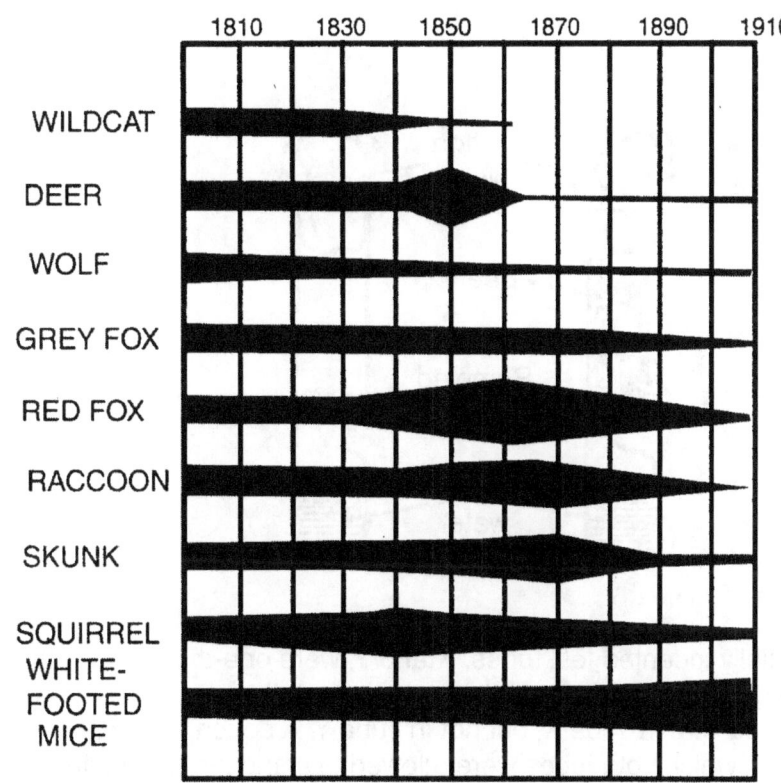

45. The cheapest and most practical way in which the population of white-footed mice could be decreased is to   45._____

    A. raise more cats
    B. spread poisoned bran in the fields
    C. put much of the crop land back in pasture
    D. set traps and hire boys to tend them
    E. encourage hawks and owls to increase by enacting protective hunting laws

46. On the basis of other data in this graph, the 1850 peak of the deer population was VERY likely   46._____

    A. due to an increase in available food
    B. due largely to increased breeding activity
    C. due in part to the decline of the wildcat-wolf population in that period
    D. unrelated to the trend of the wildcat-wolf population in 1850
    E. related directly to the increase in white-footed mice

47. The MOST probable explanation of the increase in white-footed mice in 110 years is that   47.____

    A. man considers white-footed mice harmless
    B. man is more friendly to carnivorous animals than to herbivorous animals
    C. white-footed mice have no natural enemies
    D. white-footed mice are protected by law
    E. man has greatly reduced the carnivore link of the food chain

Questions 48-50.

DIRECTIONS: Questions 48 through 50 are to be answered on the basis of the following experiment.

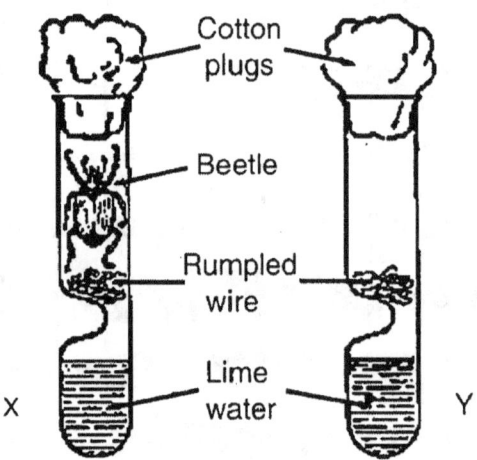

Two specially indented test tubes, X and Y, were one-third filled with limewater. A piece of rumpled wire was then lodged just above the indentation in each tube. A live beetle was placed over the rumpled wire in Tube X, but not in Tube Y. A cotton plug was inserted as a stopper in each tube, after which both tubes were allowed to stand for 20 minutes. At the end of that time, the limewater in Tube X had become cloudy, while the limewater in Tube Y remained clear.

48. This experiment provided evidence that   48.____

    A. carbon dioxide was being set free in Tube X
    B. a beetle cannot live in the presence of limewater
    C. oxygen was being used up in Tube X
    D. oxygen was being set free in Tube X
    E. carbon dioxide was being used up in Tube X

49. How would the experiment have been affected if the beetle had been placed in a cyanide   49.____
    jar before being put in Tube X?

    A. The beetle would have withstood the limewater much better.
    B. The limewater would have become more cloudy.
    C. The limewater would have turned yellow in color.
    D. The limewater would have remained clear.
    E. There would have been no appreciable change in the results.

50. A scientist would call that part of the experiment which involved test tube Y and its contents the 50.____

    A. follow-up
    B. verification
    C. reserve
    D. duplicate
    E. control

KEY (CORRECT ANSWERS)

1. B	11. B	21. E	31. E	41. E
2. C	12. D	22. B	32. C	42. D
3. D	13. A	23. D	33. A	43. E
4. C	14. E	24. C	34. C	44. B
5. D	15. C	25. D	35. E	45. E
6. A	16. C	26. A	36. A	46. C
7. A	17. E	27. D	37. D	47. E
8. D	18. C	28. E	38. B	48. A
9. B	19. D	29. A	39. B	49. D
10. D	20. B	30. A	40. C	50. E

EXAMINATION SECTION
TEST 1

DIRECTIONS: Each question or incomplete statement is followed by several suggested answers or completions. Select the one that BEST answers the question or completes the statement. *PRINT THE LETTER OF THE CORRECT ANSWER IN THE SPACE AT THE RIGHT.*

1. Which of the following statements about chemical elements is NOT true? 1.____

   A. Hydrogen usually forms only one covalent bond.
   B. Oxygen can form up to two covalent bonds.
   C. The addition of oxygen to a molecule often makes that molecule more water soluble.
   D. Nitrogen can form up to three covalent bonds.
   E. The addition of carbon to a molecule often makes that molecule more water soluble.

2. The addition of oxygen to a molecule 2.____

   A. usually makes that molecule more water soluble
   B. makes the molecule smaller
   C. always forms a double covalent bond
   D. has the same effect as adding carbon to that molecule
   E. usually requires energy, and therefore energy is added to that molecule

3. Which of the following is NOT a biologically important quality peculiar to water? 3.____

   A. Water molecules form strong hydrogen bonds with each other.
   B. Water is less dense as a solid than it is as a liquid.
   C. Water has a high heat capacity.
   D. Liquid water has a high surface tension.
   E. Water is an excellent solvent for nonpolar materials.

4. Which of the following functional groups would NOT increase the water solubility of a molecule? 4.____

   A. Hydroxyl (-OH)
   B. Amino ($-NH_2$)
   C. Methyl ($-CH_3$)
   D. Carboxyl ($-C{\overset{O}{\underset{OH}{}}}$)
   E. Phosphate ($-O-\overset{OH}{\underset{O}{P}}-O^-$)

5. Which of the following statements about carbohydrates is NOT true? 5.____

   A. Carbohydrates are composed of Carbohydrates unit (H-C-OH)
   B. Carbohydrates contain carbon, hydrogen, and oxygen at a ratio of approximately 1:2:1.

C. Carbohydrates are never used as structural material.
D. Carbohydrates with three to seven carbons are often called sugars.
E. Most carbohydrates are water soluble.

6. Which of the following is NOT a characteristic common to both five-carbon and six-carbon sugars?
They

   A. often form ring-shaped molecules
   B. are primarily composed of Carbohydrates umits ($H-\overset{|}{\underset{|}{C}}-OH$)
   C. can both be used for energy
   D. are used as structural components in nucleic acids
   E. can both be part of larger polymeric molecules

7. Which of the following is NOT a polysaccharide?

   A. Sucrose   B. Starch   C. Glucose
   D. Glycogen   E. Cellulose

8. Which of the following statements about lipids is NOT true?

   A. Lipids contain carbon and hydrogen, but very little oxygen.
   B. Lipids are soluble in water.
   C. Some lipids are used for long-term energy storage.
   D. Some lipids are components of cell membranes.
   E. Some lipids function as hormones in animals.

9. Proteins

   A. are polymers of hydrocarbon units ($H-\overset{|}{\underset{|}{C}}-H$)
   B. contain hydrogen, oxygen, nitrogen, carbon, and often sulfur
   C. store and transmit genetic information
   D. are never used as architectural material
   E. are synthesized by hydrolysis reactions

10. Which of the following is an example of the secondary structure of proteins?

    A. An alpha helix or beta pleated sheet
    B. The order of amino acids in a polypeptide
    C. A globular structure held together by disulfide covalent bonds and other weak bonds
    D. Two or more polypeptide chains held together by disulfide covalent bonds and other weak bonds
    E. An individual amino acid

11. Which of the following statements about nucleic acids is NOT true?

    A. Nucleic acids store genetic information.
    B. Nucleic acids are composed of hydrogen, oxygen, nitrogen, carbon, and phosphorus.
    C. Nucleic acids do not participate in energy metabolism.

D. Nucleic acids are polymers of nucleotides.
E. There are only five different types of nitrogenous bases in nucleic acids.

12. Which of the following would NOT be considered to be part of the cytosol?   12.____

    A. Water
    B. Enzymes
    C. Ribosomes
    D. Mitochondria
    E. Dissolved monosaccharides

13. Which of the following statements about ribosomes is NOT true?   13.____
    Ribosome(s)

    A. are macromolecular organelles
    B. synthesize proteins
    C. are composed of proteins and rRNA molecules
    D. are composed of three subunits, two small and one large
    E. components are synthesized in the nucleolus

14. Which of the following is NOT a part of the cytoskeleton?   14.____

    A. The cytosol   B. Microtubules
    C. Microfilaments   D. Tubulin subunits
    E. Actin molecules

15. Which of the following is the CORRECT sequence of movement of materials within the   15.____
    eukaryotic intracellular transport system?

    A. Golgi bodies endoplasmic reticulum secretory vesicles plasma membrane
    B. Golgi bodies endoplasmic reticulum plasma membrane ⟶ secretory vesicles
    C. Secretory vesicles endoplasmic reticulum golgi bodies plasma membrane
    D. Endoplasmic reticulum golgi bodies secretory vesicles plasma membrane
    E. Endoplasmic reticulum ⟶ secretory vesicles plasma membrane golgi bodies

16. Which of the following is NOT evidence for the endosymbiont hypothesis for the evolution   16.____
    of mitochondria, chloroplasts, and undulapodia?

    A. Mitochondria, chloroplasts, and undulapodia are similar to prokaryotic cells.
    B. Mitochondria, chloroplasts, and undulapodia all have their own DNA.
    C. Mitochondria, chloroplasts, and undulapodia all have a nucleus.
    D. Mitochondria and chloroplasts have their own prokaryotic ribosomes.
    E. Mitochondria and chloroplasts have inner membranes very similar to the plasma membranes of some bacteria.

17. Which of the following is NOT a function of cell membranes?   17.____

    A. Regulate the passage of materials into, within, and around cells
    B. Provide a surface for some metabolic reactions
    C. Participate in sending and receiving chemical messages
    D. Provide rigid support and protection for cells
    E. Form cell-to-cell connections

18. The figure at the right represents a U tube with the two sides separated by a membrane permeable to water but not to glucose. Side A contains a 2% solution of glucose in water. Side B contains a 47% solution of glucose in water. Assuming uniform temperature and pressure, which one of the following statements BEST describes what will happen in this system? Water will diffuse

    A. from side A to side B only
    B. from side B to side A only
    C. equally in both directions
    D. in both directions, with more moving from side A to side B
    E. in both directions, with more moving from side B to side A

18.____

19. Which of the following materials would probably NOT be transported by a membrane protein?

    A. Sodium ions (Na^+)
    B. Potassium ions (K^+)
    C. Small lipid molecules
    D. Chloride ions (Cl^-)
    E. Hydrogen ions (H^+)

19.____

20. Which of the following statements about active transport is NOT true?

    A. Active transport requires energy, usually in the form of ATP.
    B. Active transport and diffusion work using the same mechanisms.
    C. Sodium and potassium ions (Na^+ and K^+) can be transported by active transport.
    D. Active transport often requires a membrane protein.
    E. Active transport moves particles against their concentration gradient.

20.____

21. Which of the following statements about light is NOT true?

    A. Light is a form of electromagnetic radiation, which has properties of both particles and waves.
    B. Visible light is only a small part of the electromagnetic spectrum.
    C. White light is composed of photons of many different wavelengths, which we perceive as different colors of light.
    D. Green objects appear green because they absorb green light.
    E. The spectrum of visible light ranges from red to violet.

21.____

22. Which of the following statements about chlorophyll is NOT true?

    A. Chlorophyll is a water soluble biomolecule.
    B. Chlorophyll contains a ring of hydrocarbons, which usually surround an atom of magnesium.
    C. When a photon of red light strikes the chlorophyll, valence electrons in the magnesium atom in the chlorophyll are boosted to a higher energy level.
    D. Photons of both red and blue wavelengths can activate chlorophyll.
    E. Chlorophyll can pass energized electrons to other molecules.

22.____

23. In photosynthesis, the reduction of carbon dioxide to carbohydrate requires that both energy currency and a strong reducing substance (i.e., an electron donor) be available in ample supply. The process of noncyclic photophosphorylation provides these prerequisites, using light energy to synthesize

    A. ADP and ATP
    B. ATP and chlorophyll
    C. ATP and NADPH
    D. ADP and NADPH
    E. ATP and NADH

24. Which of the following statements about photophosphorylation is NOT true? Photophosphorylation

    A. synthesizes ATP using membrane-level phosphorylation
    B. uses sunlight energy to oxidize water
    C. must be coupled with carbohydrate synthesis
    D. does not use substrate level phosphorylation
    E. can be used to make ATP alone

25. During the transfer of electrons in noncyclic photophosphorylation, which event happens FIRST?

    A. Absorption of photon of red light of 680 nm by photo-system II
    B. Transfer of electrons from photosystem II to plasto-quinone
    C. Transfer of electrons to the cytochrome bf complex and hydrogen ions into the inner compartment of thylakoids by plastoquinone
    D. Absorption of photon of red light of 700 nm by photo-system I
    E. Transfer of electrons (and hydrogen ions) to NADP+, making NADPH

26. In the chloroplast labeled above, which of the areas would have the LOWEST pH (i.e., would be the most acidic location) when exposed to light?

    A. a   B. b   C. c   D. d   E. e

27. Which event does NOT occur during cyclic photophosphorylation?

    A. Absorption of photon of red light of 700 nm by photosystem I
    B. Transfer of electrons from photosystem I to photo-system II
    C. Transfer of electrons to plastoquinone and transfer of hydrogen ions into the inner compartment of thylakoids
    D. Transfer of electrons from plastocyanin to photo-system I
    E. Transfer of electrons (and hydrogen ions) to NADP$^+$, making NADPH

28. In the chloroplast diagrammed and labeled in Question 26 above, where would the PGAL concentration be HIGHEST?

    A. a   B. b   C. c   D. d   E. e

29. Photosynthesizing green algae are provided with carbon dioxide labeled with radioactive oxygen ($_{18}O_2$). Later analysis shows that all but one of the following compounds produced by these algae are radioactively labeled. That one EXCEPTION would probably be

    A. Glucose
    B. Ribulose diphosphate (RUDP)
    C. Oxygen gas (O_2)
    D. Phosphoglycerate (PGA)
    E. Phosphoglyceraldehyde (PGAL)

30. Which of the following is NOT made from phosphoglyceraldehyde (PGAL) produced in the Calvin Cycle?

    A. Glucose
    B. Rubulose bisphosphate
    C. NADPH
    D. Phosphoglycerate (PGA)
    E. Ribulose monophosphate

KEY (CORRECT ANSWERS)

#	Ans	#	Ans	#	Ans
1.	E	11.	C	21.	D
2.	A	12.	D	22.	A
3.	E	13.	D	23.	C
4.	C	14.	A	24.	C
5.	C	15.	D	25.	A
6.	D	16.	C	26.	B
7.	C	17.	D	27.	A
8.	B	18.	D	28.	D
9.	B	19.	C	29.	C
10.	A	20.	B	30.	C

TEST 2

DIRECTIONS: Each question or incomplete statement is followed by several suggested answers or completions. Select the one that BEST answers the question or completes the statement. *PRINT THE LETTER OF THE CORRECT ANSWER IN THE SPACE AT THE RIGHT.*

1. Which of the following statements about matter and energy is NOT true? 1.____

   A. All matter is composed of atoms.
   B. Energy is what causes matter to change or move.
   C. Atoms are composed of a nucleus, surrounded by electrons.
   D. Protons have a positive charge.
   E. Neutrons have a negative charge.

2. Which of the following statements about charged particles is NOT true? 2.____

   A. Like charges (+ and +, - and -) repel each other.
   B. Electrons are attracted to each other.
   C. Protons have a positive (+) charge.
   D. Electrons have a negative (-) charge.
   E. Unlike charges (+ and -) attract each other.

3. Which of the following statements about chemical elements is NOT true? They 3.____

   A. can be broken down without losing their unique properties
   B. are composed of atoms with the same numbers of protons
   C. can be combined to form chemical compounds
   D. can be symbolized by a one-or two-letter abbreviation
   E. have the same properties in living and nonliving things

4. What is the MAXIMUM number of electrons that can fit in the second electron shell of an atom? 4.____

   A. 2   B. 6   C. 8   D. 10   E. 18

5. Which of the following chemical bonds is formed by two atoms sharing a pair of electrons equally? 5.____

   A. Polar covalent   B. Hydrogen
   C. Ionic   D. Nonpolar covalent
   E. Hydrophobic

6. Which of the following chemical bonds is the STRONGEST in solution in water? 6.____

   A. Van der Waal's interactions
   B. Hydrophobic interactions
   C. Hydrogen bonds
   D. Ionic bonds
   E. Covalent bonds

7. Which statement BEST describes an acid? A material

   A. that releases hydrogen ions (H^+) in solution in water
   B. with a pH of 10
   C. with a pH of 8
   D. that releases hydroxide ions (OH^-) in solution in water
   E. that reacts very vigorously

8. The central nervous system differs from the peripheral nervous system in that the central nervous system

   A. is composed of neurons
   B. has no direct access sensory receptors
   C. is composed of nerves
   D. has access to motor outputs only
   E. is completely coated with several layers of myelin

9. Which of the following processes would be controlled by the somatic nervous system? The _____ of an animal.

   A. breathing rate
   B. heart rate
   C. muscle tone
   D. digestive processes
   E. movement of the legs

10. Which of the following is NOT a difference between the sympathetic and parasympathetic nervous systems of vertebrates? The

    A. sympathetic nervous system uses noradrenalin as a neurotransmitter in its synapses with various organs
    B. parasympathetic nervous system slows the heart rate
    C. sympathetic nervous system controls largely automatic processes
    D. parasympathetic nervous system has nerves that connect with the cranial and sacral regions of the spinal cord
    E. sympathetic nervous system can be stimulated directly by the hormonal system

11. In a typical simple reflex arc, which of the following is NOT usually included?

    A. Sensory inputs to the brain
    B. Motor outputs to skeletal muscles
    C. Sensory inputs to the spinal cord
    D. Synapses with interneurons in the spinal cord
    E. Sensory input from sensory receptor cells

12. Damage to which of the following parts of the vertebrate hindbrain would probably result in permanent coma? The

    A. medulla oblongata
    B. pons
    C. thalamus
    D. reticular activating system
    E. cerebellum

13. The vertebrate midbrain   13.____
    A. has become less important during the evolution of more advanced groups such as birds and mammals
    B. controls primarily automatic processes
    C. is primarily a switching center in advanced vertebrates
    D. includes the hypothalamus
    E. both A and C are correct choices

14. Which of the following parts of the vertebrate brain primarily controls emotions and motivational drives?   14.____

    A. Thalamus   B. Corpus callosum
    C. Cerebellum   D. Hypothalamus
    E. Pons

15. If you can remember the name of your kindergarten teacher, you probably accomplish this as the result of a 15.____

    A. spinal memory   B. short-term memory
    C. simple reflex arc   D. long-term memory
    E. sensory memory

16. Sensory receptors   16.____

    A. are always modified sensory neurons
    B. convert physical and chemical stimuli into action potentials
    C. are always specialized cells that have synapses with sensory neurons
    D. do not release neurotransmitters
    E. are dendrites

17. Which of the following sensory receptors of vertebrate skin does NOT respond to a physical or chemical change in the external environment? _____ receptors. 17.____

    A. Heat   B. Touch   C. Pressure
    D. Pain   E. Cold

18. Damage to the semicircular canals would most affect which of the following senses?   18.____

    A. Gravity
    B. Hearing
    C. Pain
    D. Location and position of body parts in space
    E. Balance and coordination of movement

19. _____ are sensory receptors that react primarily to chemicals dissolved or suspended in food or water.   19.____

    A. Thermoreceptors   B. Proprioceptors
    C. Pain receptors   D. Taste buds
    E. Mechanoreceptors

20. Imagine that you are walking around outdoors on a night with a bright full moon. You can distinctly see most of the objects around you, although you cannot see what color they are. These visual images are primarily sensed by

    A. rod cells
    B. cone cells
    C. corneal cells
    D. the lens of the eyes
    E. proprioceptors of the retina

21. Perception of sound ultimately depends on which of the following types of receptors?

    A. Thermoreceptors
    B. Photoreceptors
    C. Proprioceptors
    D. Mechanoreceptors
    E. Pain receptors

22. Damage to the hair cells of the organ of corti, severe enough to cause tears in the cell membranes, would result in

    A. constant white light, which would eventually disappear
    B. constant, loud sound *(ringing),* which would eventually diminish
    C. intermittent loud noises, without physical cause
    D. a continuous sensation of heat and pressure in the head
    E. loss of the sensations of taste

23. It Which of the following types of animal reproduction would resu in the GREATEST genetic diversity?

    A. Fragmentation
    B. Budding
    C. Parthenogenesis
    D. Fission
    E. Sexual reproduction

24. At the completion of oogenesis, _____ haploid egg cell(s) is/are produced per primary oocyte, whereas at the completion of spermatogenesis, _____ haploid sperm cell(s) is/are produced per primary spermatocyte.

    A. 1; 1   B. 1; 4   C. 2; 4   D. 3; 4   E. 4; 4

25. Which of the following statements about animal reproductive cycles is NOT true?

    A. Animal reproductive cycles are often seasonal.
    B. Animal reproductive cycles are often regulated by the pineal gland.
    C. Animal reproductive cycles often include periods of time during which the animals are not sexually receptive.
    D. Animal reproductive cycles are generally regulated by hormonal releases.
    E. All of these statements about animal reproductive cycles are true.

26. Which of the following structures conducts egg cells from the ovaries to the uterus? The

    A. vagina
    B. fallopian tubes
    C. urethra
    D. vas deferens
    E. seminalvesicles

27. The first division of meiosis of human egg cells occurs during _____, and the second division of meiosis occurs

    A. birth; during puberty
    B. fetal development; following fertilization
    C. puberty; following fertilization
    D. fetal development; during puberty
    E. birth; following fertilization

27.____

28. During the follicular phase of the menstrual cycle,

    A. follicle stimulating hormone (FSH) levels are very low
    B. the lining of the endometrium sloughs off
    C. follicles are converted into the corpus luteum
    D. progesterone levels are very high
    E. follicles and egg cells develop in the ovary

28.____

29. Which of the following is NOT a function of the seminiferous tubules of the testes?

    A. Production of testosterone
    B. Production of nutrient fluid for sperm
    C. Production of sperm cells
    D. Conduction of sperm cells to the epididymis
    E. All of these choices are functions of the seminiferous tubules of the testes

29.____

30. Which of the following methods of birth control does NOT involve blockage of fertilization (i.e., either egg cells or sperm cells are NOT produced in this method)?

    A. Oral contraceptives   B. Use of a condom
    C. Use of a diaphragm   D. Sterilization
    E. Use of a spermicide

30.____

KEY (CORRECT ANSWERS)

1. E	11. A	21. D
2. B	12. D	22. B
3. A	13. E	23. E
4. C	14. D	24. B
5. D	15. D	25. E
6. E	16. B	26. B
7. A	17. D	27. B
8. B	18. E	28. E
9. E	19. D	29. E
10. C	20. A	30. A

TEST 3

DIRECTIONS: Each question or incomplete statement is followed by several suggested answers or completions. Select the one that BEST answers the question or completes the statement. *PRINT THE LETTER OF THE CORRECT ANSWER IN THE SPACE AT THE RIGHT.*

1. Which of the following is NOT a macronutrient of animals? 1.____

   A. Water B. Oxygen C. Carbohydrates
   D. Sunlight E. Proteins

2. Vitamins differ from minerals in that vitamins are 2.____

   A. only needed in small quantities
   B. useually obtained as ions
   C. small organic molecules
   D. micronutrients
   E. required for metabolic and physiological processes

3. Mechanical digestion differs from chemical digestion in that mechanical digestion 3.____

   A. breaks down large food materials into smaller units
   B. begins in the mouth of vertebrates
   C. is enhanced by saliva
   D. does not require enzymes
   E. occurs before nutrient absorption

4. Pepsin 4.____

   A. functions more efficiently in an alkaline environment
   B. is secreted by the lining of the stomach
   C. participates in the digestion of lipids
   D. has no effect on proteins
   E. is a carbohydrate

5. The pancreas secretes _____ via the pancreatic duct, whereas the _____ secretes bile via the bile duct. 5.____

   A. digestive enzymes; liver and gall bladder
   B. digestive enzymes; stomach
   C. insulin; liver and gall bladder
   D. insulin; stomach
   E. lipids; esophagus

6. Which of the following processes does NOT occur primarily in the small intestine? 6.____

   A. Absorption of carbohydrate monomers
   B. Digestion of lipids
   C. Absorption of lipids
   D. Digestion of nucleic acids
   E. Absorption of vitamin K

7. Which of the following is in the correct order from the beginning to the end of the GI tract of a typical vertebrate?

   A. Small intestine stomach → large intestine rectum anus
   B. Stomach small intestine → large intestine anus → rectum
   C. Stomach → large intestine → small intestine rectum anus
   D. Stomach small intestine large intestine rectum anus
   E. Stomach small intestine → rectum large intestine anus

8. Larger animals

   A. require larger gas exchange surfaces than smaller animals
   B. require less oxygen than smaller animals
   C. have more surface area proportionately for gas exchange
   D. require less moist membranes for gas exchange
   E. do not exchange carbon dioxide

9. Which of the following statements about gills is NOT true?

   A. Gills are located on the exterior of an animal's body.
   B. Gills use countercurrent exchange.
   C. Gills are composed of gill filaments that arise from gill arches.
   D. Gas exchange via gills is restricted to fish.
   E. Gills exchange gases more efficiently than lungs do.

10. Which of the following organisms can exchange gases through both gills and lungs?

    A. Manylarvalamphibians   B. Sharks   C. Mammals
    D. Birds   E. Reptiles

11. How do insect and bird gas exchange systems differ? Only

    A. insects exchange gases through moist membranes
    B. birds take air inside their bodies, where it travels through many interior spaces
    C. birds exchange gases via blood in the circulatory system
    D. birds take in oxygen and give off carbon dioxide
    E. insects exchange gases more rapidly when they are flying

12. Hemoglobin

    A. transports oxygen, but does not transport much carbon dioxide
    B. is a quaternary protein
    C. contains one iron atom per molecule
    D. releases more oxygen at lower pHs
    E. binds oxygen when its partial pressure is low and acidity is high

13. Homeostatic regulating mechanisms

    A. affect only body temperature
    B. maintain an organism's internal conditions within a fairly narrow range, regardless of external changes
    C. do not require energy

D. allow an organism's internal conditions to nearly reproduce those of the external environment
E. affect only dissolved ion concentrations

14. Which of the following characteristics would you NOT expect in a homeothermic animal?

    A. Fur
    B. Feathers
    C. Heat exchange mechanisms
    D. Large amounts of brown fat
    E. Thermoregulatory behaviors

15. Which of the following is NOT a structure adapted for fluid regulation?

    A. A contractilevacuole   B. Kidneys   C. Nephridia
    D. The liver   E. Flame cells

16. Which of the following organs of an insect is adapted for water reabsorption?

    A. The skin   B. The liver
    C. Malpighian tubules   D. Kidneys
    E. The rectum

17. Which of the following is NOT a regulatory function of the vertebrate liver?

    A. Storage of excess glucose as glycogen
    B. Breakdown of glycogen into glucose, which is secreted into the blood
    C. Deamination of amino acids
    D. Conversion of ammonia into urea
    E. Concentration of urea

18. Of the following materials, which is NOT filtered out of the blood via the glomeruli of the vertebrate kidneys?

    A. Proteins   B. Glucose
    C. Amino acids   D. Sodium ions
    E. Water

19. Freshwater fish

    A. lose excess water by osmosis
    B. excrete nitrogenous wastes primarily in the form of ammonia
    C. excrete a very concentrated urine
    D. actively transport dissolved ions out of their gills into the surrounding water
    E. drink water almost continuously

20. Marine fish and most land vertebrates

    A. gain excess water by osmosis
    B. excrete nitrogenous wastes primarily in the form of urea
    C. excrete a concentrated urine
    D. actively transport dissolved ions out of their body tissues into their urine
    E. cannot absorb water through their digestive systems

21. In which of the following locations would the protein concentration of the blood be HIGHEST?
    In the

    A. renal arteries
    B. renal arterioles
    C. renal portal vessels
    D. vasa recta
    E. renal veins

22. Water is reabsorbed from the

    A. proximal convoluted tubules
    B. descending loop of Henle
    C. distal convoluted tubules
    D. glomerulus
    E. Bowman's capsule

23. Which of the following would probably cause a DECREASE in blood pressure?

    A. Secretion of antidiuretic hormone
    B. Prolonged lack of water (thirst)
    C. Secretion of aldosterone
    D. Intake of large amounts of salt (NaCl)
    E. Increased active transport of sodium and chloride ions from the ascending loops of Henle

24. In humans, the LARGEST amount of the carbon dioxide produced in the cells is carried to the lungs as

    A. carbaminohemoglobin
    B. CO_2 gas in solution in plasma
    C. CO_2 gas in the red blood cells
    D. bicarbonate in the plasma
    E. bicarbonate in the red blood cells

25. Which of the following would occur as a result of increased activity of the sympathetic nervous system?

    A. Accelerated digestion
    B. Decreased heart rate
    C. Increased adrenalin secretion
    D. Increased salivation
    E. Decreased glucose release by the liver

KEY (CORRECT ANSWERS)

1. D
2. C
3. D
4. B
5. A

6. E
7. D
8. A
9. D
10. A

11. C
12. B
13. B
14. D
15. D

16. E
17. E
18. A
19. B
20. C

21. C
22. A
23. B
24. D
25. C

EXAMINATION SECTION

TEST 1

DIRECTIONS: Each question or incomplete statement is followed by several suggested answers or completions. Select the one that BEST answers the question or completes the statement. *PRINT THE LETTER OF THE CORRECT ANSWER IN THE SPACE AT THE RIGHT.*

1. The atomic weight of an element is equal to the
   A. atomic weight
   B. mass number minus the number of electrons
   C. number of protons plus the number of neutrons
   D. number of protons
   E. number of bonds an atom of that element will make

   1.____

2. Which of the following pairs are isomers?
   A. ^{14}C and ^{14}N
   B. ^{16}O and ^{18}O
   C. Uranium and plutonium
   D. Glucose ($C_6H_{12}O_6$) and fructose ($C_6H_{12}O_6$)
   E. CO and CO_2

   2.____

3. How many covalent bonds would you expect silicon ($_{14}Si$) to make?
   A. One
   B. Two
   C. Three
   D. Four
   E. None; it is a strong electron acceptor and makes ionic bonds by gaining two electrons

   3.____

4. Which of the following bonds are nonpolar covalent?
   A. O=O   B. C-H   C. C-C
   D. Both C and B   E. A, B, and C

   4.____

5. Cola has a pH of 2; orange juice has a pH of 3; beer has a pH of 4; coffee has a pH of 5; and acid rain has a pH of 4.3. Which of these has the HIGHEST molar concentration of H^+?
   A. Cola   B. Orange juice   C. Beer
   D. Coffee   E. Acid rain

   5.____

6. Why is olestra considered a zero calorie fake fat?
   A. Olestra contains sucrose-fatty acid bonds which humans lack the enzyme to break.
   B. Olestra acts like fiber in the diet; we cannot break the b bonds linking the glucose monomers.
   C. Olestra contains many fat-soluble vitamins that do not provide energy when broken down.

   6.____

D. The fatty acids are shorter than normal fatty acids in the diet and thus contain less energy.
E. Olestra is made from chopped-up rice and oat hulls, containing only cellulose, which we are unable to digest.

7. Maltose is made from joining two glucose molecules in a condensation reaction. What is the molecular formula for this disaccharide?
   A. $C_6H_{12}O_6$
   B. $C_{12}H_{24}O_{12}$
   C. $C_{12}H_{24}O_{13}$
   D. $C_{12}H_{22}O_{11}$
   E. $C_{10}H_{20}O_{10}$

8. Which of these bonds or molecular interactions is the WEAKEST? A(n)
   A. ionic bond in a dry crystal
   B. ionic bond in a molecule dissolved in water
   C. hydrogen bond
   D. hydrophobic interaction
   E. covalent bond

Questions 9-11.

DIRECTIONS: Use these functional groups to answer Questions 9 through 11.

a. $-OH$ b. $-CH_3$ c. $-C(=O)OH$ d. $-NH$ e. $C=O$

9. Which functional group(s) is(are) nonpolar?
   A. a
   B. b
   C. c
   D. b and d
   E. e

10. Which functional groups would be involved in condensation reactions to form a fat?
    A. a and c
    B. a and e
    C. b and c
    D. b and e
    E. c and d

11. Which functional group(s) would be found in a monosaccharide?
    A. a
    B. b
    C. a and c
    D. a and e
    E. a, c, and e

12. Which of the following is an energy storage molecule common in plants?
    A. Starch
    B. Glycogen
    C. Cellulose
    D. Chitin
    E. Amino sugars

Questions 13-16.

DIRECTIONS: Questions 13 through 16 are to be answered on the basis of the following figures.

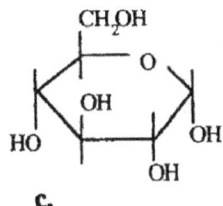

13. Which of the above molecules would be found in DNA?
    A. a   B. b   C. c   D. d   E. e

14. Which of the above molecules has a peptide bond?
    A. a   B. b   C. c   D. d   E. e

15. Which of the following molecules are hydrophobic?
    A. a and b   B. b and d   C. a, b, and e
    D. c and d   E. c, d, and e

16. Which of the above molecules is a monomer of glycogen?
    A. a   B. b   C. c   D. d   E. e

17. If you have started to exercise more, stopped smoking, and decreased the quantity of French fries, hamburgers, and ice cream in your diet, what are you hoping to do?
    A. Lose weight
    B. Reduce your LDLs and raise your HDLs
    C. Raise your LDLs and reduce your HDLs
    D. Increase your level of atherosclerosis
    E. Decrease the proportion of calories in your diet from carbohydrates

18. An alpha helix region in a protein is held in its coiled shape by
    A. peptide bonds   B. hydrogen bonds
    C. interactions between R groups   D. disulfide bridges
    E. hydrophobic interactions

19. If the nucleotide sequence on one strand of DNA is GCCTAA, what would the base sequence be on the mRNA molecule made from that DNA template?
    A. GCCTAA
    B. CGGATT
    C. AATCCG
    D. CGGUTT
    E. CGGAUU

20. Frog eggs are unusually large cells that may be 2 mm in diameter. How many µm is that?
    A. 200
    B. 2×10^3
    C. 2×10^{-3}
    D. 2×10^6
    E. 2×10^{-6}

21. How would you describe what happens to glucose ($C_6H_{12}O_6$) when it is converted to CO_2 and H_2O?
    A. Glucose is reduced.
    B. Glucose is oxidized.
    C. Glucose and O_2 are the reactants in this endergonic reaction, and CO_2 and H_2O are the products.
    D. Both A and C are correct.
    E. Both B and C are correct.

22. Which of these labeled lines indicates the activation energy of the reaction
    A + B → C + D
    when it is NOT catalyzed by an enzyme?
    A. a
    B. b
    C. c
    D. d
    E. e

23. ATP can decrease the activity of an early enzyme in the metabolic pathway that breaks down glucose for energy. What would you call this type of effect?
    A. Negative feedback
    B. Feedback activation
    C. Competitive inhibition
    D. Noncompetitive inhibition
    E. Denaturation

24. Which of the following are NOT found in bacteria?
    A. Ribosomes
    B. DNA as genetic material
    C. Cell walls
    D. Mitochondria
    E. Enzymes

25. Which of the following chimpanzees is the only one to have lived through the entire 38-year period that Jane Goodall has observed the chimpanzees at Gombe National Park?
    A. Figan
    B. Fifi
    C. Flo
    D. Goliath
    E. David Greybeard

26. Which of the following statements about Jane Goodall's research into the ecology and behavior of African chimpanzees is NOT true?
    A. Chimpanzees have distinct personalities, just like humans.
    B. Chimpanzees are subject to the same diseases as humans.
    C. The most fertile females are also the most successful in terms of reproductive success and longevity.
    D. Chimpanzees form male-dominated hierarchies.
    E. The chimpanzee population at Gombe National Park is sufficiently large to ensure the long-term survival of the chimpanzees in that ecosystem.

27. A U-tube is set up with a solution of 1.0M glucose separated from a solution of 1.0M sucrose by a membrane that is permeable to glucose and water, but not to sucrose. Which of the following statements BEST describes this U-tube experiment after it reaches equilibrium?
    A. The two sides are isotonic and there is no net movement of water.
    B. Side A becomes hypertonic to B, and water moves into side A.
    C. Side B becomes hypertonic to A, and the water moves into side B.
    D. The water level rose in side A because A becomes hypotonic to B.
    E. Even though the two sides are isotonic, water moves into side B because sucrose molecules are bigger than glucose.

28. K^+ is more concentrated inside a nerve cell than outside the cell. What process does the cell use to move K^+ into the cell?
    A. Simple diffusion
    B. Facilitated diffusion
    C. Active transport
    D. Phagocytosis
    E. Exocytosis

29. What result would you observe in the cells of a pond plant if you move a leaf into a 15% NaCl solution?
    The cells would
    A. plasmolyze
    B. become more turgid
    C. lyse
    D. crenate
    E. not change in appearance because they would be isotonic to the solution

30. According to the endosymbiotic theory,
    A. cells transport most large macromolecules into the cell by receptor-mediated endocytosis
    B. mitochondria and chloroplasts may have originated from bacteria that were engulfed by an ancestral bacterial cell
    C. all of a cell's internal membranes are related by the flow of membranes from the nuclear envelope, through the endoplasmic reticulum, Golgi apparatus, transport vesicles, to the plasma membrane

D. procaryotes existed for approximately 2 billion years before the evolution of eucaryotes
E. life began when abiotically synthesized organic molecules became surrounded by membranes that allowed the internal environment to differ from the external environment

31. Which one of the following is INCORRECTLY paired with its function? 31._____
    A. Lysosomes – contain the enzyme catalase that breaks down H_2O_2
    B. Mitochondria – produce ATP by oxidative respiration
    C. Cytoskeleton – cellular support, movement
    D. Nucleolus – synthesize ribosomal RNA and assemble ribosome components
    E. Smooth endoplasmic reticulum – lipid synthesis

32. Which structure would synthesize a protein secreted by a cell? 32._____
    A. Golgi apparatus   B. Free ribosome
    C. Ribosome bound to rough ER C. Transport vesicle
    D. Peripheral protein

33. How does a plant cell communicate with its neighboring cells? 33._____
    A. Through the middle lamella
    B. Via the cytoplasmic connections of its plasmodesmata
    C. By recognizing each cell's glycoproteins and glycolipids
    D. By interactions involving its glycocalyx
    E. Through their shared cellulose fibrils

34. Which of these molecules is the MOST reduced? 34._____
    A. O_2
    B. Phosphoglyceric acid (PGA)
    C. Diphosphoglyceric acid (diPGA)
    D. Glyceraldehyde 3-phosphate (G3P)
    E. Glucose

35. In glycolysis, which of the following materials is NOT phosphorylated (i.e., has phosphate added to it)? 35._____
    A. Glucose
    B. Glucose 6-phosphate
    C. Glyceraldehyde 3-phosphate (G3P)
    D. Oxidized nicotine adenine dinucleotide (NAD^+)
    E. Adenosine diphosphate (ADP)

36. In glycolysis, 36._____
    A. electrons are donated to PGAL by NADH
    B. oxygen is necessary for ATP production
    C. the end product is always lactic acid (lactate)
    D. a gross total of four ATPs are produced per glucose
    E. there is an increase in free energy overall

37. Which of the following intermediates in glycolysis contains the LARGEST amount of potential energy (i.e., how much ATP can be made from each one)?
    A. PGAL in the absence of oxygen
    B. PGA in the absence of oxygen
    C. PGA in the absence of oxygen
    D. Pyruvate in the presence of oxygen
    E. Lactate in the presence of oxygen

38. Which of the following statements about fermentation is TRUE?
    It
    A. occurs in the same way in animals and plants
    B. produces a net total of 2 ATPs
    C. is simply a way of recycling NAD^+
    D. is more efficient in animals than yeast in the absence of oxygen
    E. requires ATP

39. The function of the Krebs Cycle is primarily to
    A. make carbon dioxide
    B. synthesize ATP
    C. synthesize NADH and $FADH_2$
    D. oxidize pyruvic acid
    E. recycle NAD^+

40. Which of the following statements about the Krebs Cycle is NOT true?
    A. It requires oxygen directly.
    B. It releases carbon dioxide.
    C. Coenzyme A adds acetic acid (acetate) to the cycle.
    D. It occurs inside the inner membrane of mitochondria.
    E. It is similar to the Calvin Cycle run backwards.

41. Which of the following statements about oxidative phosphorylation in mitochondria is NOT true?
    A. NADH donates electrons and protons to the cytochrome electron transport system.
    B. The cytochrome electron transport system acts as a hydrogen ion pump.
    C. A hydrogen ion gradient is used to synthesize ATP.
    D. NAD^+ and FAD are recycled.
    E. Oxygen is necessary as an electron donor.

Questions 42-44.

DIRECTIONS: Questions 42 through 44 are to be answered on the basis of the following diagram of a mitochondrion.

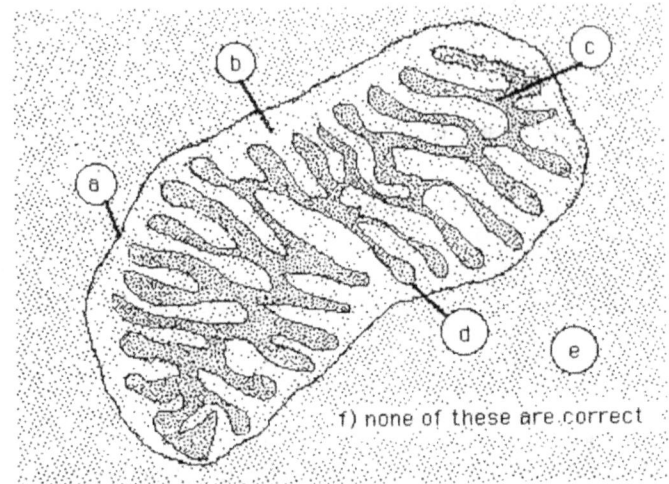

f) none of these are correct

42. Which of the labeled areas would have the lowest pH (i.e., the highest H⁺ concentration)? 42.____
    A. A   B. B   C. C   D. D   E. E

43. In which of the labeled areas would you be MOST likely to find NADH? 43.____
    A. A   B. B   C. C   D. D   E. E

44. The cyctochrome electron transport system is located in 44.____
    A. A   B. B   C. C   D. D   E. E

45. Which of the following materials is NOT produced during fermentation in either animal or yeast cells? 45.____
    A. Carbon dioxide   B. ATP   B. Ethanol
    D. NAD⁺   E. Lactic acid

KEY (CORRECT ANSWERS)

1.	D	11.	D	21.	B	31.	A	41.	E
2.	D	12.	A	22.	C	32.	C	42.	B
3.	D	13.	A	23.	A	33.	B	43.	C
4.	E	14.	E	24.	D	34.	E	44.	D
5.	A	15.	B	25.	B	35.	D	45.	B
6.	A	16.	C	26.	E	36.	D		
7.	D	17.	B	27.	C	37.	E		
8.	D	18.	B	28.	C	38.	C		
9.	B	19.	E	29.	A	39.	C		
10.	A	20.	B	30.	B	40.	A		

TEST 2

DIRECTIONS: Each question or incomplete statement is followed by several suggested answers or completions. Select the one that BEST answers the question or completes the statement. *PRINT THE LETTER OF THE CORRECT ANSWER IN THE SPACE AT THE RIGHT.*

1. The basis premise of the article DARWINIANA by Thomas H. Huxley, published in 1894, was that
    A. Darwin's theory of evolution is justified by the fossil record
    B. scientific discovery is the only way to establish philosophical truths
    C. the inductive and deductive techniques of scientific inquiry are the same methods of reasoning that we all employ in our everyday life
    D. all living organisms are composed of cells and originate from other cells
    E. all of life is built on a hierarchy of organizational levels

    1.____

2. Potassium has an atomic number of 19 and a mass number of 39. How many electrons would a potassium ion (K^+) have?
    A. 18   B. 19   C. 20   D. 38   E. 39

    2.____

3. Sulfur has an atomic number of 16 and a mass number of 32. What is its bonding capacity (i.e., how many covalent bonds will it form)?
    A. 0; it will form ionic bonds   B. 2
    C. 3   D. 4
    E. 6

    3.____

4. In which of the following are hydrogen bonds NOT typically found?
    A. Proteins (helping to form the secondary and tertiary structure)
    B. DNA (holding the two polynucleotide strands together)
    C. Unsaturated fats (helping to maintain the kinks that keep oils liquid)
    D. Cellulose (holding parallel cellulose molecules together to form strong fibrils)
    E. Water (producing some of water's unusual and important properties)

    4.____

5. Radioactive isotopes can be used in medical diagnosis because
    A. their radioactivity can be detected within the body and help pinpoint a problem area
    B. their half-life allows a physician to determine the amount of time that a process takes
    C. their extra protons allow a technician to locate them within the body
    D. isotopes cannot participate in the normal chemical reactions of the body and will accumulate in problem areas
    E. they are more reactive than normal atoms and will speed the processes that the physician is interested in studying

    5.____

6. Water is an excellent solvent because
    A. it can exist as a liquid, solid, and gas
    B. water molecules are polar and can surround and dissolve polar and ionic molecules

    6.____

C. a water molecule can hydrogen bond with four other water molecules
D. it can dissociate to form H⁺ and OH⁻ and, depending on the concentration of these ions, can be acidic or basic
E. it can move by osmosis through a selectively permeable membraned

7. Normally, rain has a pH of about 5.6. Some rain in the Northeast has been measured at a pH of 3.6. Compared to normal rain, this acid rain has ____ H⁺ than normal rain.
   A. 2 times more
   B. 2 times less
   C. 10 times more
   D. 100 times more
   E. 1,000 times more

8. What are the monomers of polysaccharides?
   A. Hydroxyl groups and a carbonyl group
   B. Isomers
   C. CH₂O groups joined by dehydration synthesis
   D. Monosaccharides
   E. Carbohydrates

Questions 9-11.

DIRECTIONS: Questions 9 through 11 are to be answered on the basis of the following diagrams.

9. Which of the above molecules looks like cholesterol?
   A. a   B. b   C. c   D. d   E. e

10. Which of the above molecules is a nucleotide?
    A. a   B. b   C. c   D. d   E. e

11. Which of the above molecules would provide the MOST energy when oxidized (most kcal/g)?
    A. a   B. b   C. c   D. d   E. e

12. Which of the following would tend to INCREASE the level of HDLs in your blood?   12.____
    A. Exercise
    B. A diet rich in eggs and meat
    C. Smoking
    D. A diet rich in proteins
    E. Both B and C

13. Olestra is a(n)   13.____
    A. brand of potato chips that may cause digestive problems and may reduce the absorption of important fat soluble vitamins and carotenoids
    B. unsaturated fat that contains fewer calories and is less of a health risk than saturated fats
    C. oleomargarine that has been hydrogenated to keep it solid at room temperature
    D. sucrose molecule with attached fatty acids that is used to make nonfat foods because it passes through the intestines without being digested
    E. high-calorie but low-fat diet food that should help people reduce the quantity of cholesterol in their diet

14. Which letter refers to a peptide bond?   14.____
    A. a
    B. b
    C. c
    D. d
    E. e

15. By what process would this peptide bond shown in Question 14 be broken?   15.____
    A. Dehydration synthesis
    B. Change in pH
    C. Hydrolysis
    D. Condensation
    E. Denaturation

16. What effect do R groups have on a protein?   16.____
    A. They create its primary structure.
    B. Hydrogen bonds between them produce its secondary structure.
    C. Their interactions (H bonding, ionic, and hydrophobic interactions, disulfide bridges) determine its tertiary structure.
    D. They determine the specificity of an active site for its substrate when the protein is an enzyme.
    E. Both C and D are correct.

17. What is RNA?   17.____
    A. The nucleotide that functions as ATP when two additional phosphate groups are added
    B. The molecule that makes up genes
    C. The second nucleotide strand in a DNA molecule

D. A protein with quaternary structure that is the major component of ribosomes
E. An intermediary that translates DNA into the amino acid sequence of proteins

18. The LARGEST number of bound ribosomes would be found in a cell that
    A. needs a great deal of ATP
    B. detoxifies poisons
    C. produces digestive enzymes for export from the cell
    D. moves with cilia
    E. moves by amoeboid motion

18._____

19. Which of the following is(are) NOT found in a prokaryotic cell?
    A. Plasma membrane   B. DNA   C. Ribosomes
    D. Mitochondria   E. Both C and D

19._____

20. What type of microscope would show in the greatest detail the shape and arrangement of the numerous cilia on the surface of a protist?
    A. Compound light   B. Dissecting
    C. Video   D. Transmission electron
    E. Scanning electron

20._____

21. Which of the following is(are) composed entirely of protein?
    A. Chromatin   B. The cell wall of fungi
    C. The endoplasmic reticulum   D. Mitochondria
    E. Microtubules and microfilaments

21._____

22. The endosymbiotic (or *big gulp*) hypothesis explains the origin of
    A. ribosomes   B. phagocytosis
    C. mitochondria and chloroplasts   D. lysosomes and food vacuoles
    E. peroxisomes

22._____

23. The fossil record first shows evidence of prokaryotes about _____ years ago.
    A. 4.5 million   B. 3.5 billion   C. 2 billion
    D. 1.5 billion   E. 3.0 million

23._____

24. You estimate the size of a nucleus of a cheek cell to be 5 μm. What would that measurement be in mm?
    A. 0.005   B. 0.05   C. 0.5   D. 500   E. 5000

24._____

25. Facilitated diffusion across a cellular membrane requires _____ and moves a substance _____ its concentration gradient.
    A. energy and transport proteins; down
    B. energy and transport proteins; up (against)
    C. energy; up
    D. transport proteins; down
    E. transport proteins; up

25._____

26. The extracellular fluids that surround the cells of a multicellular animal must be
    A. buffers
    B. isotonic
    C. hypotonic
    D. hypertonic
    E. homotonic

27. A U-tube is set up with a solution of 1.0M glucose and 2.0M maltose separated from a solution of 3.0M glucose and 2.0M maltose by a membrane that is permeable to glucose and water, but not to maltose. Which of the following statements BEST describes the results of this U-tube experiment after equilibrium is reached?

    Experimental U-tube Set-up
    A   B
    1.0 M glucose
    2.0 M maltose
    3.0 M glucose
    2.0 M maltose
    membrane permeable to water and glucose but not to maltose

    A. Glucose diffuses to side A and water moves into this now hypertonic side, raising the level in side A.
    B. Even though side B is initially hypertonic to A, glucose diffuses into A and the two sides become isotonic; no net movement of water occurs.
    C. Side A becomes hypotonic to B, and the water moves into side A.
    D. Side B becomes hypotonic to A, and the water moves into side B.
    E. The water level rises in side B because it is hypertonic to side A.

28. LDLs (low density lipoproteins) enter animal cells by
    A. diffusion through the lipid bilayer
    B. receptor-mediated endocytosis
    C. exocytosis
    D. pinocytosis
    E. diffusion through transport proteins

29. The fluid mosaic model describes biological membranes as consisting of
    A. two layers of phospholipids with proteins sandwiched between them
    B. two layers of phospholipids with proteins coating the outside of them
    C. a phospholipid bilayer with proteins embedded in it
    D. a protein bilayer with phospholipids embedded in it
    E. a bilayer of cholesterol with proteins embedded in the hydrophobic center

30. Which of the following statements concerning energy is NOT true?
    A. Fireflies can convert the potential energy in their food to the kinetic energy of light and heat.
    B. During photosynthesis, plants convert the kinetic energy of light into the chemical energy of glucose.
    C. Energy transformations in cells are accompanied by an increase in entropy shown by the release of heat.

D. Living systems convert heat energy into kinetic energy in order to reduce entropy.
E. The potential energy of a H⁺ gradient in the inner compartment of a mitochondrion can be converted to the chemical energy of ATP, which can be transformed into kinetic energy when a flagellum moves.

31. In an exergonic reaction,
    A. activation energy must be added to start the reaction
    B. no enzymes are required for the reaction to occur rapidly because the reactants have more energy than the products
    C. the products have more energy than the reactants
    D. energy is released
    E. both A and D are correct

32. According to Jane Goodall, chimpanzees do all of the following EXCEPT
    A. form family ties
    B. use tools
    C. have a prolonged period of childhood during which they are dependent on their mothers
    D. form long-lasting monogamous pairs that cooperatively raise offspring
    E. defend their territory

33. What is the GREATEST threat to the chimpanzee populations of Africa?
    A. Habitat destruction and poaching
    B. Territorial conflicts between neighboring chimpanzee populations
    C. Mange, polio, and other human diseases
    D. The breakdown of traditional family values
    E. The scientific study of chimpanzees in the wild

34. An enzyme called _____ catalyzes the oxidation of G3P (glyceraldehyde 3-phosphate), and _____ serves as a coenzyme for the reaction and becomes reduced.
    A. dehydrogenase; NAD⁺   B. phosphofructokinase; zinc
    C. peroxidase; NADH   D. ATP synthase; coenzyme A
    E. NADH; NAD⁺

35. Why is glycolysis considered to be an older pathway than the Krebs Cycle? It
    A. involves fermentation, which is an anaerobic process
    B. is only found in prokaryotes, whereas the Krebs Cycle is only found in eukaryotes
    C. is nearly universal, takes place in the cytosol, and does not involve O₂
    D. produces only 2 ATP by substrate level phosphorylation, whereas the Krebs Cycle produces all its ATP by chemosis
    E. does not involve enzymes that are regulated by feedback inhibition, whereas most of the enzymes of the Krebs Cycle are regulated that way

36. What is the function of O_2 in your body?
    It
    A. provides the energy to produce ATP
    B. is used to reduce glucose in CO_2
    C. is used as an electron acceptor and shuttle to carry electrons to the electron transport chain
    D. serves as the final electron acceptor for the electron transport chain
    E. recycles NAD^+ to NADH so that cellular respiration can continue

Questions 37-39.

DIRECTIONS: Questions 37 through 39 are to be answered on the basis of the following diagram.

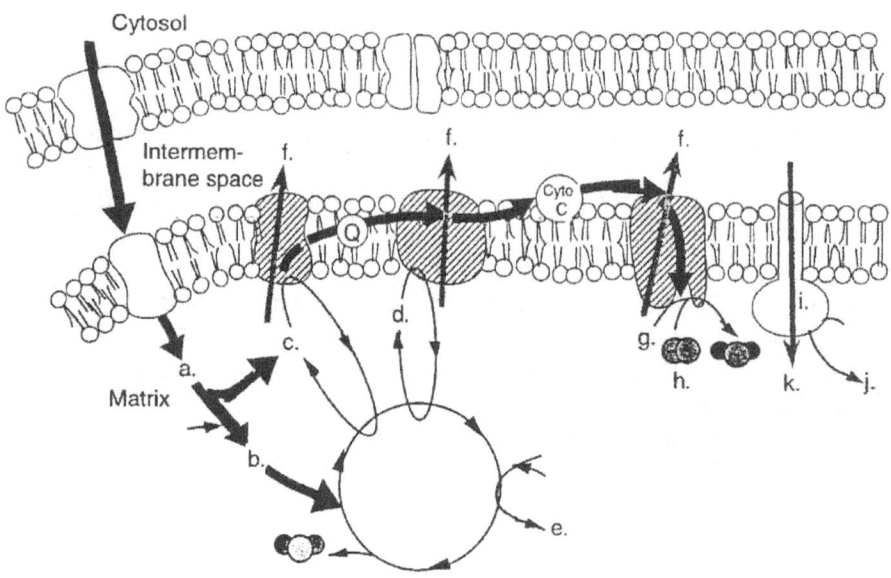

37. Which letter represents NADH?
    A. a   B. b   C. c   D. d   E. e

38. Which of the following letters represent ATP?
    A. c, d
    B. e, j
    C. f, g, k
    D. j only
    E. i, k

39. The letter k represents the
    A. movement of electrons through the electron transport chain
    B. transfer of electrons to O_2 to form H_2O
    C. pumping of H^+ against its concentration gradient
    D. flow of H^+ down its concentration gradient through ATP synthase to form ATP
    E. transport of NADH from glycolysis into the matrix of the mitochondrion

40. Individuals who begin drinking alcohol before age 15
    A. are alcoholics
    B. are less likely to become alcohol abusers
    C. are more likely to become alcohol dependent
    D. show signs of fatty livers
    E. are also illicit drug users

41. How are fats used in cellular respiration?
    A. They are converted to glycogen and then undergo glycolysis.
    B. They are deaminated and then converted into intermediates of the Krebs Cycle.
    C. They are oxidized into cholesterol and then used as cell membrane components.
    D. Their glycerol component is converted into G3P and the fatty acids are broken down to acetyl CoA molecules, which then enter the Krebs Cycle.
    E. They are not broken down to yield ATP but are transformed to fat storage in the body.

42. Which of the following vitamin or mineral is mismatched with its function?
    A. Vitamin E – antioxidant
    B. Vitamin K – blood clotting
    C. Calcium – component of bones
    D. Vitamin C – antioxidant; connective tissue production
    E. Iron – component of thyroid hormone

43. Vegetarians usually combine several different protein sources in a meal in order to
    A. obtain all the essential amino acids needed for protein synthesis at the same time
    B. obtain sufficient calories so that they do not suffer from malnutrition
    C. make sure they get all their essential vitamins and minerals
    D. provide for a more varied and interesting diet
    E. make sure that at least one of the foods contains complete proteins with all the essential fatty acids

44. Most B vitamins
    A. function as coenzymes
    B. are fat soluble
    C. function as antioxidants
    D. are obtained by fats
    E. are metal ions that function as cofactors or components of the proteins in the electron transport chain

45. All of the following are part of or explained by the theory of evolution by natural selection EXCEPT which one?
    A. Each species has its own special set of adaptations that have evolved by natural selection.
    B. Individuals who are best adapted to their environment will be the strongest and will kill all their competitors.

C. The existence of common metabolic pathways, DNA, and a common genetic code gives evidence for the evolutionary relatedness of all organisms.
D. The higher reproductive success of organisms best adapted to their environment leads to the gradual accumulation of favorable traits in a population.
E. All of life traces back to a common ancestor, from which have gradually evolved the many diverse life forms. Thus, there is unity in diversity.

KEY (CORRECT ANSWERS)

1. C	11. E	21. E	31. E	41. D
2. A	12. A	22. C	32. D	42. E
3. B	13. D	23. B	33. A	43. A
4. C	14. B	24. A	34. A	44. A
5. A	15. C	25. D	35. C	45. B
6. B	16. E	26. B	36. D	
7. D	17. E	27. B	37. C	
8. D	18. C	28. B	38. B	
9. C	19. D	29. C	39. D	
10. A	20. E	30. D	40. C	

TEST 3

DIRECTIONS: Each question or incomplete statement is followed by several suggested answers or completions. Select the one that BEST answers the question or completes the statement. *PRINT THE LETTER OF THE CORRECT ANSWER IN THE SPACE AT THE RIGHT.*

1. What is a gastrovascular cavity? 1.____
    A. A type of open circulatory system found in mollusks
    B. The circulatory system found in annelids (worms)
    C. The intracellular digestive system found in protists and sponges
    D. The digestive cavity with a single opening found in hydra and flatworms
    E. The extracellular digestive system used by fungi

2. Which of the following is NOT descriptive of a type of epithelial tissue? 2.____
    A. Scattered cells that secrete fibers and extracellular matrix
    B. Tightly joined cells that line body surfaces
    C. A thin layer of cells specialized for absorption
    D. Multiple layers of cells that function in protection (i.e., skin)
    E. Mucus membranes that line the respiratory tract

3. What happens in your pharynx? 3.____
    A. Peristalsis moves food down the esophagus.
    B. Inhaled air is warmed and moistened.
    C. Air moving past the vocal cords produces speech.
    D. The paths of air and food cross.
    E. The epiglottis protects the opening to the esophagus so you do not swallow air.

4. What is the function of villi and microvilli? 4.____
    A. Sweep mucus and trapped particles out of the respiratory tract
    B. Protect the stomach lining from acidic gastric juice
    C. Secrete gastric juice in response to the presence of food in the stomach
    D. Mechanically break down food by the contraction of these folds in the small intestine
    E. Increase the surface area for absorption of digested nutrients

5. Which of the following groups of enzymes would be MOST involved in the digestion of a large order of French fries (deep fat-fried potatoes)? 5.____
    A. Lipase, amylase, maltase
    B. Pepsin, trypsin, chymotrypsin
    C. Bile, starchase, sucrose
    D. Endopeptidases, exopeptidases, amylase
    E. Disaccharidases attached to brush border, pepsin, pancreatic amylase

6. Digested macromolecules enter the intestinal epithelial cells as _____ and are transported to the liver through the hepatic _____.
   A. small monomers; portal vein
   B. small monomers; artery
   C. large macromolecules; portal vein
   D. large macromolecules; artery
   E. large macromolecules; vein

7. Why are insects able to function with a relatively inefficient open circulatory system?
   A. They utilize anaerobic respiration to obtain their energy.
   B. Their gastrovascular cavity circulates oxygen-rich fluid throughout their bodies.
   C. Their heart has a double pump that separates oxygenated blood from deoxygenated blood.
   D. Their tracheal system branches throughout the body and efficiently delivers O_2 to active tissues.
   E. They have high concentrations of hemoglobin in their body fluids.

8. The countercurrent exchange between the external flow of water and the internal flow of blood in a fish gill
   A. maintains a favorable concentration gradient for diffusion of O_2 across the gill
   B. enables fish to separate their pulmonary from their systemic blood circulation
   C. is used to actively pump salts across the gill epithelium
   D. increases the velocity of blood flow through the capillaries of the gill
   E. is necessary because the gill is an evagination rather than an invagination of the fish's body wall

9. In your respiratory system, O_2 and CO_2 exchange occurs in the
   A. nasal cavity B. trachea C. bronchioles
   D. alveoli E. all of the above

10. Blood that is in the hepatic artery will pass through _____ capillary beds before it returns to the left atrium of the heart.
    A. one B. two C. three D. four E. five

11. The doctor tells you your blood pressure is 112/70. What does the 70 refer to?
    A. The velocity of blood during diastole
    B. The systolic pressure from the ventricular contraction
    C. The diastolic pressure from the recoil of the arteries
    D. The venous pressure caused by the compression of the blood pressure cuff
    E. Your heart rate

12. What causes the filtration of fluid out of the arterial end of a capillary?
    A. The hydrostatic pressure of the blood entering the capillary
    B. The osmotic pressure of the surrounding interstitial fluid
    C. Endocytosis through vesicles
    D. The opening of sphincters
    E. Vasoconstriction of the arterial walls

13. Which of the following would cause an INCREASE in your breathing rate? A(n)
    A. *increase* in the O_2 content of the inspired air
    B. *increase* in the pH of your blood due to a buildup of bicarbonate ions
    C. *decrease* in blood pH due to an increased level of CO_2
    D. *increase* in the blood osmolarity
    E. *decrease* in the blood osmolarity

14. Which of the following would NOT be a possible function of a blood plasma protein?
    A. Oxygen transport by hemoglobin   B. Buffer
    C. Lipid transport   D. Clotting agent
    E. Antibody

Questions 15-17.

DIRECTIONS: Questions 15 through 17 are to be answered on the basis of the following diagram.

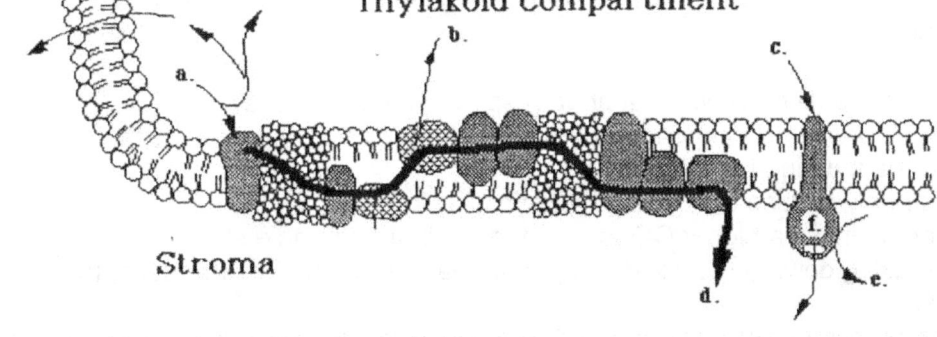

15. What molecule would be produced at letter d?
    A. H_2O B. O_2 C. CO_2 D. NADPH   E. ATP

16. Which letter represents the movement of H^+ across the membrane against its concentration gradient?
    A. a   B. b   C. c   D. d   E. e

17. What structure does letter f represent?
    A. Photosystem II and noncyclic electron flow
    B. Antenna complex
    C. Photosystem I and cyclic electron flow
    D. ATP synthase complex
    E. Electron transport chain

18. What processes are associated with the thylakoids? The
    A. light-dependent reactions (photophosphorylation)
    B. transfer of electrons from H_2O to NADPH
    C. generation of a H^+ gradient
    D. release of O_2
    E. all of the above

19. The _____ of an illuminated plant cell would be expected to have the lowest pH.
    A. central vacuole   B. Golgi apparatus   C. chloroplast
    D. stroma   E. thylakoid interior

20. Rubisco is
    A. combined with CO_2 to form a temporary 6 carbon intermediate in the Calvin Cycle
    B. regenerated after 3 turns of the Calvin Cycle
    C. the first stable product of the Calvin Cycle
    D. perhaps the most abundant protein on earth, but a lousy enzyme
    E. used in the biosynthesis of other carbohydrates, fats, proteins, and nucleic acids

21. C_4 plants are able to avoid most photorespiration because they
    A. fix carbon into 4-carbon organic acids at night so they can close their stomata during the day
    B. use only rubisco to add atmospheric CO_2 to RuBP
    C. can maintain a higher CO_2 concentration in their bundle sheath cells by breaking down a 4-carbon compound that was formed in the mesophyll cells
    D. have enzymes that are more efficient at higher temperatures
    E. close their stomata during hot and dry weather

22. Most mineral nutrients of plants are
    A. actively transported as ions from the soil solution into the roots
    B. produced by synthetic bacteria housed in their roots
    C. inorganic ions that enter through the stomata of leaves
    D. absorbed in organic form from decomposing organic material in the soil
    E. not needed because plants produce their own food

23. Mycorrhizae are
    A. symbiotic associations of nitrogen-fixing bacteria within root nodules of legumes
    B. root hair extensions that greatly increase the surface area available for water and mineral absorption
    C. the fibrous root systems typical of grasses
    D. symbiotic associations of fungi and plant roots that increase the surface area for water and mineral absorption
    E. transport tissues that carry water and dissolved minerals to the leaves

24. On the way from the soil to the xylem, water is forced to enter the cytoplasm of plant roots by a waxy barrier in the walls of the
    A. root hairs   B. endodermis   C. epidermis
    D. cortex   E. xylem

25. Suppose you are measuring the diameter of a tree with a very accurate device and the ground is very dry. You water the ground thoroughly. What will happen?
    A. Nothing
    B. The diameter of the tree will increase
    C. The diameter of the tree will decrease
    D. The diameter of the tree will increase and then decrease
    E. The height of the tree will increase

26. Which of the following statements concerning transport in xylem and transport in phloem is FALSE?
    A. Both occur in the vascular bundles of the root, stem, and leaves
    B. Both involve the movement of water
    C. Both involve transport from high pressure to low pressure
    D. In both, the end walls of the conducting cells are either missing or perforated with a large holes
    E. Carbohydrates are transported in both systems

27. The overall pattern of sucrose transport in plants is from
    A. the leaf, downward to the roots
    B. the soil, upward to the leaves
    C. mature leaves to immature leaves
    D. sink to source
    E. regions of carbohydrate synthesis to regions of carbohydrate use

28. In the phloem of plants, the sieve elements have a much higher concentration of sugars than do surrounding cells. They are kept from bursting by the strong cell walls that surround them.
    What establishes and maintains this high concentration of sugar in sieve elements?
    A. Diffusion   B. Photosynthesis   C. Osmosis
    D. Active transport   E. Transpiration

29. What mechanism is involved in the opening of stomata so that gas exchange can occur?
    A. Active transport of K⁺ into guard cells, followed by osmosis and the buckling apart of the turgid cells
    B. Secondary transport of sucrose into the guard cells following the active pumping of protons out of the cells
    C. Transpiration of water pulled up from the roots by tension
    D. The diffusion of Cl⁻ from a source to a sink in the guard cells, followed by osmosis
    E. The action of accessory pigments that produce glucose, increasing the osmotic concentration within the guard cells so that water moves into the cells

Questions 30-31.

DIRECTIONS: Questions 30 and 31 are to be answered on the basis of the following diagram of a nephron.

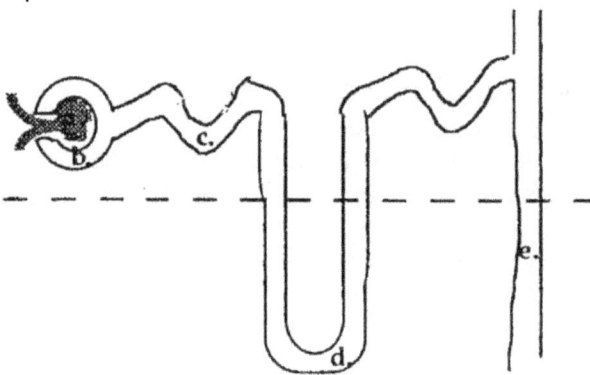

30. Which letter indicates the glomerulus?
    A. a   B. b   C. c   D. d   E. e

31. Which of the following occurs in the region indicated by letter c?
    A. Reabsorption of nutrients and H_2O
    B. Secretion of glucose and ions
    C. Filtration of small molecules and urea
    D. Excretion of urea
    E. Production of hypertonic urine

32. What is the DIRECT cause of a stroke?
    A. The lodging of a blood clot in a coronary artery supplying the heart
    B. High blood pressure
    C. The blocking of an artery in the brain by a thrombus or embolus
    D. Smoking and a buildup of CO in the blood
    E. A high cholesterol diet

33. What is lymph?
    A. A plasma protein that regulates osmotic balance between the blood and the interstitial fluid
    B. Excess interstitial fluid that is being returned to the circulatory system through lymph vessels
    C. A solution of leukocytes that phagocytize bacteria
    D. Fragments of cells that initiate the complex process of blood clotting
    E. Edema (swelling of tissues due to interstitial fluid accumulation)

34. One of the advantages of the production of uric acid by birds is that uric acid
    A. takes little energy to produce
    B. is very soluble in water
    C. can be produced in the nephron
    D. has low toxicity and can be safely stored in the egg
    E. requires a moderate loss of water to excrete

35. Which of the following sets of osmoregulatory adaptations would be found in a freshwater fish?
    A. Drink lots of water, produce lots of dilute urine, pump salts in through gills
    B. Do not drink water, produce lots of dilute urine, pump salts in through gills
    C. Do not drink water, produce small amounts of urine, pump salts in through gills
    D. Drink lots of water, produce concentrated urine, pump salts out through gills
    E. Do not drink water, produce small amounts of isotonic urine, pump salts out through gills

36. All of the following are adaptations for conserving heat EXCEPT
    A. fur   B. burrowing   C. feathers
    D. sweating   E. subcutaneous fat

37. Which of the following animals would have the HIGHEST metabolic rate?
    A. A large ectotherm, such as a shark
    B. A small ectotherm, such as a frog
    C. A large endotherm, such as an elephant
    D. A small endotherm, such as a mouse
    E. These would all have approximately the same metabolic rate

38. What is the effect of the secretion of ADH (antidiuretic hormone) from the posterior pituitary?
    A. Breathing rate and heart rate increase
    B. Diuresis (increased excretion of urine)
    C. Blood pressure is lowered
    D. A more dilute urine is formed
    E. A more concentrated urine is formed

39. What kinds of hormones are secreted by the anterior pituitary gland?   39._____
    A. Releasing factors: small polypeptides that regulate the synthesis and secretion of hormones from the hypothalamus
    B. Steroid hormones that act by negative feedback to stop release of specific pituitary hormones
    C. Hormones that are released in response to direct nervous stimulation
    D. Hormones that are produced by the hypothalamus, stored in the posterior pituitary, and secreted in response to changes in blood plasma composition
    E. Hormones that regulate the activity of another endocrine gland, such as the thyroid

40. All of the following are effects of levels of insulin that are too low EXCEPT   40._____
    A. high blood-glucose levels
    B. excretion of glucose in the urine
    C. increased uptake of glucose by muscle and fat cells
    D. increase in protein and fat hydrolysis
    E. excess urine production, dehydration, and pH imbalance

41. Which of the following hormones prepares the body for *flight or fight* by increasing heart rate, increasing blood glucose, and dilating vessels to muscles and heart?   41._____
    A. Anabolic steroids   B. Thyroxin
    C. Growth hormone   D. Epinephrine
    E. Glucagon

42. Which one of the following statements about animal chemical control systems is NOT true?   42._____
    A. They usually produce much slower responses than nervous systems.
    B. They occur in virtually all multicellular animals.
    C. The chemical message is always lipid soluble.
    D. The carrier for the message is usually the circulatory system.
    E. Some cells have internal chemical messengers also.

43. For many mammalian physiological processes, the ULTIMATE control center is the   43._____
    A. hypothalamus   B. adrenal cortex   C. anterior pituitary
    D. pancreas   E. posterior pituitary

44. In many mammalian hormonal control pathways, there are several steps between the receipt of a stimulus and the production of a response. For example, in the control of metabolic rate, the SECOND step is   44._____
    A. secretion of thyroid releasing hormone (TRH) by the hypothalamus
    B. secretion of thyroid stimulating hormone (TSH) by the anterior pituitary
    C. secretion of thyroid hormone (thyroxine) releasing hormone by the thyroid
    D. binding of thyroxine to receptors on the plasma membranes of target cells
    E. modification of the rate of electron transport in the mitochondria

45. When epinephrine stimulates a cell, which of the following materials would you expect to find INSIDE the stimulated cell?
    A. Epinephrine
    B. Cyclic AMP
    C. Epinephrine receptors
    D. Epinephrine releasing hormone
    E. Adrenocorticotrophic hormone

KEY (CORRECT ANSWERS)

1. D	11. C	21. C	31. A	41. D
2. A	12. A	22. A	32. C	42. C
3. D	13. C	23. D	33. B	43. A
4. E	14. A	24. B	34. D	44. B
5. A	15. D	25. D	35. B	45. B
6. A	16. B	26. E	36. D	
7. D	17. D	27. E	37. D	
8. A	18. E	28. D	38. E	
9. D	19. E	29. A	39. E	
10. B	20. D	30. A	40. C	

TEST 4

DIRECTIONS: Each question or incomplete statement is followed by several suggested answers or completions. Select the one that BEST answers the question or completes the statement. *PRINT THE LETTER OF THE CORRECT ANSWER IN THE SPACE AT THE RIGHT.*

1. The _____ system plays the central role of assisting the other four systems as they contribute to maintaining homeostasis in your body.
    A. respiratory
    B. circulatory
    C. digestive
    D. endocrine
    E. excretory

    1.____

2. Which of the following describes connective tissue?
    A. Tightly joined cells that connect all the organs of the body
    B. Striated cells composed primarily of protein fibers that can contract
    C. Sparse cells that secrete protein fibers and a matrix
    D. Elongated cells that can communicate between different tissue layers
    E. Cells that produce the interstitial fluid that surrounds all body cells

    2.____

3. The purpose of digestion is to
    A. obtain proteins, carbohydrates, lipids, and nucleic acids in prefabricated form
    B. obtain inorganic nutrients that cells can use to build their own macromolecules
    C. break food into small enough pieces so that it can be swallowed
    D. store food in a stomach or crop so that an animal does not have to eat continuously
    E. hydrolyze polymers into monomers that can be absorbed by cells

    3.____

4. The digestion of starch is begun in the mouth by salivary amylase. Why is the breakdown of starch to maltose not completed by this enzyme in the stomach?
    A. Food moves through the stomach too rapidly for digestion to occur.
    B. The mucous lining prevents the disaccharides from reaching the enzymes embedded in the epithelium of the stomach.
    C. There is not sufficient surface area present in the stomach.
    D. The acid pH denatures proteins and pepsin begins to digest them, so that the enzyme salivary amylase can no longer function.
    E. The function of the stomach is only storage and mechanical breakdown of food.

    4.____

5. Nutrients such as glucose and amino acids that are absorbed from the small intestine
    A. are transported from the capillaries of the small intestine through the hepatic portal vessel to the liver
    B. are transferred to the circulatory system by way of the lymphatic system
    C. enter the capillaries by endocytosis and exit to the body cells by exocytosis

    5.____

100

D. enter capillaries and are carried to the heart in the hepatic portal vessel
E. enter capillaries in the villi, are carried through the intestinal vein to the inferior vena cava, and delivered to the right atrium of the heart.

6. The gas exchange surfaces of all terrestrial multicellular animals must have all of the following characteristics EXCEPT
   A. a thin cell layer across which gases diffuse
   B. a large surface area for exchange
   C. a moist surface
   D. a circulatory system for distributing O_2 throughout the body
   E. protection from injury and desiccation

6.____

7. It is important for fish to have a countercurrent flow of water past the blood flowing through the gills in order to
   A. maximize heat exchange and maintain a stable internal temperature
   B. maximize gas exchange because fish do not have a circulatory system to supply O_2-rich blood to their body
   C. pump water across the gills because water is harder to move than air
   D. maximize gas exchange since water contains less O_2 than air and O_2 diffuses more slowly in water
   E. put hydrostatic pressure on the capillaries so that blood flow is maintained to the rest of the body

7.____

8. Which of the following structures is INCORRECTLY paired with its function or description?
   A. Pharynx – region where paths of food and air cross
   B. Larynx – voice box; contains vocal cords
   C. Epiglottis – protective flap that closes off entrance to the esophagus
   D. Alveoli – multilobed gas exchange sacs
   E. Mucus–coated cilia on cells lining bronchioles – sweep trapped particles out of respiratory tract

8.____

9. Which of the following is(are) NOT associated with the inflation of your lungs (inspiration)?
   A. Peristalsis
   B. Contraction of diaphragm and rib muscles
   C. Increase in pressure in the chest cavity
   D. Increase in volume in the chest cavity
   E. Both A and C

9.____

10. A gastrovascular cavity is
    A. a body cavity that serves both digestive and circulatory functions in simple animals such as hydra
    B. a circulatory system in which blood is pumped through some vessels but is otherwise free in the body cavity
    C. the mouth of a fish through which water flows past the gills and food enters the esophagus

10.____

D. a common heart chamber in amphibians that pumps blood to both the gas exchange surface and the rest of the body
E. a common exit for the digestive and excretory system found in insects

11. Breathing rate will increase when _____ CO_2 in the blood causes a _____ in pH, which is sensed by the medulla.
    A. increased; rise
    B. increased; drop
    C. decreased; rise
    D. decreased; drop
    E. It is a decrease in the level of O_2 in the blood that signals the medulla to increase breathing rate

12. Blood is pumped to the systemic circuit from the
    A. pulmonary artery
    B. right atrium
    C. left atrium
    D. left ventricle
    E. right ventricle

13. What causes the *lub* of the heartbeat that occurs during systole?
    A. The pacemaker (SA node) signaling the atria to contract
    B. The snapping open of the semilunar valves
    C. The closing of the atrioventricular (AV) valves
    D. Electrical changes in the heart that can be measured by an EKG
    E. A heart murmur caused by leaking AV valves

14. Blood that is in the pulmonary vein will usually pass through how many capillary beds before it reaches the pulmonary artery?
    A. One
    B. Two
    C. Three
    D. Four, if it goes through a portal system
    E. Five, if it travels through both the liver and kidney on the way back to the heart

15. What causes the return of fluid to the capillaries at the venous end of a capillary bed?
    A. Filtration
    B. Forced by muscle contraction through one-way valves
    C. Active transport
    D. A hydrostatic pressure that is greater than the osmotic pressure
    E. An osmotic pressure that is greater than the hydrostatic pressure of the blood in the capillaries

16. The velocity of blood flow is the SLOWEST in
    A. the capillaries
    B. the arteries in the extremities (arms and legs)
    C. lymphatic capillaries
    D. the right atrium
    E. the veins

17. What is the MAIN function of hemoglobin?
    A. Blood clotting
    B. Binding to and transporting O_2
    C. Osmotic balance
    D. Producing antibodies for defense
    E. Providing nutrients and O_2 to fetal circulation

17.____

18. You have a friend who is a *couch potato*, lying around on the couch most of the day, eating potato chips, smoking cigarettes, drinking a beer or two, and watching cartoons. Of these many bad habits, which would you encourage your friend to change FIRST (i.e., which one is shown by statistics to be the most harmful)?
    Stop
    A. smoking
    B. eating potato chips and start eating more fruits and vegetables
    C. lying on the couch and get some exercise
    D. drinking beer
    E. watching cartoons and start studying biology

18.____

19. According to scientific articles and studies on diet drugs
    A. echocardiograms show that obesity is linked with heart valve problems
    B. the diet drug combination fenfluramine-phentermine has been linked to heart valve damage
    C. the fen-phen combination has proven ineffective in helping obese people lose weight
    D. doctors working for the FDA monitored the fen-phen combination and recognized its potential harmful effects just after the drugs came on the market
    E. the FDA would never approve a drug that could cause lung disease or heart damage

19.____

20. Which of the following would help an ectotherm maintain a relatively high and constant body temperature?
    A. Going into a daily torpor
    B. Conserving body heat by layers of fat, fur, or feathers
    C. Increasing its metabolic rate with hormones
    D. Living in the tropics and moving in and out of the sun as necessary
    E. Metabolizing brown fat

20.____

21. A camel crossing a desert uses all of the following osmoregulatory and thermoregulatory adaptations EXCEPT
    A. producing very hypertonic urine
    B. breathing through extensive respiratory turbinates
    C. sweating profusely to maintain a lower body temperature
    D. metabolizing fats to obtain metabolic water
    E. producing very dry feces

21.____

22. When your hypothalamus senses a decrease in body temperature below the set point, it initiates
    A. sweating and vasodilation of surface blood vessels
    B. shivering and vasodilation of surface vessels
    C. shivering and vasoconstriction of surface vessels
    D. vasodilation of blood vessels running to your hands and feet
    E. goose bumps, shivering, and a drop in your metabolic rate

22.____

23. What is the original source of the electrons used to reduce CO_2 in photosynthesis?
    A. H_2O
    B. O_2
    C. Sunlight
    D. The accessory pigments in photosystem II
    E. Photosystem I

23.____

24. C_4 plants and CAM plants
    A. have higher rates of photosynthesis than do C_3 plants
    B. use a more efficient enzyme than rubisco to combine CO_2 with RuBP (ribulose bisphosphate)
    C. are able to perform the Calvin Cycle at night and thus avoid unnecessary water loss
    D. have adaptations that allow them to avoid photorespiration by providing rubisco with a relatively high concentration of CO_2
    E. are able to produce G3P (glyceraldehyde 3-phosphate) using less ATP than do C_3 plants

24.____

Questions 25-26.

DIRECTIONS: Questions 25 and 26 are to be answered on the basis of the following diagram of the light reactions.

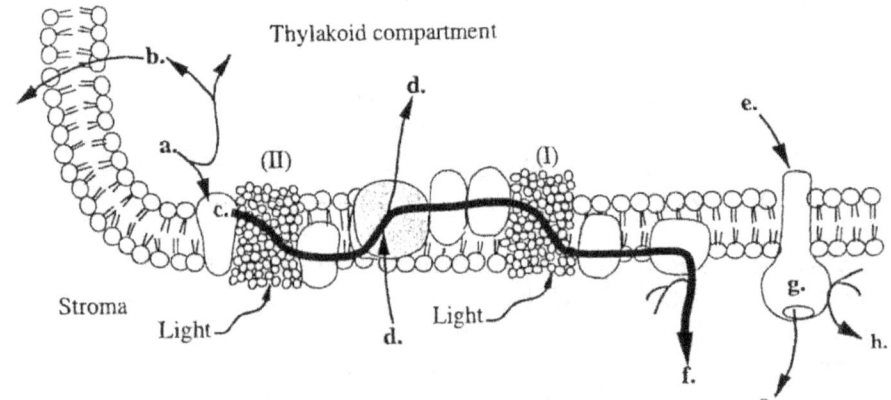

25. What is produced at letter f?
    A. H^+ B. O_2 C. H_2O D. ATP E. NADPH

25.____

26. Which letter represents electrons?
    A. a   B. b   C. c   D. d   E. e

Questions 27-28.

DIRECTIONS: Questions 27 and 28 are to be answered on the basis of the following diagram.

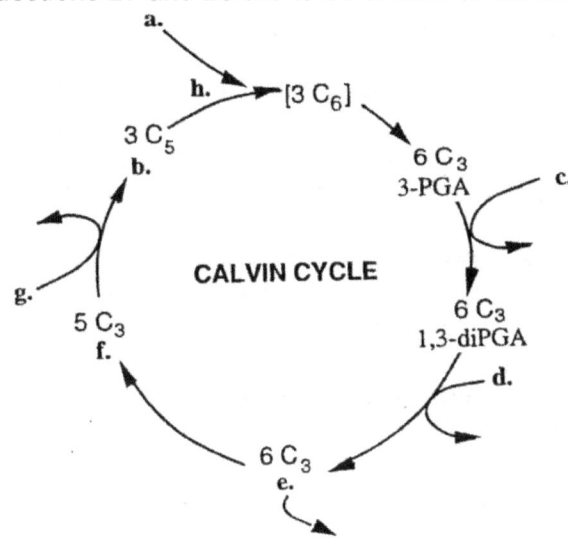

27. Which of the following letters represent molecules of ATP?
    A. c, g
    B. c, d, g
    C. c, d, g, h
    D. d
    E. d, e

28. What does a represent?
    A. NADPH
    B. RuBP (ribulose bisphosphate)
    C. G3P (glyceraldehyde 3-phosphate)
    D. CO_2
    E. Rubisco

29. Plants need nitrate, phosphate, and sulfate in order to
    A. help transport sucrose through the plant
    B. maintain a proper osmotic balance in their cells
    C. produce their amino acids and nucleic acids
    D. balance the uptake of cations (positive ions) from the soil
    E. provide micronutrients needed as cofactors for many enzymatic reactions

30. Plants use ATP to drive proton pumps that create H^+ concentrations. These proton pumps are used in all of the following EXCEPT
    A. cation exchange
    B. cotransport of anions (negative ions) into root cells
    C. ATP formation by chemiosmosis in the thylakoids
    D. secondary active transport of sucrose into phloem
    E. all of the above use ATP-driven proton pumps

31. Symbiotic associations of bacteria and the roots of legumes
    A. are root nodules that increase the surface area for absorption of nitrogen from the soil
    B. provide fixed nitrogen to the plant and carbohydrates to the bacteria
    C. provide protection from the increasing acidity of the soil caused by acid rain
    D. help the plant root break down organic matter in the soil in order to obtain inorganic nutrients
    E. are good examples of the competitive nature of interspecific interactions

31.____

32. Despite falling levels in the emission of acidic air pollutants, acid rain remains a serious environmental threat. Which of these situations has added to the acid rain problem?
    A. Taller smoke stacks have spread pollution over wider areas.
    B. Dust particles are washed down by acid rain and the cation exchange resulting from their cations is release H$^+$ in the soil and decreasing the pH of soil waters
    C. Atmospheric dust particles have not been reduced sufficiently and their cations are contributing to the acidity of the rain
    D. Atmospheric bases, which neutralize acid rain and contribute to cation supplies in the soil, have declined due to emission regulations on dust particles
    E. Acid rain interacts with dust particles, releasing new acids and further lowering the pH of rain and increasing the pollutants that are poisoning vegetation

32.____

33. The function of the Casparian strip is
    A. to enlarge surface area of root available for absorption of water and minerals
    B. to pump ions into the central vascular bundle of a root
    C. the outer wall of dead xylem cells that provides mechanical support to a stem
    D. the site of proton pump that helps to load ions and water into the xylem of a root
    E. the waterproof barrier that assures that all absorbed minerals pass through a selective plasma membrane

33.____

34. Which of the following is NOT a reason why plants need an ample water supply?
    A. The osmotic loss of water from guard cells opens stomata for gas exchange.
    B. Mineral ions are transported through the plant dissolved in water.
    C. Water is one of the reactants in photosynthesis.
    D. Water is used for cell elongation during plant growth.
    E. Plants use water for evaporative cooling.

34.____

35. A decrease in the diameter of the trunk of a tree that is actively transporting water provides evidence that
    A. transpiration is the mechanism of transporting water up a tree
    B. water is under pressure within the xylem of a tree trunk
    C. water is under tension when it is transported up a tree
    D. water is moving through the nonliving cavities of xylem cells
    E. secondary active transport of sucrose is driving water transport

36. Translocation involves the
    A. passive flow of sucrose from where it is less concentrated to where it is more concentrated
    B. cotransport of sucrose with Na^+ moving down its concentration gradient from one phloem cell to the next
    C. secondary active transport of glucose from source to sink
    D. pressure-driven movement of dissolved sucrose from source to sink
    E. evaporation of water from the sink, resulting in the cohesive pull on water molecules flowing from the source

37. Which of the following processes would you expect to find happening in the gills of a marine (salt-water) fish?
    A. Diffusion of ammonia from gills into water
    B. Osmotic loss of water and active pumping of salts out of gills into water
    C. Osmotic gain of water and active pumping of salts out of gills into water
    D. Both A and B
    E. Both A and C

38. Which of the following is NOT a true statement concerning urea?
    Urea
    A. is easily and safely transported in blood and is removed from the blood by the nephrons of the kidney
    B. is the waste product produced by insects and most reptiles
    C. takes more energy to produce than does ammonia, but less energy than needed to produce uric acid
    D. is produced in the liver from ammonia, which is formed from the deamination of amino acids
    E. requires a moderate loss of water to excrete

39. Drinking alcohol blocks the release of ADH (antidiuretic hormone) from the posterior pituitary. Without ADH,
    A. more water moves into the collecting duct by osmosis and a more dilute urine is produced
    B. more water is reabsorbed from the collecting duct and a more concentrated urine is produced
    C. less water is reabsorbed from the collecting ducts, and the body produces a larger quantity of dilute urine
    D. the hypothalamus does not signal the body to drink, urine production decreases, and dehydration produces the effects of a hangover
    E. the kidney cannot reabsorb salts and H^+, and the osmotic balance and pH of the body is disturbed

40. Which of the following hormones have antagonistic (opposite) effects?
    A. ACTH (adrenocorticotropic hormone) – epinephrine
    B. Thyroid hormone – TSH (thyroid-stimulating hormone)
    C. Glucocorticoids – glucagon
    D. Melatonin – prolactin
    E. Insulin - glucagon

40.____

41. All of the following are descriptive of a peptide hormone EXCEPT that it
    A. binds with a specific receptor attached to the inside of the plasma membrane
    B. produces a fast, but not necessarily long-lasting, effect
    C. often amplifies a hormonal message by a cascade of enzyme activations
    D. may use membrane-bound relay proteins and enzymes to produce a second messenger
    E. often uses cAMP as the second messenger to carry the message throughout the cytoplasm

41.____

42. Which organ is responsible for adjusting nutrient levels of the blood, detoxifying drugs and alcohol, and producing urea?
    A. Pancreas   B. Liver   C. Small intestine
    D. Kidney   E. Hypothalamus

42.____

43. Glucocorticoids are produced in response to
    A. high blood-glucose levels
    B. releasing hormones from the anterior pituitary
    C. an inflammatory immune stimulus
    D. long-term, physiological stress
    E. nervous stimulation from the hypothalamus

43.____

44. What regulates the level of thyroid hormones (TH) in the body?
    A. A feedback loop in which TSH (thyroid-stimulating hormone) and TH inhibit the release of TRH
    B. A feedback loop in which excess TRH (TSH-releasing hormone) inhibits its own release
    C. An adequate supply of iodine
    D. A balance between growth hormone and TSH, both of which are produced by the anterior pituitary
    E. The temperature-control center of the hypothalamus which increases the release of TSH when the body temperature drops

44.____

45. A portal vessel is a
    A. vessel that carries urea-loaded blood from the liver to the kidney for processing
    B. vessel that connects the capillary beds of the kidney to the renal vein
    C. vessel that connects two capillary beds without the blood first returning to the heart to be repumped
    D. vein that transports oxygen-rich blood instead of oxygen-poor blood
    E. lymphatic vessel that returns excess interstitial fluid to the circulatory system

45.____

KEY (CORRECT ANSWERS)

1.	B	11.	B	21.	C	31.	B	41.	A
2.	C	12.	D	22.	C	32.	D	42.	B
3.	E	13.	C	23.	A	33.	E	43.	D
4.	D	14.	A	24.	D	34.	A	44.	A
5.	A	15.	E	25.	E	35.	C	45.	C
6.	D	16.	A	26.	C	36.	D		
7.	D	17.	B	27.	A	37.	D		
8.	C	18.	A	28.	D	38.	B		
9.	E	19.	B	29.	C	39.	C		
10.	A	20.	D	30.	C	40.	E		

TEST 5

DIRECTIONS: Each question or incomplete statement is followed by several suggested answers or completions. Select the one that BEST answers the question or completes the statement. *PRINT THE LETTER OF THE CORRECT ANSWER IN THE SPACE AT THE RIGHT.*

1.

a)
```
      H
      |
  H — C — O
      |
      O
       \
        H
```

b)
```
      H
      |
  H — C — H
      ||
  H — C — H
      |
  H — C — H
      |
      H
```

c)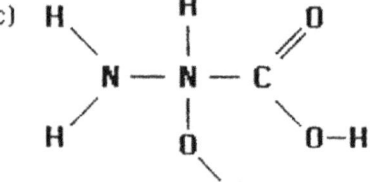

d)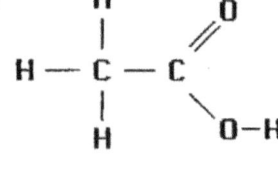

e)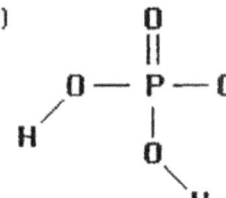

1.___

   Which of the above structures is drawn CORRECTLY?
   A. a   B. b   C. c   D. d   E. e

2. Which of the following arrangements of chemical bonds indicates the relative strengths of chemical bonds in molecules in solution in water from strongest to weakest?
   A. Covalent – hydrogen – ionic – hydrophobic
   B. Hydrogen – covalent – ionic – hydrophobic
   C. Ionic – covalent – hydrophobic – hydrogen
   D. Hydrophobic – hydrogen – covalent – ionic
   E. Covalent – ionic – hydrogen - hydrophobic

2.___

3. Which of the following molecules would you expect to find in the interior of a globular protein?

   A.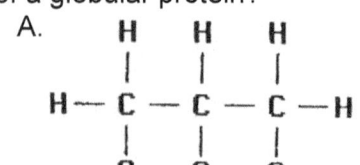

   B.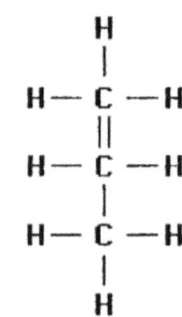

3.___

C.

H   H   O
 \ | //
  N—C—C
 / | \
H   O   O—H
    |
    H

D.

H   H   O
 \ | //
  N—C—C
 / | \
H   H—C—H O—H
    |
    H—C—H
    |
    H

E.

O   O—H
 \\ /
  C
  |
H—C—H
  |
H—C—H
  |
H—C—H
  |
H—C—H
  |
H—C—H
  |
  H

4. The figure at the right represents a U-tube with the two sides separated by a membrane permeable to water but not to glucose. Side A contains a 2% solution of glucose in water. Side B contains a 47% solution of glucose in water. Assuming uniform temperature and pressure, which one of the following statements BEST describes what will happen in this system?
Water will move
   A. from side A to side B only
   B. from side B to side A only
   C. equally in both directions
   D. in both directions, with more moving from side A to side B
   E. in both directions, with more moving from side B to side A

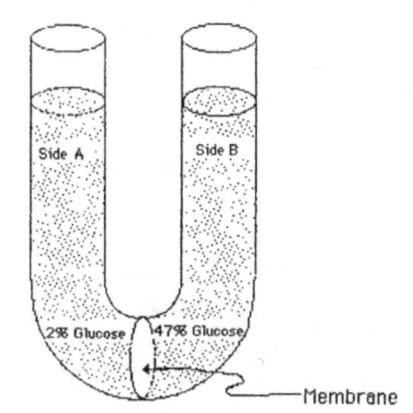

4.____

Questions 5-6.

DIRECTIONS: Questions 5 and 6 are to be answered on the basis of the following graph.

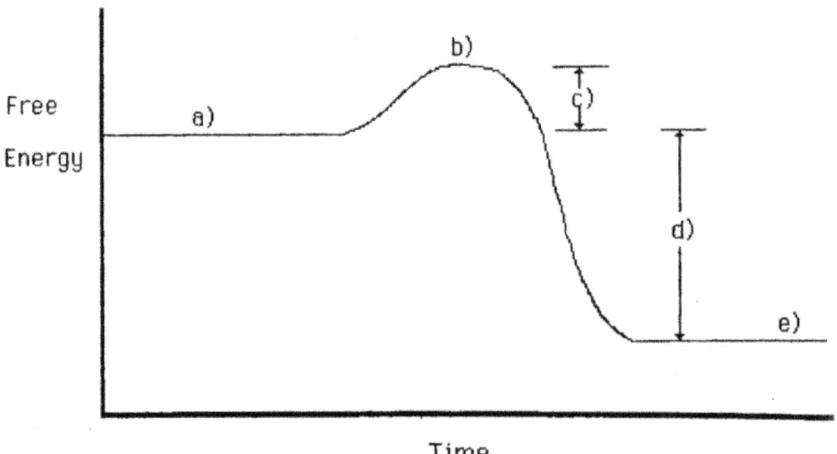

5. Enzymes act so as to change which of the components in the above graph?
   A. a   B. b   C. c   D. d   E. e

6. In the above graphed reaction, energy was _____; therefore, this must have been an _____ reaction.
   A. released; exergonic
   B. required; exergonic
   C. released; endergonic
   D. required; endergonic
   E. neither released nor required; enzyme catalyzed

7. In glycolysis, which of the following materials is NOT phosphorylated (i.e., has phosphate added to it)?
   A. Glucose
   B. Glucose 6-phosphate
   C. Glyceraldehyde 3-phosphate (G3P)
   D. Pyruvate
   E. Adenosine diphosphate (ADP)

8. Which of the following components of glycolysis contains the LARGEST amount of potential energy (i.e., how much ATP can be made from each one)?
   A. G3P in the absence of oxygen
   B. Glucose in the absence of oxygen
   C. NADH in the presence of oxygen
   D. Pyruvate in the presence of oxygen
   E. Acetyl CoA in the presence of oxygen

Questions 9-10.

DIRECTIONS: Questions 9 and 10 are to be answered on the basis of the following diagram.

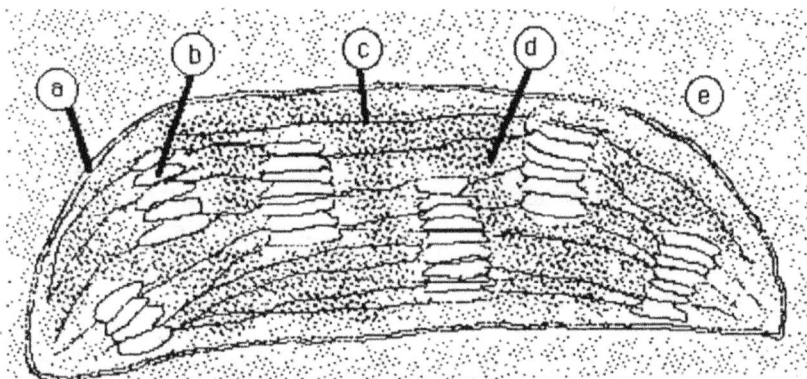

9. In the chloroplast labeled above, in which of the areas would oxygen be produced when exposed to light?
   A. In the outer membrane of the chloroplast
   B. Inside a thylakoid
   C. In a connecting lamella
   D. In the stroma
   E. Outside the chloroplast

9._____

10. In the chloroplast diagrammed and labeled above, where would the NADPH concentration be HIGHEST?
    A. In the outer membrane of the chloroplast
    B. Inside a thylakoid
    C. In a connecting lamella
    D. In the stroma
    E. Outside the chloroplast

10._____

11.

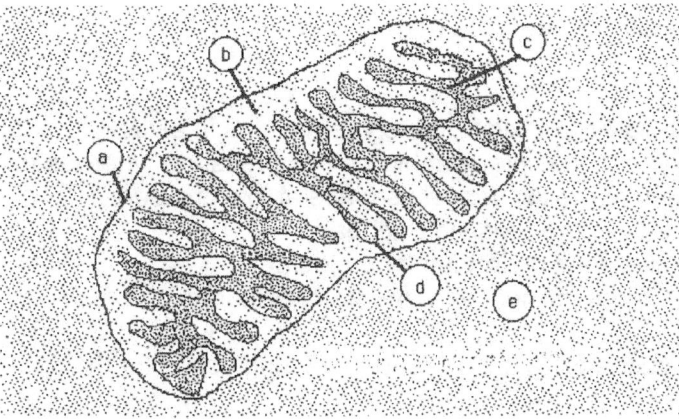

11._____

Which of the labeled areas of the above mitochondrion would contain acetyl-CoA?
A. Outer membrane   B. Outer compartment
C. Inner compartment (matrix) D. Inner membrane
E. Outside the mitochondrion

12. Which of the following statements about oxidative phosphorylation is NOT true?
    A. It occurs in the inner membrane of mitochondria.
    B. It produces much more ATP than glycolysis.
    C. If blocked, it results in the accumulation of NADH.
    D. It uses carbohydrates directly to make ATP by substrate level phosphorylation.
    E. It is exergonic overall.

13. Of the following, which nutrients are required by animals, but NOT by plants?
    A. Oxygen   B. Carbohydrates
    C. Sodium   D. Water
    E. All except D are correct choices

14. A person consumes large numbers of vitamin supplements over a long period of time. A sample of fatty tissue from this person would contain significant quantities of all of the following EXCEPT vitamin
    A. A   B. C   C. D   D. E   E. K

15. Which of the following materials do NOT begin digestion with enzymes produced by the pancreas?
    A. Carbohydrates   B. Lipids   C. Proteins
    D. Nucleic acids   E. Both A and C

16. Which of the following statements about gas exchange is NOT true?
    A. In plants, the largest amount of gas exchange occurs in the spongy mesophyll.
    B. In plants, the largest amount of gas exchange occurs in leaves during the day.
    C. Gas exchange in animals involves countercurrent exchange mechanisms when the demand for oxygen is low compared to the supply.
    D. Exchange of oxygen is generally easier on land than in the water.
    E. It often involves either water loss or gain.

17. In fish
    A. the exchange of carbon dioxide and oxygen occurs in alveoli
    B. the intake of oxygen takes place at high blood pressure, whereas the delivery of oxygen to the tissues takes place at low pressure
    C. carbon dioxide leaves the cells via tracheae
    D. oxygen is carried in solution in the blood plasma
    E. gas exchange is more efficient at higher temperatures

18. A(n) _____ would have the SMALLEST amount of lung tissue for their body size.
    A. elephant   B. horse   C. dog
    D. mouse   E. frog

19. Which of the following processes provides the motive force for transport in the phloem?
    A. Evaporation
    B. Cohesion of water
    C. Adhesion of water to cellulose
    D. Diffusion of mineral ions
    E. Secondary active cotransport of sucrose

19.____

20. A red blood cell is in the left ventricle of the heart. What is the MAXIMUM number of capillary beds it would have to pass through before passing through the left atrium?
    A. None   B. One   C. Two   D. Three   E. Four

20.____

21. In mammals, the contraction of the ventricles is stimulated by the
    A. medulla of the brain   B. central nervous system
    C. nodes of Ranvier   D. sinoatrial (SA) node
    E. atrioventricular (AV) node

21.____

22. Which of the following organisms might use a contractile vacuole to excrete wastes?
    A. Salamander larva   B. Amoeba
    C. Grasshopper   D. Flatworm
    E. Earthworm

22.____

23. A fish living in the Finger Lakes of New York would probably excrete most of its nitrogenous wastes in the form of
    A. ammonia   B. urea   C. uric acid
    D. amino acids   E. nitrogen gas

23.____

Questions 24-25.

DIRECTIONS: Questions 24 and 25 are to be answered on the basis of the following diagram.

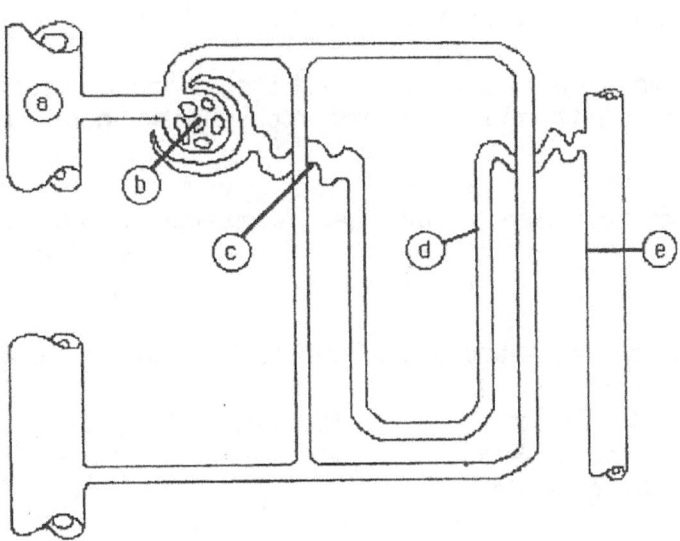

24. In the nephron diagrammed above, where would you expect to find the HIGHEST hydrostatic (i.e., fluid) pressure?
    A. a	B. b	C. c	D. d	E. e

25. In the nephron diagrammed above, where would glucose be reabsorbed?
    A. a	B. b	C. c	D. d	E. e

26. Which one of the following statements about animal chemical control systems is NOT true?
    A. They usually produce much slower responses than nervous systems.
    B. They occur in virtually all multicellular animals.
    C. The chemical message is always lipid soluble.
    D. The carrier for the message is usually the circulatory system.
    E. Some cells have internal chemical messengers also.

27. For many mammalian physiological processes, the ULTIMATE control center is the
    A. hypothalamus
    B. anterior pituitary
    C. posterior pituitary
    D. adrenal cortex
    E. pancreas

28. Which of the following hormones maintains the uterus for implantation and pregnancy?
    A. Estrogen
    B. Prostaglandin
    C. Testosterone
    D. Follicle stimulating hormone
    E. Progesterone

29. Which of the following is the CORRECT sequence for the hormonal releases involved in the regulation of the male reproductive cycle?
    A. Gonadotropin releasing hormone → follicle stimulating hormone → testosterone
    B. Gonadotropin releasing hormone → leutinizing hormone → testosterone
    C. Gonadotropin releasing hormone → follicle stimulating hormone → estrogen
    D. Gonadotropin releasing hormone → leutinizing hormone → estrogen
    E. Follicle stimulating hormone → gonadotropin releasing hormone → testosterone

30. Which of the following animals has the LEAST centralized nervous system?
    A. Sponge	B. Hydra	C. Flatworm
    D. Insect	E. Vertebrate

31. During the course of vertebrate evolution, the position of the chief control over behavior has shifted from the
    A. cerebrum to the hindbrain
    B. forebrain to the cerebellum
    C. cerebellum to the cerebrum
    D. cerebrum to the cerebellum
    E. hindbrain to the cerebrum

32. Short-term memories are converted into long-term memories by the
    A. cerebellum
    B. medulla oblongata
    C. hypothalamus
    D. hippocampus
    E. reticular activating system

33. The sympathetic nervous system
    A. promotes *fight or flight* responses
    B. acts to inhibit the sinoatrial (S-A) node of the heart
    C. usually has only one neurotransmitter
    D. usually stimulates the organs of digestion
    E. is part of the central nervous system

34. Which of the following statements about the parasympathetic nervous system is NOT true?
    A. It opposes the effects of the sympathetic nervous system.
    B. It tends to slow the breathing and heart rate.
    C. The principal transmitter is acetylcholine.
    D. It generally stimulates digestive organs.
    E. It is part of the central nervous system.

Questions 35-36.

DIRECTIONS: Questions 35 and 36 are to be answered on the basis of the following diagram.

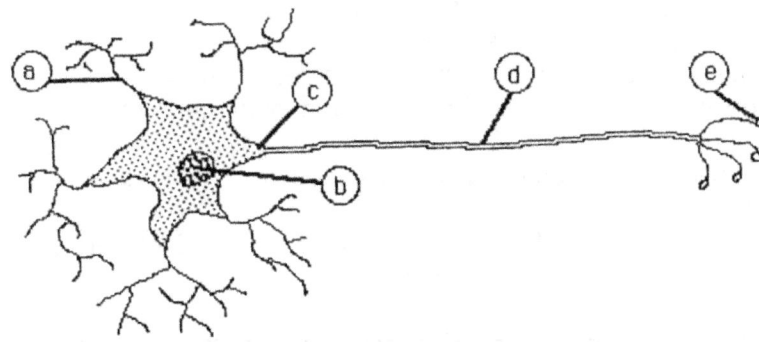

35. In the neuron diagrammed above, where are action potentials usually generated?
    A. a   B. b   C. c   D. d   E. e

36. In the neuron diagrammed above, where would you expect to find channels for calcium ions (Ca^{++})?
    A. a   B. b   C. c   D. d   E. e

Questions 37-38.

DIRECTIONS: Questions 37 and 38 are to be answered on the basis of the following diagram.

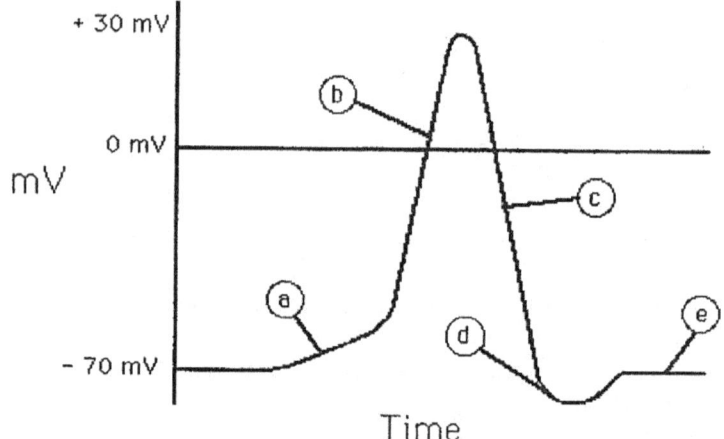

37. In the above diagram, which part of the graph corresponds to the flow of potassium ions OUT through ion channels in the axonal membrane?
    A. a   B. b   C. c   D. d   E. e

    37.____

38. The above diagram is a graph of
    A. an action potential
    B. an inhibitory post-synaptic potential (IPSP)
    C. neurotransmitter release in a synapse
    D. electrical activity across the membrane of a dendrite
    E. the change in voltage measured outside an axonal membrane

    38.____

39. Synaptic transmission at neuromuscular junctions usually involves the neurotransmitter
    A. adrenalin   B. acetylcholine   C. noradrenalin
    D. histamine   E. seratonin

    39.____

40. Which of the following would NOT slow or stop synaptic transmission?
    A. Blocking the release of neurotransmitter
    B. Lowering the body temperature
    C. Competitively inhibiting the neurotransmitter receptors
    D. Competitively inhibiting the reuptake of the neurotransmitter
    E. Blocking the breakdown of transmitter fragments by the presynaptic end bulb

    40.____

41. Curaré competes with acetylcholine for the active site(s) in the acetylcholine receptor in neuromuscular junctions. The effects of curare on a mammal would be to
    A. block action potentials in its sensory neurons
    B. make it go blind
    C. paralyze its skeletal muscles
    D. slow its heart rate
    E. block nervous transmission in its central nervous system

    41.____

42. The photoreceptor cells in a human eye is contained in the
    A. lens   B. sclera   C. choroid
    D. cornea   E. retina

43. Which of the following statements about human eyes is NOT true?
    A. They have flexible lenses.
    B. They cannot normally detect ultraviolet light.
    C. They accommodate by moving the lens in and out.
    D. They can detect both the intensity and wavelength of light.
    E. Light is perceived by two different types of receptor cells.

44. Which of the following sensory inputs is detected by a modified dendrite, rather than by a specialized sensory receptor cell?
    A. Taste   B. Pain   C. Gravity
    D. Sight   E. Sound

45. Which of the following would MOST likely cause a complete loss of hearing?
    A. Puncture of the tympanic membrane
    B. Blockage of the Eustachian tubes
    C. Calcification of the ear ossicles (*bones*)
    D. Puncture of the round window of the cochlea
    E. Loss of hair cells in the organ of Corti in the narrow end of the cochlea

46. During sensory transduction, which of the following processes does NOT always occur?
    A. Conversion of stimulus energy into biochemical changes in the receptor cells
    B. Production of a receptor potential in sensory receptor cells
    C. Production of action potentials in sensory neurons
    D. Transmission of sensory inputs to the central nervous system
    E. Production of motor responses in motor circuits

47. During the generation of a motor response, how many of the following processes directly require calcium ions (Ca^{++})?
    - Transmission of action potentials along motor axons
    - Release of acetylcholine at neuromuscular junctions
    - Binding of acetylcholine to receptors in the sarcolemma
    - Generation of action potentials in the sarcolemma and T tubules
    - Binding of myosin to actin

    A. 1   B. 2   C. 3   D. 4   E. 5

48. Which of the following statements about muscle contraction is NOT true?
    A. It requires large amounts of ATP.
    B. It requires calcium ions (Ca^{++}).
    C. It occurs in the same way in all types of muscles.
    D. In a single muscle fiber, there is an *all-or-none* response.
    E. It is under complete voluntary control only in skeletal muscle.

49. During the stages of the contraction of myofibrils in muscle fibers, which of the following processes requires the binding of a phosphate ion (obtained from ATP)?
    A. Acetylcholine release by motor neurons
    B. Depolarization of the sarcolemma and T tubules
    C. Exposure of actin binding sites to myosin
    D. Binding of myosin cross bridges to actin
    E. Swiveling and then release of the myosin-actin cross-bridge

49.____

50. Which of the following statements about skeletal systems is NOT true?
    A. In vertebrates, they are the primary reservoir for calcium.
    B. They act as lever systems along with the contraction of muscles.
    C. They serve a protective as well as locomotory function in both invertebrates and vertebrates.
    D. In vertebrates, they are composed entirely of non-living components.
    E. They are one of the principal factors limiting the size of animals.

50.____

KEY (CORRECT ANSWERS)

1.	D	11.	C	21.	E	31.	E	41.	C
2.	E	12.	D	22.	B	32.	D	42.	E
3.	D	13.	E	23.	A	33.	A	43.	C
4.	D	14.	B	24.	A	34.	E	44.	B
5.	C	15.	E	25.	C	35.	C	45.	D
6.	A	16.	C	26.	C	36.	E	46.	E
7.	D	17.	B	27.	A	37.	C	47.	B
8.	D	18.	E	28.	E	38.	A	48.	C
9.	B	19.	E	29.	B	39.	B	49.	E
10.	D	20.	D	30.	B	40.	D	50.	D

EXAMINATION SECTION
TEST 1

DIRECTIONS: Each question or incomplete statement is followed by several suggested answers or completions. Select the one that BEST answers the question or completes the statement. *PRINT THE LETTER OF THE CORRECT ANSWER IN THE SPACE AT THE RIGHT.*

1. In an Ameba, materials are taken from its environment and then moved throughout its cytoplasm.
   These processes are known as

   A. absorption and circulation
   B. food processing and energy release
   C. energy release and synthesis
   D. coordination and regulation

   1.____

2. In which kingdom is an organism classified if it lacks a membrane separating MOST of its genetic material from its cytoplasm?

   A. Protist   B. Monera   C. Plant   D. Animal

   2.____

3. Which is TRUE of organisms that are classified in the same genus?
   They must be

   A. in the same phylum but may be of different species
   B. of the same species but may be in different phyla
   C. in the same phylum but may be in different kingdoms
   D. in the same kingdom but may be in different phyla

   3.____

4. According to the cell theory, which statement is CORRECT?

   A. Viruses are true cells.
   B. Cells are basically unlike in structure.
   C. Mitochondria are found only in plant cells.
   D. Cells come from pre-existing cells.

   4.____

5. To transplant a nucleus from one cell to another cell, a scientist would use

   A. an electron microscope
   B. an ultracentrifuge
   C. microdissection instruments
   D. staining techniques

   5.____

6. A student using a compound microscope measured the diameter of several red blood cells and found that the average cell length was 0.008 millimeter.
   What is the AVERAGE length of a single red blood cell in micrometers?

   A. 0.8   B. 8   C. 80   D. 800

   6.____

7. MOST cellular respiration in plants takes place in organelles known as

   A. chloroplasts   B. stomates
   C. ribosomes   D. mitochondria

   7.____

8. Which organic compound is CORRECTLY matched with the sub-unit that composes it?

    A. Maltose - amino acid
    B. Starch - glucose
    C. Protein - fatty acid
    D. Lipid - sucrose

9. A fruit fly is classified as a heterotroph, rather than as an autotroph, because it is unable to

    A. transport needed materials through the body
    B. release energy from organic molecules
    C. manufacture its own food
    D. divide its cells mitotically

10. The diagram at the right illustrates phases of a specific life activity being carried on by a cell. Which process is occurring at phase 3?

    A. Intracellular digestion
    B. Extracellular digestion
    C. Ingestion
    D. Excretion

11. At optimum light intensity, which atmospheric gas MOST directly influences the rate of photosynthesis?

    A. Nitrogen
    B. Oxygen
    C. Carbon dioxide
    D. Hydrogen

12. Which physical factor associated with upward movement in vascular plants is MOST affected when leaves are shed in the autumn?

    A. Transpirational pull
    B. Capillary action
    C. Root pressure
    D. Active transport

13. A red blood cell placed in distilled water will swell and burst due to the diffusion of

    A. salt from the red blood cell into the water
    B. water into the red blood cell
    C. water from the blood cell into its environment
    D. salts from the water into the red blood cell

14. Carbohydrate molecules A and B come in contact with the cell membrane of the same cell. Molecule A passes through the membrane readily, but molecule B does not. It is MOST likely that molecule A is a(n)

    A. protein and B is a lipid
    B. polysaccharide and B is a monosaccharide
    C. amino acid and B is a monosaccharide
    D. monosaccharide and B is a polysaccharide

15. Most animals make energy available for cell activity by transferring the potential energy of glucose to ATP. This process occurs during

A. aerobic respiration *only*
B. anaerobic respiration *only*
C. both aerobic and anaerobic respiration
D. neither aerobic nor anaerobic respiration

16. Nitrogenous waste products are produced from the complete metabolism of

    A. water   B. sugars   C. starches   D. proteins

17. What do the tracheal tubes of the grasshopper and the air spaces of a geranium leaf have in common?
    They

    A. regulate the flow of urea into and out of the organism
    B. are the major sites for the ingestion of nutrients
    C. contain enzymes that convert light energy to chemical bond energy
    D. are surrounded by moist internal surfaces where gas exchange occurs

18. Which of the following processes releases the GREATEST amount of energy?
    The

    A. oxidation of one glucose molecule to lactic acid molecules
    B. oxidation of one glucose molecule to carbon dioxide and water molecules
    C. conversion of two glucose molecules to a maltose molecule
    D. conversion of one glucose molecule to alcohol and carbon dioxide molecules

19. Which organism is CORRECTLY paired with its excretory structure?

    A. Earthworm - nephridium   B. Ameba - skin
    C. Grasshopper - nephron   D. Hydra - Malpighian tube

20. In the diagram of two neurons shown above, at which point would a substance that interferes with the action of a neurotransmitter be MOST effective?

    A. 1   B. 2   C. 3   D. 4

21. The structure and function of the nervous system of the earthworm are MOST similar to those of the

    A. Ameba   B. Hydra
    C. grasshopper   D. Paramecium

22. Tropisms in plants MOST directly result from the

    A. unequal distribution of auxins
    B. transpirational pull of water
    C. transmission of impulses by acetylcholine
    D. excitation of chlorophyll molecules by light

23.

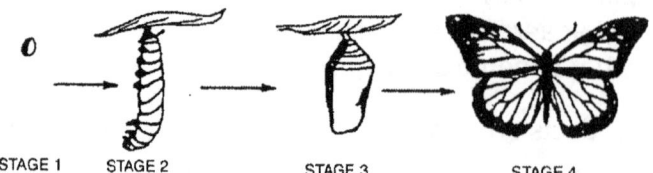

STAGE 1   STAGE 2   STAGE 3   STAGE 4

The above diagram represents four stages of development in an arthropod. Which substances MOST directly regulate the process illustrated in the diagram?

    A. Auxins   B. Hormones   C. Vitamins   D. Minerals

24. Which life function is MOST closely associated with structure A in the cross-sectional diagram of an earthworm shown at the right?

    A. Locomotion
    B. Respiration
    C. Transport
    D. Excretion

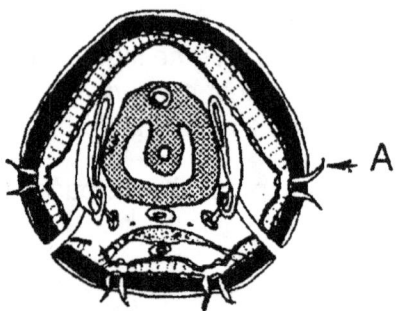

25. Which two organisms are able to move due to the interaction of muscular and skeletal systems?

    A. Earthworm and human   B. Grasshopper and Hydra
    C. Hydra and earthworm   D. Grasshopper and human

26. Which is NOT a major function of cartilage tissues in a human adult?

    A. Giving pliable support to body structures
    B. Cushioning joint areas
    C. Adding flexibility to joints
    D. Providing skeletal levers

27. Which is a CORRECT route of an impulse in a reflex arc?

    A. Receptor → sensory neuron → interneuron → motor neuron → effector
    B. Effector → receptor → motor neuron → sensory neuron → interneuron
    C. Sensory neuron → effector → motor neuron → receptor → interneuron
    D. Motor neuron → sensory neuron → interneuron → effector

28. In addition to water, the PRINCIPAL components of urine are

    A. amino acids and fatty acids
    B. urea and salts
    C. ammonia and bile
    D. hydrochloric acid and bases

29. MOST carbon dioxide is carried in the plasma in the form of

    A. hydrogen ions   B. bicarbonate ions
    C. lactic acid   D. oxyhemoglobin

30. Which cells are able to carry on the process of phagocytosis? _____ cells.   30.____

    A. Nerve
    B. Epidermal
    C. Red blood
    D. White blood

KEY (CORRECT ANSWERS)

1. A	16. D
2. B	17. D
3. A	18. B
4. D	19. A
5. C	20. C
6. B	21. C
7. D	22. A
8. B	23. B
9. C	24. A
10. A	25. D
11. C	26. D
12. A	27. A
13. B	28. B
14. D	29. B
15. C	30. D

TEST 2

DIRECTIONS: Each question or incomplete statement is followed by several suggested answers or completions. Select the one that BEST answers the question or completes the statement. *PRINT THE LETTER OF THE CORRECT ANSWER IN THE SPACE AT THE RIGHT.*

1. The thin-walled vessels of the circulatory system where most oxygen and carbon dioxide are exchanged are

   A. alveoli   B. arteries   C. capillaries   D. veins

   1.____

2. Small lymphatic vessels which extend into the villi are

   A. veins   B. lacteals   C. nodes   D. capillaries

   2.____

3.

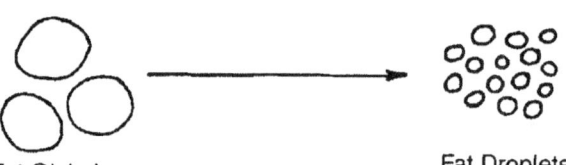

Fat Globules → Fat Droplets

Which process is represented by the above diagram?

   A. Emulsification   B. Excretion
   C. Absorption   D. Peristalsis

   3.____

4. The following list describes some of the events associated with normal cell division:
   - A. - Nuclear membrane formation around each set of newly formed chromosomes
   - B. - Separation of centromeres
   - C. - Replication of each chromosome
   - D. - Movement of single-stranded chromosomes to opposite ends of the spindle

   What is the NORMAL sequence in which these events occur?

   A. A → B → C → D   B. C → B → D → A
   C. C → D → B → A   D. D → C → A → B

   4.____

5.

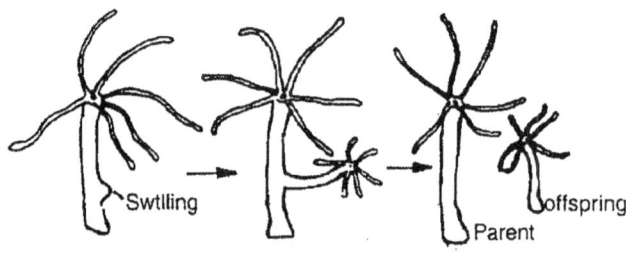

Swtlling   Parent   offspring

Which process, carried out by a Hydra, is illustrated by the series of above drawings?

   A. Binary fission   B. Budding
   C. Vegetative propagation   D. Spore formation

   5.____

126

6. During the normal meiotic division of a diploid cell, the change in chromosome number that occurs is represented as

   A. $4n \rightarrow n$ B. $2n \rightarrow 4n$ C. $2n \rightarrow n$ D. $n \rightarrow 1/2\, n$

7. In animals, polar bodies are formed as a result of cell division in _____.

   A. meiotic; females
   B. meiotic; males
   C. mitotic; females
   D. mitotic; males

8. In mammals, the placenta is essential to the embryo for

   A. nutrition, reproduction, and growth
   B. nutrition, respiration, and excretion
   C. locomotion, respiration, and excretion
   D. nutrition, reproduction, and excretion

9. The diagram at the right illustrates the important stages in the life cycle of an organism that reproduces sexually. Which processes result in the formation of cells with the monoploid number of chromosomes?

   A. 1 and 2
   B. 2 and 3
   C. 3 and 4
   D. 4 and 5

10. In a flowering plant, the ovule develops within a part of the

    A. style B. anther C. pistil D. stigma

11. Which embryonic structure supplies nutrients to a germinating bean plant?

    A. Pollen tube
    B. Hypocotyl
    C. Epicotyl
    D. Cotyledon

12. Polydactyly is a human characteristic in which a person has six fingers per hand. The trait for polydactyly is dominant over the trait for five fingers.
    If a man who is heterozygous for this trait marries a woman with the normal number of fingers, what are the chances that their child would be polydactyl?

    A. 0% B. 50% C. 75% D. 100%

13. Which statement describes how two organisms may show the same trait, yet have different genotypes for that phenotype?

    A. One is homozygous dominant and the other heterozygous.
    B. Both are heterozygous for the dominant trait.
    C. One is homozygous dominant and the other homozygous recessive.
    D. Both are homozygous for the dominant trait.

14. A child with blood type O has a mother with blood type A and a father with blood type B. The parental genotypes for blood types must be

    A. I^AI^A and I^BI^B
    B. I^Ai and I^BI^B
    C. I^AI^B and I^Bi
    D. I^Ai and I^Bi

15. Two pea plants, hybrid for a single trait, produce 60 pea plants. Approximately how many of the pea plants are expected to exhibit the recessive trait?

    A. 15   B. 45   C. 30   D. 60

16. Which statement CORRECTLY describes the normal number and type of chromosomes present in human body cells of a particular sex?

    A. Males have 22 pairs of autosomes and 1 pair of sex chromosomes known as XX.
    B. Females have 23 pairs of autosomes.
    C. Males have 22 pairs of autosomes and 1 pair of sex chromosomes known as XY.
    D. Males have 23 pairs of autosomes.

17. Based on the pattern of inheritance known as sex linkage, if a male is a hemophiliac, how many genes for this trait are present on the sex chromosomes in each of his diploid cells?

    A. 1   B. 2   C. 3   D. 0

18. To help to insure the maintenance of a desirable trait in a particular species of plant, a farmer would make use of

    A. binary fission
    B. mutagenic agents
    C. vegetative propagation
    D. natural selection

19. Which substances are components of a DNA nucleotide?

    A. Phosphate, deoxyribose, and uracil
    B. Phosphate, ribose, and adenine
    C. Thymine, deoxyribose, and phosphate
    D. Ribose, phosphate, and uracil

20. The diagram at the right represents a section of undisturbed rock and the general location of fossils of several closely related species. According to currently accepted evolutionary theory, which is the MOST probable correct assumption to be made concerning species A, B, C, and D?

    | species | C a D |
    | species | C |
    | species | AaBaC |
    | species | AaB |
    | species | A |

    A. A is the ancestor of B, C, and D.
    B. B was already extinct when C evolved.
    C. C evolved more recently than A, B, and D.
    D. D is the ancestor of A, B, and C.

21. If a rabbit is sensitized to human blood, the blood of the rabbit will react to chimpanzee blood very much the way it does to human blood.
This is an example of which type of evidence supporting the theory of evolution? Comparative

   A. habitat
   B. anatomy
   C. embryology
   D. biochemistry

21.____

22. Structures having a similar origin but adapted for different purposes, such as the flipper of a whale and arm of a human, are called _____ structures.

   A. homozygous
   B. identical
   C. homologous
   D. embryological

22.____

23. An athlete explains that his muscles have become well-developed through daily activities of weightlifting. He believes that his offspring will inherit this trait of well-developed muscles.
This belief would be MOST in agreement with the theory set forth by

   A. Darwin
   B. Lamarck
   C. Weismann
   D. Mendel

23.____

24. Natural selection can BEST be defined as

   A. survival of the strongest organism
   B. elimination of the smallest organisms by the largest organisms
   C. survival of those organisms genetically best adapted to the environment
   D. survival and reproduction of those organisms that occupy the largest area in an environment

24.____

25. Many modern evolutionists have accepted much of Darwin's theory of evolution, but have added genetic information that gives a scientific explanation of

   A. overproduction
   B. the struggle for existence
   C. the survival of the fittest
   D. variations

25.____

26. As a result of sexual reproduction, the rate of evolutionary change in the plant and animal kingdoms has been greatly speeded up because

   A. the offspring show more diversity than in asexual reproduction
   B. characteristics change less frequently than in asexual reproduction
   C. environmental changes never affect organisms produced by asexual reproduction
   D. two parents have fewer offspring than one parent

26.____

27. The heterotroph hypothesis is an attempt to explain

   A. how the Earth was originally formed
   B. why simple organisms usually evolve into complex organisms
   C. why evolution occurs very slowly
   D. how life originated on the Earth

27.____

28. Which sequence shows increasing complexity of levels of ecological organization?   28.____

    A. Biosphere, ecosystem, community
    B. Biosphere, community, ecosystem
    C. Community, ecosystem, biosphere
    D. Ecosystem, biosphere, community

29. In a freshwater pond community, a carp eats decaying material from around the bases of underwater plants, while a snail scrapes algae from the leaves and stems of the same plants.   29.____
    They can survive at the same time because they occupy

    A. the same niche, but different habitats
    B. the same habitat, but different niches
    C. the same habitat and the same niche
    D. different habitats and niches

30. Which term describes the bird and the cat in the following pattern of energy flow?   30.____
    sun → grass → grasshopper → bird → cat

    A. Herbivores   B. Saprophytes
    C. Predators   D. Omnivores

KEY (CORRECT ANSWERS)

1.	C	16.	C
2.	B	17.	A
3.	A	18.	C
4.	B	19.	C
5.	B	20.	A
6.	C	21.	D
7.	A	22.	C
8.	B	23.	B
9.	A	24.	C
10.	C	25.	D
11.	D	26.	A
12.	B	27.	D
13.	A	28.	C
14.	D	29.	B
15.	A	30.	C

TEST 3

DIRECTIONS: Each question or incomplete statement is followed by several suggested answers or completions. Select the one that BEST answers the question or completes the statement. *PRINT THE LETTER OF THE CORRECT ANSWER IN THE SPACE AT THE RIGHT.*

1. Which food chain relationship illustrates the nutritional pattern of a primary consumer? 1.____

    A. Seeds and fruits eaten by a mouse
    B. An earthworm eaten by a mole
    C. A mosquito eaten by a bat
    D. A mold growing on a dead frog

2. The elements stored in living cells of organisms in a community will eventually be returned to the soil for use by other living organisms. 2.____
   The organisms which carry out this process are

    A. producers   B. herbivores
    C. carnivores   D. decomposers

3. The natural replacement of one community with another until a climax stage is reached is known as 3.____

    A. ecological balance   B. organic evolution
    C. dynamic equilibrium   D. ecological succession

4. Recent evidence indicates that lakes in large areas of New York State are being affected by acid rain. 4.____
   The MAJOR effect of acid rain in the lakes is

    A. an increase in game fish population levels
    B. the stimulation of a rapid rate of evolution
    C. the elimination of many species of aquatic life
    D. an increase in agricultural productivity

5. Bacillus popilliae is a bacterium which causes *milky disease* in the Japanese beetle. 5.____
   Using bacillus popilliae to decrease a Japanese beetle population is an example of the

    A. abiotic control of insect pests
    B. use of biological control of insect pests
    C. use of artificial insecticides
    D. destruction of the abiotic environment

Questions 6-9.

DIRECTIONS: For each statement in Questions 6 through 9, select the process, chosen from the list below, that is BEST described by that statement.

Biological Processes

    A. Anaerobic respiration
    B. Aerobic respiration
    C. Photochemical reactions of photosynthesis
    D. Carbon-fixation reactions of photosynthesis

131

6. Light energy is absorbed by organic pigment molecules.   6.___

7. The oxidation of a glucose molecule results in the synthesis of ATP, water, and carbon dioxide.   7.___

8. Lactic acid accumulates in the muscle tissues of humans during vigorous activity.   8.___

9. PGAL is synthesized.   9.___

Questions 10-13.

DIRECTIONS: Questions 10 through 13 are to be answered on the basis of the chemical equation below and on your knowledge of biology.

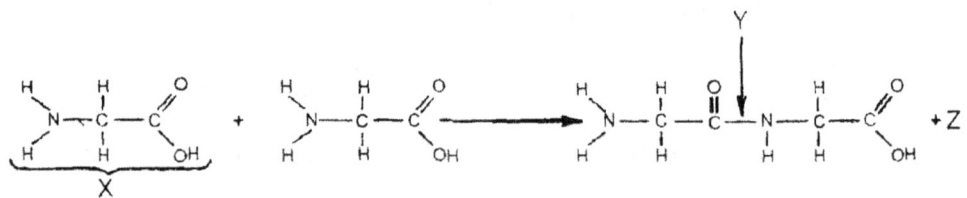

10. The chemical reaction represented by the equation is known as   10.___

    A. hydrolysis   B. digestion
    C. dehydration synthesis D. carbon fixation

11. The substance represented by X is a(n) _____ molecule.   11.___

    A. glucose   B. amino acid
    C. glycerol   D. fatty acid

12. Which substance is represented by letter Z?   12.___

    A. Water   B. Carbon dioxide
    C. Oxygen   D. Salt

13. Letter Y represents a(n)   13.___

    A. peptide bond   B. hydrogen bond
    C. polymer   D. enzyme

14. If the test tubes represented in the diagrams below were allowed to stand at room temperature for several hours, which test tube would MOST likely contain the GREATEST amount of alcohol and carbon dioxide?   14.___

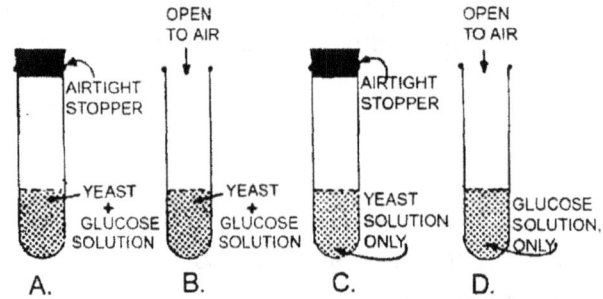

15. Which represents a carbohydrate molecule?

    A. $C_6H_6O_6$ B. $C_{12}H_{12}O_6$ C. $C_6H_{12}O_5$ D. $C_6H_{12}O_6$

Questions 16-19.

DIRECTIONS: For each function in Questions 16 through 19, select the organ, chosen from the list below, which is MOST closely associated with that function. (A letter may be used more than once or not at all.)

> Organs
>
> A. Kidney
> B. Liver
> C. Lung
> D. Stomach
> E. Skin

16. Removal of CO_2 from the blood.

17. Extracellular hydrolysis of protein.

18. Storage of glycogen.

19. Production of urea.

20. A type of *heart attack* in which a narrowing of the coronary artery causes an inadequate supply of oxygen to reach the heart muscle is known as

    A. anemia
    B. leukemia
    C. angina pectoris
    D. cerebral palsy

21. In humans, circulation to and from the lungs is known as _____ circulation.

    A. systemic
    B. pulmonary
    C. coronary
    D. lymphatic

22. The somatic nervous system contains nerves that run from the central nervous system to the

    A. muscles of the skeleton
    B. heart
    C. smooth muscles of the gastrointestinal tract
    D. endocrine glands

23. A person who consumes large amounts of saturated fats may increase his or her chances of developing

    A. meningitis
    B. hemophilia
    C. viral pneumonia
    D. cardiovascular disease

24. Which gland does NOT secrete hormones? _____ gland.

    A. Pituitary   B. Thyroid   C. Sex   D. Salivary

25. Which of the following contains the GREATEST amount of skeletal muscle tissue?   25.____

    A. Cerebrum   B. Small intestine
    C. Kidney   D. Foot

Questions 26-30.

DIRECTIONS: Questions 26 through 30 are to be answered on the basis of the diagram below which represents some stages in the embryonic development of a specific vertebrate.

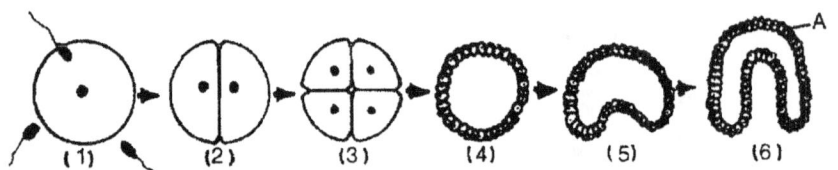

26. In humans, stage 1 NORMALLY occurs in the   26.____

    A. ovary   B. oviduct   C. vagina   D. uterus

27. Structures 2 and 3 are formed as a direct result of   27.____

    A. meiosis   B. gastrulation
    C. cleavage   D. differentiation

28. The structure in stage 4 represents a   28.____

    A. zygote   B. blastula   C. gastrula   D. follicle

29. The cells of layer A give rise to the   29.____

    A. digestive system and liver
    B. excretory system and muscles
    C. circulatory system and gonads
    D. nervous system and skin

30. Which cells are NOT represented in the diagrams?   30.____
    _____ cells.

    A. Endoderm   B. Mesoderm
    C. Diploid   D. Monoploid

KEY (CORRECT ANSWERS)

1.	A	16.	C
2.	D	17.	D
3.	D	18.	B
4.	C	19.	B
5.	B	20.	C
6.	C	21.	B
7.	B	22.	A
8.	A	23.	D
9.	D	24.	D
10.	C	25.	D
11.	B	26.	B
12.	A	27.	C
13.	A	28.	B
14.	A	29.	D
15.	D	30.	B

TEST 4

DIRECTIONS: Each question or incomplete statement is followed by several suggested answers or completions. Select the one that BEST answers the question or completes the statement. *PRINT THE LETTER OF THE CORRECT ANSWER IN THE SPACE AT THE RIGHT.*

Questions 1-3.

DIRECTIONS: For each of the processes in Questions 1 through 3, choose the stage of the human menstrual cycle, chosen from the list below, during which that process occurs. (A letter may be used more than once or not at all.)

Human Menstrual Cycle Stages

A. Ovulation
B. Follicle stage
C. Menstruation
D. Corpus luteum stage

1. The lining of the uterus is shed.   1.___

2. An egg is released from an ovary.   2.___

3. An egg matures in an ovary   3.___

4. Which type of fertilization and development is exhibited by birds and many reptiles? _____ fertilization and _____ development.   4.___

   A. External; external   B. Internal; internal
   C. External; internal   D. Internal; external

5. Which structure is a source of food for embryos which develop externally?   5.___

   A. Yolk   B. Placenta   C. Chorion   D. Amnion

Questions 6-9.

DIRECTIONS: For each phrase in Questions 6 through 9, select the type of nucleic acid, chosen from the list below, which is BEST described by that phrase. (A letter may be used more than once or not at all.)

Types of Nucleic Acid
A. DNA
B. Messenger RNA
C. Transfer RNA

6. Genetic material responsible for the individuality of an organism that is passed from parent to offspring.   6.___

7. Carries genetic information from the cell nucleus to the ribosomes.   7.___

8. Contains thymine instead of uracil.   8.___

9. Carries amino acid molecules to the ribosomes.   9.___

136

10. By which process can a group of genetically identical plants be rapidly produced from the cells of a single plant? 10.____

    A. Screening
    B. Chromosomal karyotyping
    C. Genetic engineering
    D. Cloning

11. Which is a genetic disorder in which abnormal hemoglobin leads to fragile red blood cells and obstructed blood vessels? 11.____

    A. Phenylketonuria
    B. Sickle-cell anemia
    C. Leukemia
    D. Down's syndrome

12. During the replication of a DNA molecule, separation or *unzipping* of the DNA molecule will normally occur when hydrogen bonds are broken between 12.____

    A. thymine and thymine
    B. guanine and uracil
    C. adenine and cytosine
    D. cytosine and guanine

13. Which set of conditions would MOST likely cause a change in gene frequency in a sexually reproducing population? 13.____

    A. Mutations and small populations
    B. Large populations and no migrations
    C. Random matings and large populations
    D. No mutations and no migrations

14. In humans, a gene mutation results from a change in the 14.____

    A. sequence of the nitrogenous bases in DNA
    B. chromosome number in a sperm
    C. chromosome number in an egg
    D. sequence of the sugars and phosphates in DNA

15. The genetic code for one amino acid molecule consists of 15.____

    A. five sugar molecules
    B. two phosphates
    C. three nucleotides
    D. four hydrogen bonds

Questions 16-18.

DIRECTIONS: Questions 16 through 18 are to be answered on the basis of the information below.

A scientist studied a river and forest area downstream from a large city with an increasing human population. During the study, the scientist made many observations that could be classified as:

   A. Most likely a negative result of human activity
   B. Most likely a positive result of human activity
   C. Probably not being influenced by human activity to any extent.

For each observation in Questions 16 through 18, select the phrase, chosen from the list above, which BEST fits that observation. (A letter may be used more than once or not at all.

16. Measurement of the levels of nitrates and phosphates in the river that flows through the forest showed the following results: 16._____

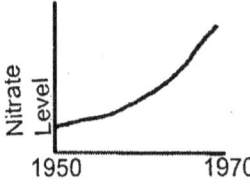 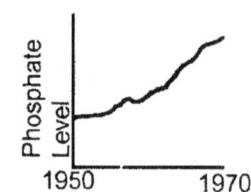

17. After 1970, the concentration of dissolved oxygen in the river increased, while the concentration of suspended particles decreased.   17._____

18. The population of hawks declined, while their food sources increased. High levels of insecticides were found in the reproductive tissues of hawks.   18._____

19. Compared to other organisms, humans have had the GREATEST ecological impact on the biosphere due to their   19._____

   A. internal bony skeleton
   B. homeostatic regulation of metabolism
   C. adaptations for respiration
   D. ability to modify the environment

20. The rapid rise of the human population level over the past few hundred years has been due MAINLY to   20._____

   A. increasing levels of air and water pollution
   B. loss of topsoil from our farmable lands
   C. removal of natural checks on population growth
   D. increasing resistance level of insect species

21. Which land biome is characterized by conifers, which include spruce and fir, as the dominant vegetation?   21._____

   A. Taiga   B. Tundra
   C. Desert   D. Grassland

22. Which two groups of organisms are MOST likely to be pioneer organisms?   22._____

   A. Songbirds and squirrels   B. Lichens and algae
   C. Deer and black bears   D. Oak and hickory trees

23. The diagram to the right illustrates some of the essential steps in   23._____

   A. the reproductive cycle
   B. the process of photosynthesis
   C. animal respiration
   D. the nitrogen cycle

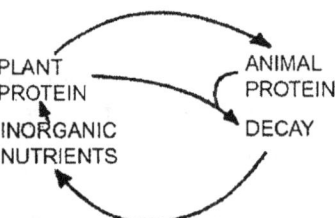

24. Which diagram BEST represents the usual relationships of biomass in a stable community?   24.____

   Key:
   C - Carnivores
   H - Herbivores
   P - Producers

   A.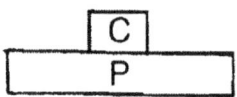
   B.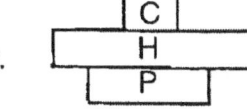
   C.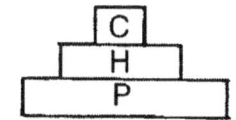
   D.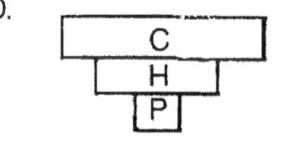

25. Bacteria which live in the human intestine derive their nutrition from digested foods. From these nutrients digested by the human, the bacteria synthesize vitamins usable by the human. This relationship demonstrates   25.____

   A. commensalism
   B. saprophytism
   C. mutualism
   D. parasitism

Questions 26-28.

DIRECTIONS: Questions 26 through 28 are to be answered on the basis of the information and chart below and on your knowledge of biology. The chart shows some indicators that are used in biological work to determine the presence of various substances in chemical compounds. The numbers on the chart represent missing information from Columns I and II. Record the letter of the choice, chosen from the lists below, which provides the information missing from the spaces numbered 26 through 28.

Column I Choices
A. Disaccharides
B. Simple sugar
C. Oxygen
D. Starch

Column II Choices
A. Brown color
B. Blue-black color
C. Milky-white color
D. Yellow color

Indicator Chart

Indicator	Column I Test for the Presence of	Column II Positive Result of the Test
Benedict's Solution	26	Red-orange color
Iodine Solution	27	Blue-black color
Bromthymol Blue Solution	Carbon dioxide	28

29. The diagram at the right shows a moss plant and a metric ruler. How tall is the moss plant in millimeters?

   A. 1.5
   B. 15
   C. 150
   D. 1,500

29. ___

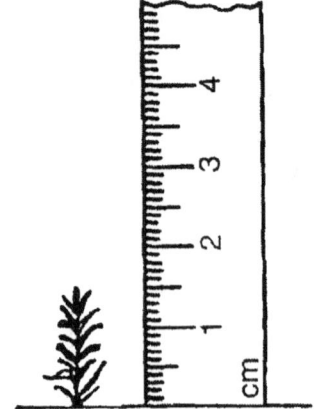

30. Which group of measurement units is CORRECTLY arranged in order of increasing size?   30. ___

   A. Micrometer, millimeter, centimeter, meter
   B. Millimeter, micrometer, centimeter, meter
   C. Meter, micrometer, centimeter, millimeter
   D. Micrometer, centimeter, millimeter, meter

KEY (CORRECT ANSWERS)

1.	C	16.	A
2.	A	17.	B
3.	B	18.	A
4.	D	19.	D
5.	A	20.	C
6.	A	21.	A
7.	B	22.	B
8.	A	23.	D
9.	C	24.	B
10.	D	25.	C
11.	B	26.	B
12.	D	27.	D
13.	A	28.	D
14.	A	29.	B
15.	C	30.	A

EXAMINATION SECTION
TEST 1

DIRECTIONS: Each question or incomplete statement is followed by several suggested answers or completions. Select the one that BEST answers the question or completes the statement. *PRINT THE LETTER OF THE CORRECT ANSWER IN THE SPACE AT THE RIGHT.*

1. To collect mitochondria from cells and study their structure in fine detail, which instruments would a scientist MOST likely use?

    A. Microdissection apparatus and compound light microscope
    B. Ultracentrifuge and electron microscope
    C. Microdissection apparatus and dissecting microscope
    D. Ultracentrifuge and compound light microscope

1.____

Questions 2-4.

DIRECTIONS: Questions 2 through 4 are to be answered on the basis of the information below and on your knowledge of biology.

A student observed a green plant cell under the low-power objective of her microscope and noted the movement of organelles as shown in diagram A. She then added three drops of a 10% salt solution to the slide, waited a few minutes, and observed the cell as shown in diagram B.

2. The organelles observed were MOST likely

    A. centrosomes   B. chloroplasts
    C. mitochondria   D. ribosomes

2.____

3. The movement of these organelles as shown in diagram A is known as

    A. ingestion   B. transpiration
    C. pinocytosis   D. cyclosis

3.____

4. The appearance of the clumped material as shown in diagram B is due to _____ the cell.

    A. loss of water from   B. loss of salt from
    C. addition of water into   D. addition of salt into

4.____

5.

ELEMENTS	COMPOUND			
	A	B	C	D
bromine	X			
carbon		X		X
fluorine				X
hydrogen	X	X		X
lead			X	
nitrogen			X	
oxygen		X	X	

The chart above shows the elements present in four different chemical compounds (A, B, C, and D). An X indicates the presence of a particular element. Which compound could be a carbohydrate?

A. A B. B C. C D. D

6. A student using a compound microscope estimated the diameter of a cheek cell to be 50 micrometers (μm).

What is the diameter of this cheek cell in millimeters?
_____ mm.

A. 0.050 B. 0.500 C. 5.00 D. 50.9

7. A characteristic of all known living things is that they

A. use atmospheric oxygen
B. use carbon dioxide
C. carry on metabolic activities
D. are capable of locomotion

8. The mosquito, *Anopheles quadrimaculatus*, is MOST closely related in structure to

A. Aedes sollicitans   B. Culex pepiens
C. Aedes aegypti   D. Anopheles punctulatus

9. Blue-green algae lack a membrane separating their nuclear material from their cytoplasm.
On this basis, these organisms are classified as

A. fungi   B. protists   C. monerans   D. plants

10. Which word equation represents the process of photosynthesis?

A. Carbon dioxide + water → glucose + oxygen + water
B. Glucose → alcohol + carbon dioxide
C. Maltose + water → glucose + glucose
D. Glucose + oxygen → carbon dioxide + water

11. Which is a polysaccharide associated with the cells of a tomato plant, but not with the cells of a grasshopper?

A. Hemoglobin   B. Glycogen
C. Protease   D. Cellulose

12. The openings on the lower surface of some leaves, which allow for the exchange of gases, are called

    A. stomates
    B. guard cells
    C. lenticels
    D. vascular bundles

13. What are the end products of carbohydrate hydrolysis?

    A. Amino acids
    B. Simple sugars
    C. Glycerol
    D. Fatty acids

14. A common characteristic of animals and fungi is their ability to carry on

    A. heterotrophic nutrition
    B. alcholic fermentation
    C. auxin production
    D. transport through vascular tissue

15. Which function is performed by both an ameba and a maple tree?

    A. Chlorophyll synthesis
    B. Locomotion
    C. Auxin secretion
    D. Intracellular digestion

16. The net movement of molecules into cells is MOST dependent upon the

    A. selectivity of the plasma membrane
    B. selectivity of the cell wall
    C. number of lysosomes
    D. number of chromosomes

17. The diagram at the right represents a leaf. The structure indicated by the arrow contains

    A. lenticels
    B. pollen grains
    C. xylem cells
    D. pistils

18. Which organism has a specialized organ system for transport?

    A. Ameba
    B. Hydra
    C. Earthworm
    D. Paramecium

19. The site of aerobic cellular respiration is the

    A. nucleus
    B. ribosome
    C. chromosome
    D. mitochondrion

20. Green plants use molecular oxygen for

    A. ATP production during anaerobic respiration
    B. ATP production during aerobic respiration
    C. light absorption during photosynthesis
    D. the hydrolysis of starch during intracellular digestion

21. Which organism carries on gas exchange in a terrestrial environment?

    A. Ameba
    B. Shark
    C. Hydra
    D. Grasshopper

22. Which statement BEST describes the excretion of nitrogenous wastes from Paramecia?

    A. Urea is excreted by nephrons.
    B. Uric acid is excreted by nephridia.
    C. Ammonia is excreted through cell membranes.
    D. Urea and uric acid are excreted through Malpighian tubules.

23. The central nervous system of a grasshopper is MOST similar in structure to the central nervous system of a(n)

    A. earthworm   B. human   C. Ameba   D. Hydra

24. A chemical injected into a tadpole caused the tadpole to undergo rapid metamorphosis into a frog.
    This chemical was MOST probably a(n)

    A. enzyme
    B. neurohumor
    C. hormone
    D. blood protein

25. Setae are structural adaptations for

    A. digestion in the Hydra
    B. locomotion in the earthworm
    C. reproduction in the grasshopper
    D. transport in the Ameba

KEY (CORRECT ANSWERS)

1. B
2. B
3. D
4. A
5. B
6. A
7. C
8. D
9. C
10. A
11. D
12. A
13. B
14. A
15. D
16. A
17. C
18. C
19. D
20. B
21. D
22. C
23. A
24. C
25. B

TEST 2

DIRECTIONS: Each question or incomplete statement is followed by several suggested answers or completions. Select the one that BEST answers the question or completes the statement. *PRINT THE LETTER OF THE CORRECT ANSWER IN THE SPACE AT THE RIGHT.*

1. According to the fluid mosaic model, a cell membrane is described as a structure composed of a 1.____

    A. protein layer in which large lipids are found
    B. carbohydrate structure in a *sea of lipids*
    C. double lipid layer in which proteins float
    D. phospholipid layer divided by carbohydrates

2. The MOST common food reserves in humans are fat and 2.____

    A. hemoglobin B. maltose
    C. DNA D. glycogen

3. The PRINCIPAL function of mechanical digestion is the 3.____

    A. hydrolysis of food molecules for storage in the liver
    B. production of more surface area for enzyme action
    C. synthesis of enzymes necessary for food absorption
    D. breakdown of large molecules to smaller ones by the addition of water

4. Phagocytosis and the production of antibodies are functions associated with specialized 4.____

    A. white blood cells B. red blood cells
    C. platelets D. neurons

5. Which compounds are produced in human muscle cells as a result of the oxidation of glucose in the absence of oxygen? 5.____

    A. Lipase and water
    B. sucrase and carbon dioxide
    C. Ethyl alcohol and ATP
    D. Lactic acid and ATP

6. Nitrogenous wastes may be produced as a result of the metabolism of 6.____

    A. glucose B. glycogen
    C. fatty acids D. amino acids

7. The breathing rate of humans is PRINCIPALLY regulated by the concentration of _____ in the blood. 7.____

    A. carbon dioxide B. oxygen
    C. platelets D. white blood cells

8. Compared to blood entering the human kidney, blood leaving the kidney NORMALLY contains a lower concentration of 8.____

    A. red cells B. proteins
    C. white cells D. urea

9. Which part of the human central nervous system is involved PRIMARILY with sensory interpretation and thinking?

    A. Spinal cord   B. Medulla
    C. Cerebrum   D. Cerebellum

10. Each of the two daughter cells that result from the normal mitotic division of the original parent cell contains number of chromosomes _____ those of the parent cell.

    A. the same; but has genes different from
    B. the same; and has genes identical to
    C. one-half of the; but has genes different from
    D. one-half of the; and has genes identical to

11.

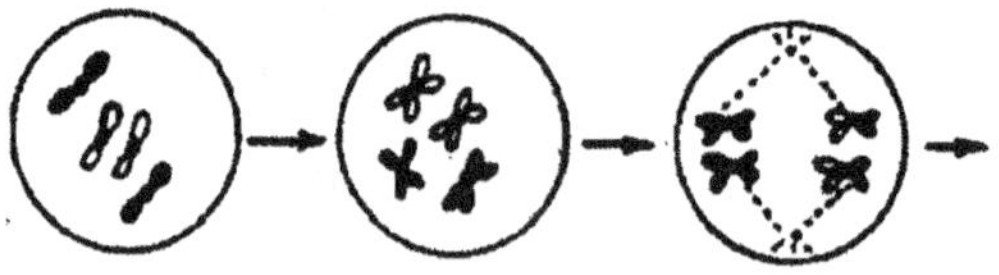

(A)   (B)   (C)   (D)

The diagrams above represent the sequence of events in a cell undergoing normal meiotic cell division.
Which diagram MOST likely represents stage D of this sequence?

A.    B.    C.    D.

12.

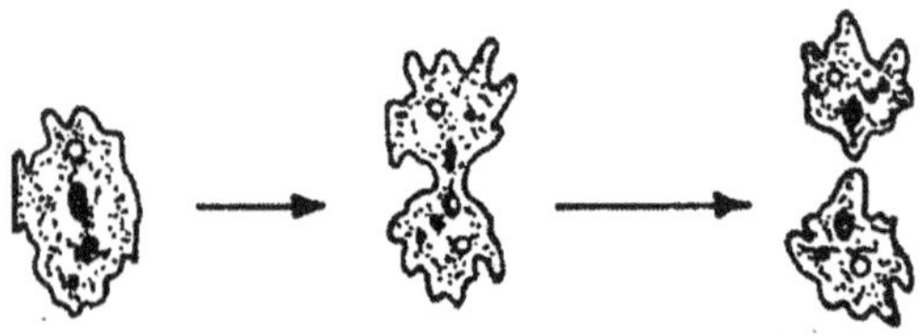

What specific type of reproduction is shown in the diagrams above of an Ameba?

    A. Vegetative propagation   B. Binary fission
    C. Budding   D. Meiosis

13. Which reproductive structures are produced within the ovaries of plants?

    A. Pollen grains   B. Sperm nuclei
    C. Egg nuclei   D. Pollen tubes

14. In the diagrams below, 2n represents the diploid number of chromosomes in a cell of an organism and n represents the monopoloid number. Which diagram represents fertilization?

    A. $2n \rightarrow \begin{matrix} n \\ n \end{matrix}$ B. $n \rightarrow \begin{matrix} 2n \\ 2n \end{matrix}$

    C. $\begin{matrix} n \\ n \end{matrix} \rightarrow 2n$ D. $\begin{matrix} 2n \\ 2n \end{matrix} \rightarrow n$

15. In most species of fish, a female produces large numbers of eggs during a reproductive cycle.
This would indicate that reproduction in fish is MOST probably characterized by _____ fertilization and _____ embryonic development.

   A. internal; internal
   B. internal; external
   C. external; internal
   D. external; external

15.____

16. The embryos of marsupials, such as the kangaroo and opossum, complete their development externally.
What is the source of nutrition for the last stages of a marsupial embryo's development?

   A. Milk from maternal mammary glands
   B. Diffusion of nutrients through the uterine wall
   C. Concentrated food in the yolk stored in the egg
   D. Food gathered from the environment and fed to the embryo

16.____

17. In apple blossoms, the function of the stigma is to

   A. produce the pollen
   B. receive the pollen
   C. form sperm nuclei
   D. pollinate the ovule

17.____

18. Curly hair in humans, white fur in guinea pigs, and needle-like spines in cacti all partly describe each organism's

   A. alleles
   B. autosomes
   C. chromosomes
   D. phenotype

18.____

19. The appearance of a recessive trait in offspring of animals MOST probably indicates that

   A. both parents carried at least one recessive gene for that trait
   B. one parent was homozygous dominant and the other parent was homozygous recessive for that trait
   C. neither parent carried a recessive gene for that trait
   D. one parent was homozygous dominant and the other parent was hybrid for that trait

19.____

20. Sexually reproducing species show greater variation than asexually reproducing species due to

   A. lower rates of mutation
   B. the occurrence of polyploidy
   C. environmental changes
   D. the recombination of alleles

20.____

21. Which parental pair could produce a colorblind female?
_____ mother and _____ father.

   A. Homozygous normal-vision; colorblind
   B. Colorblind; normal-vision
   C. Heterozygous normal-vision; normal-vision
   D. Heterozygous normal-vision; colorblind

21.____

22. A man heterozygous for blood type A marries a woman with blood type AB. 22.____
    The blood type of their offspring could NOT be

    A. A   B. B   C. O   D. AB

23. Identical twins were separated at birth and brought together after thirteen years. They 23.____
    varied in height by two inches and in weight by 20 pounds.
    The MOST probably explanation for these differences is that

    A. their environments affected the expression of their traits
    B. their cells did not divide by mitotic cell division
    C. they developed from two different zygotes
    D. they differed in their genotypes

24. Which series is arranged in CORRECT order according to decreasing size of structures? 24.____

    A. DNA, nucleus, chromosome, nucleotide, nitrogenous base
    B. Nucleotide, chromosome, nitrogenous base, nucleus, DNA
    C. Nucleus, chromosome, DNA, nucleotide, nitrogenous base
    D. Chromosome, nucleus, nitrogenous base, nucleotide, DNA

25. Which assumption is the basis for the use of the fossil record as evidence for evolution? 25.____

    A. Fossils have been found to show a complete record of the evolution of all mammals.
    B. In undisturbed layers of the Earth's crust, the oldest fossils are found in the lowest layers.
    C. All fossils can be found embedded in rocks.
    D. All fossils were formed at the same time.

KEY (CORRECT ANSWERS)

1. C
2. D
3. B
4. A
5. D

6. D
7. A
8. D
9. C
10. B

11. C
12. B
13. C
14. C
15. D

16. A
17. B
18. D
19. A
20. D

21. D
22. C
23. A
24. C
25. B

TEST 3

DIRECTIONS: Each question or incomplete statement is followed by several suggested answers or completions. Select the one that BEST answers the question or completes the statement. *PRINT THE LETTER OF THE CORRECT ANSWER IN THE SPACE AT THE RIGHT.*

1.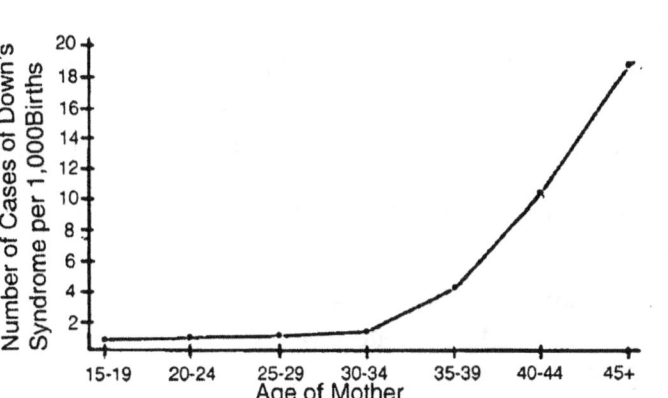

    The above graph shows the relationship between the number of cases of children with Down's syndrome per 1,000 births and maternal age. According to the graph, the incidence of Down's syndrome

    A. generally decreases as maternal age increases
    B. is about nine times greater at age 45 than at age 30
    C. stabilizes at 2 per 1,000 births after age 35
    D. is greater at age 15 than at age 35

2. Which is an example of evidence of evolution based on comparative biochemistry?

    A. Sheep insulin can be substituted for human insulin.
    B. The structure of a whale's flipper is similar to that of a human hand.
    C. Human embryos have a tail-like structure at one stage in their development.
    D. Both birds and bats have wings.

3. One weakness in Darwin's theory of evolution was that he was NOT able to

    A. explain selection of favorable traits
    B. account for an increase in population
    C. explain the genetic basis for variation in populations
    D. understand competition among individuals of a species

4. A supporter of the evolutionary theory set forth by Lamarck would PROBABLY theorize that the giraffe evolved a long neck due to

    A. need and inheritance of acquired traits
    B. mutations and genetic recombination
    C. variations and survival of the fittest
    D. overproduction and struggle for survival

5. According to the heterotroph hypothesis, the earliest heterotrophs carried out what type of energy-releasing process?

A. Protein synthesis B. Photosynthesis
C. Anaerobic respiration D. Aerobic respiration

6. The theory of continental drift hypothesizes that Africa and South America were once a single landmass, but have drifted apart over millions of years. The *Old World* monkeys of Africa, although similar, show several genetic differences from the *New World* monkeys of South America.
Which factor is probably the MOST important for maintaining these differences?

    A. Fossil records B. Comparative anatomy
    C. Use and disuse D. Geographic isolation

7. A change in the frequency of any mutant allele in a population MOST likely depends on the _____ mutant allele.

    A. size of the organisms possessing the
    B. adaptive value of the trait associated with the
    C. degree of dominance of the
    D. degree of recessiveness of the

8. Which would be considered a biotic factor in a pond ecosystem?

    A. Snails B. Water C. Oxygen D. Sunlight

9. All of the different species within an ecosystem are collectively referred to as the

    A. niche B. community
    C. consumers D. population

10. The number of African elephants has been drastically reduced by poachers who kill the animals for the ivory in their tusks.
This negative aspect of human involvement in the ecosystem could BEST be described as

    A. poor land use management
    B. importation of organisms
    C. poor agricultural practices
    D. exploitation of wildlife

11. Nitrogen-fixing bacteria living on the roots of legumes are examples of a nutritional relationship known as

    A. parasitism B. mutualism
    C. commensalism D. saprophytism

Questions 12-15.

DIRECTIONS: Questions 12 through 15 are to be answered on the basis of the following diagram and on your knowledge of biology. The diagram represents different species of organisms interacting with each other in and around a pond environment.

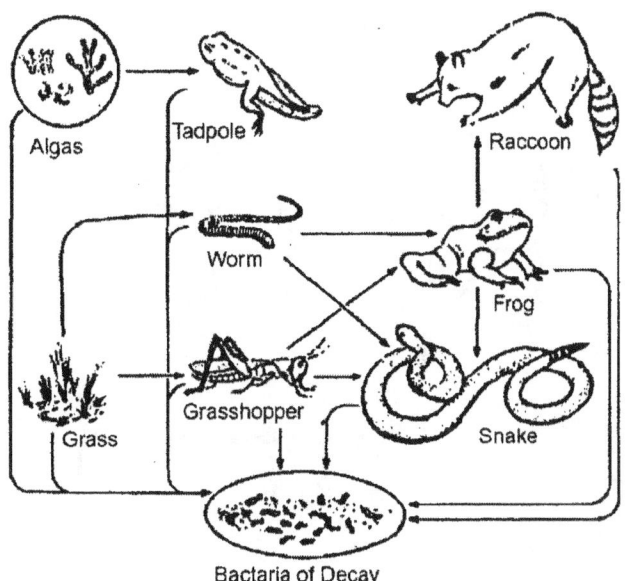

12. The adult frog represents a type of consumer known as a 12.____

    A. producer B. carnivore
    C. saprophyte D. parasite

13. Which organisms are classified as herbivores? 13.____

    A. Algae, tadpole, raccoon
    B. Worm, snake, bacteria
    C. Tadpole, worm, grasshopper
    D. Grasshopper, bacteria, frog

14. Which statement about the algae and grass is TRUE? 14.____
    They

    A. are classified as omnivores
    B. parasitize the animals that consume them
    C. contain the greatest amount of stored energy
    D. decompose nutrients from dead organisms

15. The interactions among organisms shown in this diagram illustrate 15.____

    A. a food web B. geographic isolation
    C. abiotic factors D. organic evolution

Questions 16-18.

DIRECTIONS: Questions 16 through 18 are to be answered on the basis of the structural representations below.

Structural Formulas

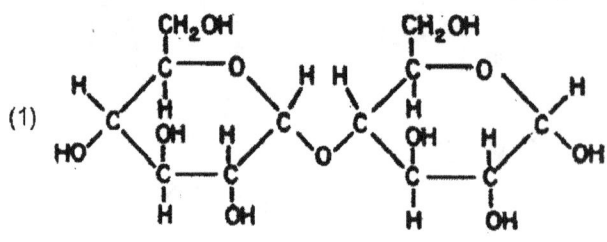

16. Which represents a disaccharide molecule?

    A. 1   B. 2   C. 3   D. 4

17. Which represents a building block molecule for enzymes?

    A. 1   B. 2   C. 3   D. 4

18. Which represents a molecule that, when combined with three fatty acids, forms a lipid molecule?

    A. 1   B. 2   C. 5   D. 4

19. The summary word equation shown below represents a set of reactions occurring in photosynthesis:

    water $\xrightarrow{\text{chlorophyll}/\text{light}}$ hydrogen + oxygen

    These reactions are known as _____ reactions.

    A. carbon fixation   B. photochemical
    C. dark   D. fermentation

20. Which process produces peptide bonds?

    A. Digestion   B. Hydrolysis
    C. Dehydration synthesis D. Enzyme deactivation

21. In humans, anaerobic respiration of glucose is a less efficient energy-releasing system than aerobic respiration of glucose.
One of the reasons for this is that in anaerobic respiration

    A. lactic acid contains much unreleased potential energy
    B. water contains much released potential energy
    C. oxygen serves as the final hydrogen acceptor
    D. chlorophyll is hydrolyzed into PGAL molecules

21.____

22.

The above diagram represents an enzyme-catalyzed reaction. Which substance is represented by letter X?

    A. Maltase   B. Sucrase   C. Lipase   D. Protease

22.____

23. What is represented by the grouping of atoms shown at the right? _____ group.

    A. Carboxyl
    B. Amino
    C. Methyl
    D. Phosphate

23.____

24. Examples of polymers which contain repeating units known as nucleotides are

    A. hemoglobin and maltase
    B. starch and glycogen
    C. fats and oils
    D. DNA and RNA

24.____

25. The *lock-and-key* model of enzyme action illustrates that a particular enzyme molecule

    A. forms a permanent enzyme-substrate complex
    B. may be destroyed and resynthesized several times
    C. interacts with a specific type of substrate molecule
    D. reacts at identical rates under all environmental conditions

25.____

KEY (CORRECT ANSWERS)

1.	B	11.	B
2.	A	12.	B
3.	C	13.	C
4.	A	14.	C
5.	C	15.	A
6.	D	16.	A
7.	B	17.	D
8.	A	18.	B
9.	B	19.	B
10.	D	20.	C

21. A
22. D
23. A
24. D
25. C

TEST 4

DIRECTIONS: Each question or incomplete statement is followed by several suggested answers or completions. Select the one that BEST answers the question or completes the statement. *PRINT THE LETTER OF THE CORRECT ANSWER IN THE SPACE AT THE RIGHT.*

Questions 1-3.

DIRECTIONS: For each phrase in Questions 1 through 3, select the food nutrient, chosen from the list below, that is described by that phrase.

<u>Food Nutrients</u>
A. Carbohydrates
B. Saturated fat
C. Unsaturated fat
D. Protein
E. Water molecules

1. Serve as major sources of energy and also provide roughage. 1.____

2. Provide a transport medium and help to regulate body temperature. 2.____

3. Composed of amino acids and needed to maintain and repair body tissues. 3.____

4. An injury to a blood vessel may result in the formation of a blood clot when 4.____

   A. bone marrow cells decrease platelet production
   B. kidney tubules synthesize clotting factors
   C. ruptured platelets release enzyme molecules
   D. white blood cells release antibodies

5. The right ventricle is the chamber of the heart which contains _____ blood and pumps this blood to the _____. 5.____

   A. deoxygenated; lungs   B. deoxygenated; brain
   C. oxygenated; lungs   D. oxygenated; brain

6. A student's blood pressure measures 116/70. 6.____
   The number 116 or systolic number refers to the amount of blood pressure exerted on the walls of the student's

   A. veins   B. lymph glands
   C. capillaries   D. arteries

7. Which organ is NOT correctly matched with its functional subunits? 7.____

   A. Brain - neurons   B. Intestine - cilia
   C. Kidney - nephrons   D. Lung - alveoli

Questions 8-10.

DIRECTIONS: For each phrase in Questions 8 through 10, select the malfunction, chosen from the list below, that is described by that statement.

155

Malfunctions of the Human Body

A. Ulcer
B. Gout
C. Allergies
D. Leukemia
E. Emphysema

8. Characterized by reduced functional surfaces of alveoli. 8.____

9. Characterized by an erosion of the lining of the stomach. 9.____

10. Characterized by body responses generally due to the release of histamines following an antigen-antibody reaction. 10.____

Questions 11-13.

DIRECTIONS: Questions 11 through 13 are to be answered on the basis of the diagram below which represents a stage in human development.

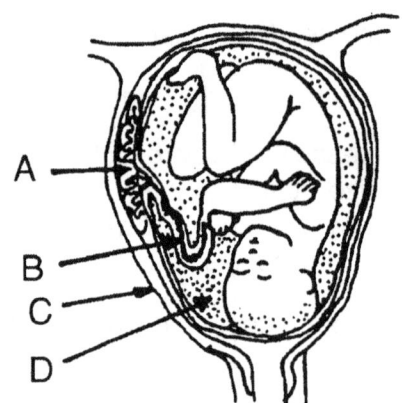

11. The exchange of oxygen, food, and wastes between mother and fetus occurs at 11.____

    A. A   B. B   C. C   D. D

12. What is the function of the fluid labeled D? 12.____

    A. Nourishment   B. Protection
    C. Excretion   D. Respiration

13. The structure labeled C, within which development occurs, is known as the 13.____

    A. oviduct   B. birth canal
    C. uterus   D. placenta

Questions 14-15.

DIRECTIONS: Questions 14 and 15 are to be answered on the basis the diagram below of the internal view of a bean seec and on your knowledge of biology.

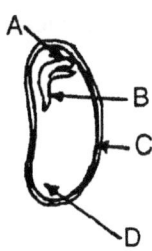

14. In which structure would MOST of the stored food for the embryo be found?

    A. A   B. B   C. C   D. D

15. The epicotyl and the hypocotyl are represented by

    A. A and C   B. B and D   C. C and D   D. A and B

16. Which embryonic membrane of a bird's egg contains metabolic wastes?

    A. Allantois   B. Amnion
    C. Placenta   D. Yolk sac

17. In nonplacental animals, MOST of the food for the embryo is found in the

    A. uterus   B. umbilical cord
    C. amniotic sac   D. yolk of the egg

18. In the early development of a zygote, the number of cells increases without an increase in mass by a process known as

    A. ovulation   B. cleavage
    C. germination   D. metamorphosis

19. The hollow-ball stage in the development of an invertebrate embryo is known as the

    A. blastula   B. ectoderm
    C. gastrula   D. endoderm

20. The technique of uniting a sperm cell with an egg cell in a test tube is an example of

    A. in vitro fertilization   B. internal fertilization
    C. gametogenesis   D. artificial ovulation

21. In the diagram at the right, what is represented by the letter x?

    A. Ribose
    B. Deoxyribose
    C. Phosphate
    D. Adenine

Questions 22-25.

DIRECTIONS: For each phrase in Questions 22 through 25, select the type of molecule, chosen from the list below, that is MOST closely associated with that phrase.

Molecules

A. DNA *only*
B. Messenger RNA *only*
C. Transfer RNA *only*
D. Messenger and transfer RNA *only*

22. Carries a specific code from the nucleus to the site of protein synthesis. 22.____

23. Carries amino acids to the site of protein synthesis. 23.____

24. May contain the nitrogenous base uracil. 24.____

25. Contains the hereditary information passed on from generation to generation in humans. 25.____

KEY (CORRECT ANSWERS)

1. A
2. E
3. D
4. C
5. A

6. D
7. B
8. E
9. A
10. C

11. A
12. B
13. C
14. D
15. D

16. A
17. D
18. B
19. A
20. A

21. C
22. B
23. C
24. D
25. A

TEST 5

DIRECTIONS: Each question or incomplete statement is followed by several suggested answers or completions. Select the one that BEST answers the question or completes the statement. *PRINT THE LETTER OF THE CORRECT ANSWER IN THE SPACE AT THE RIGHT.*

1. Which principal actions of genes insure homeostatic control of life processes and continuity of hereditary material? 1.____

    A. Oxidation and hydrolysis
    B. Enzyme synthesis and replication
    C. Oxygen transport and cyclosis
    D. Pinocytosis and dehydration synthesis

2. Human disorders such as PKU and sickle-cell anemia, which are defects in the synthesis of individual proteins, are MOST likely the result of 2.____

    A. gene mutations B. nondisjunction
    C. crossing-over D. polyploidy

3. The formation of recombinant DNA results from the 3.____

    A. addition of messenger RNA molecules to an organism
    B. transfer of genes from one organism to another
    C. substitution of a ribose sugar for a deoxyribose sugar
    D. production of a polyploid condition by a mutagenic agent

4. Which technique can be used to examine the chromosomes of a fetus for possible genetic defects? 4.____

    A. Pedigree analysis B. Analysis of fetal urine
    C. Karyotyping D. Cleavage

5. The gene pool in a population of Rana pipiens in a pond remained constant for many generations. 5.____
   The MOST probable reason for this stable gene pool is that

    A. it was a small population with nonrandom mating and many mutations
    B. random mating occurred in a small population with many mutations
    C. no mutations occurred in a large, migrating population
    D. no migration occurred in a large population with random mating

Questions 6-9.

DIRECTIONS: Questions 6 through 9 are to be answered on the basis of the diagrams below which represent different land biomes and on your knowledge of biology.

6. The biome represented by diagram D is known as a 6.____

   A. desert
   B. temperate deciduous forest
   C. taiga
   D. tundra

7. Daily changes in temperature would be GREATEST in the biome represented in diagram 7.____

   A. A   B. B   C. C   D. D

8. Which biome has the GREATEST annual rainfall? 8.____

   A. A   B. B   C. C   D. D

9. Which of the biomes represented is located at the highest altitudes and/or the highest latitudes? 9.____

   A. A   B. B   C. C   D. D

Questions 10-12.

DIRECTIONS: Questions 10 through 12 are to be answered on the basis of the graphs below showing data on some environmental factors acting in a large lake.

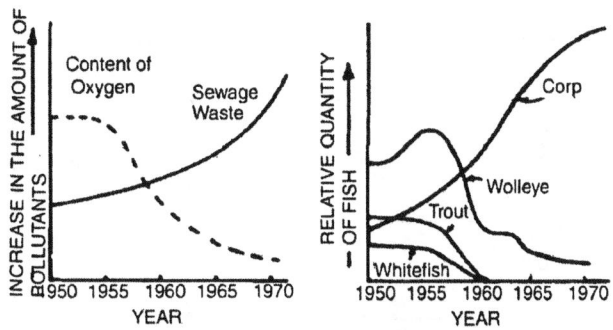

10. Which relationship can be CORRECTLY inferred from the data presented?   10.____

    A. As sewage waste increases, oxygen content decreases.
    B. As sewage waste increases, oxygen content increases.
    C. As oxygen content decreases, carp population decreases.
    D. As oxygen content decreases, trout population increases.

11. The GREATEST change in the lake's whitefish population occurred in the years between   11.____

    A. 1950 and 1955   B. 1955 and 1960
    C. 1960 and 1965   D. 1965 and 1970

12. Which of the fish species appears able to withstand the GREATEST degree of oxygen depletion?   12.____

    A. Trout   B. Carp   C. Walleye   D. Whitefish

13. In a community, the MOST severe competition develops among those organisms which   13.____

    A. are active only during the night
    B. belong to two different genera
    C. depend upon autotrophs for food
    D. occupy the same ecological niche

14. Gypsy moth infestations of rural areas of New York State may pose a potentially serious threat to many forested areas.   14.____
    Which would probably be the MOST ecologically sound method of gypsy moth control?

    A. Widespread application of DDT
    B. Introduction of a biological control
    C. Removal of its forest habitat
    D. Contamination of its food sources

15. Following a major forest fire, an area that was once wooded is converted to barren soil. Which of the following schemes describes the MOST likely sequence of changes in vegetation in the area following the fire?   15.____

    A. Shrubs → maples → pines → grasses
    B. Maples → pines → grasses → shrubs
    C. Pines → shrubs → maples → grasses
    D. Grasses → shrubs → pines → maples

16.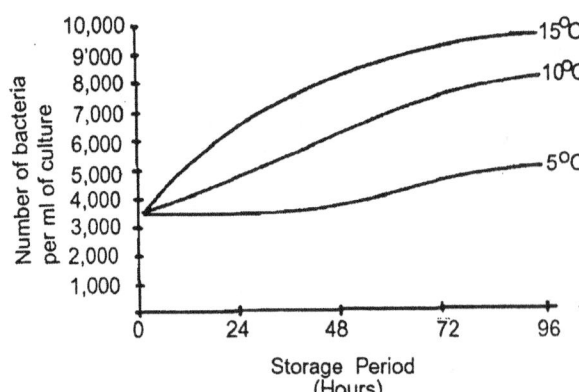

The above graph was developed as a result of an investigation of bacterial counts of three identical cultures grown at different temperatures. Which conclusion might be CORRECTLY drawn from this graph?

A. The culture contains no bacteria.
B. Refrigeration retards bacterial reproduction.
C. Temperature is unrelated to the bacteria reproduction rate.
D. Bacteria cannot grow at a temperature of 5° C.

Questions 17-18.

DIRECTIONS: Questions 17 and 18 are to be answered on the basis of the information below and on your knowledge of biology.

Laboratory investigations were performed to determine the effect of temperature on the hydrolysis of starch by the enzyme amylase. The data obtained are recorded in the table below.

Data Table

Temperature (°C)	Grains of Starch Hydrolyzed Per Minute
0	0.0
10	0.2
20	0.4
30	0.8
40	1.0
50	0.3
60	0.2

17. Which conclusion would be the LEAST reliable based upon the information in the Data Table?

A. Starch hydrolysis declines as the temperature is increased from 50° C to 60° C.
B. Starch hydrolysis declines as the temperature is decreased from 40° C to 30° C.
C. Starch hydrolysis at 25° C would be greater than starch hydrolysis at 20° C.
D. There is no starch hydrolysis above 60° C.

18. According to the data, at what temperature (°C) is the enzyme amylase MOST active? 18.____

   A. 0°   B. 20°   C. 40°   D. 60°

Questions 19-20.

DIRECTIONS: Questions 19 and 20 are to be answered on the basis of the diagram below and on your knowledge of biology.

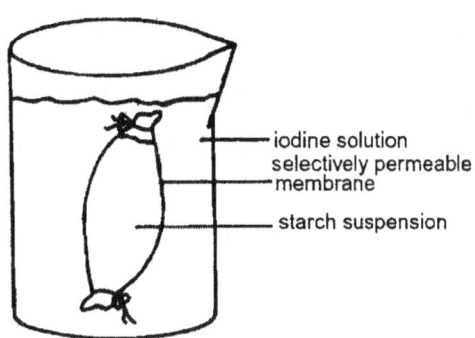

19. If iodine molecules passed through the membrane into the starch suspension, the 19.____

   A. starch suspension would turn blue-black
   B. starch suspension would turn brick-red
   C. membrane would dissolve
   D. membrane would become impermeable

20. What process accounts for the movement of the iodine? 20.____

   A. Diffusion   B. Osmosis
   C. Phagocytosis   D. Pinocytosis

21. Which piece of equipment should be used to transfer a Hydra onto a microscope slide? 21.____

   A.    B.

   C.    D.

22. For safety purposes, which piece of equipment should be used when a liquid is heated in a test tube? 22.____

   A.    B.

   C. 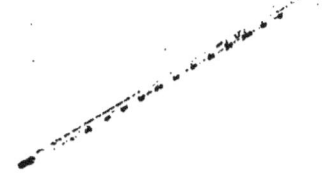   D.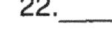

23.

sugar + yeast + water   Bromthymol blue solution

The above diagram represents a setup at the beginning of a laboratory investigation. Which hypothesis could MOST likely be supported by observing and collecting data from this investigation?

A. The fermentation of a yeast-sugar solution results in the production of carbon dioxide.
B. Yeast cells contain simple sugars.
C. Oxygen is released when a yeast-sugar solution is illuminated with green light.
D. Yeast cells contain starches.

24. Dissection of an earthworm is normally begun with a cut along a dorsal surface. What is an advantage of beginning the cut here?
The

A. four-chambered heart will remain in place
B. kidneys will be clearly exposed
C. backbone would be damaged by any other incision
D. ventral nerve cord will not be damaged

25. Which would make the nucleus of an onion skin more visible under a microscope?

A. Heat the slide over a burner.
B. Add a drop of iodine solution to the slide.
C. Soak the onion skin tissue in alcohol.
D. Add a drop of salt solution.

KEY (CORRECT ANSWERS)

1. B
2. A
3. B
4. C
5. D

6. C
7. A
8. C
9. D
10. A

11. B
12. B
13. D
14. B
15. D

16. B
17. D
18. C
19. A
20. A

21. C
22. A
23. A
24. D
25. B

EXAMINATION SECTION
TEST 1

DIRECTIONS: Each question or incomplete statement is followed by several suggested answers or completions. Select the one that BEST answers the question or completes the statement. *PRINT THE LETTER OF THE CORRECT ANSWER IN THE SPACE AT THE RIGHT.*

1. If a protein contains 80 amino acids, its corresponding gene must contain AT LEAST how many nucleotides?

    A. 40 B. 120 C. 240 D. 360 E. 480

2. Which one of the following is characteristic ONLY of mitosis and NOT of meiosis?

    A. Synapsis occurs
    B. Cells with identical genotypes are produced
    C. Splitting of centromeres takes place
    D. Homologous chromosomes separate
    E. Spindle fibers are formed

3. The PRIMARY role of oxygen in respiration is to

    A. yield energy in the form of ATP as it is passed down the respiratory chain
    B. act as an acceptor for electrons and hydrogen ions to form water
    C. combine with carbon to form CO_2
    D. combine with lactic acid to form pyruvic acid
    E. catalyze the reactions of glycolysis

4. Fetal cells sloughed off into the amniotic fluid can be collected and cultured. The cultured cells CANNOT be used for prenatal diagnosis of

    A. identical twinning
    B. paternity
    C. genetic diseases whose metabolic basis is known
    D. the sex of the fetus
    E. aneuploidy

5. The function of the Loop of Henle is to

    A. rid the body of excess urea and ammonia
    B. rid the body of excess hydrogen ions
    C. return reusable nutrients to the blood
    D. produce a sugar gradient capable of concentrating urine
    E. produce a salt gradient capable of concentrating urine

6. The cells of the testis that are MOST like the follicle cells of the ovary in that they respond to the pituitary hormone LH by producing steroid hormones are

    A. spermatids   B. endometrial cells
    C. stem cells   D. interstitial cells
    E. germ cells

167

7. Bacteriophages are

    A. organelles
    B. organisms
    C. prokaryotes
    D. bacteria
    E. viruses

8. When an aerobic organism is temporarily deprived of O_2, it obtains its chemical energy from

    A. the substrate level of ATP synthesis in glycolysis
    B. the oxidation of pyruvic acid to acetyl-CoA
    C. the respiratory electron transport chain
    D. chemiosmotic coupling
    E. metabolism of succinic acid in the TCA cycle

9. Examination of the eukaryotic cell surface by the electron microscope reveals that the plasma membrane

    A. is composed of a single layer of molecules approximately 75 Angstrom units in thickness
    B. is composed exclusively of phospholipids
    C. invaginates into the cellular cytoplasm to form canals and vesicles
    D. invaginates to form cristae on which are arranged the electron transport systems
    E. is composed exclusively of proteins

10. In a research project, a chemical was introduced to developing embryos that selectively destroyed the mesoderm germ layer.
    Which of the following structures would be absent in the fetus?

    A. Brain
    B. Pectoralis muscle
    C. Epidermis
    D. Intestinal mucosa
    E. Adrenal medulla

11. A restriction endonuclease produces a break in

    A. DNA at a specific base sequence
    B. tRNA at a specific base sequence
    C. any nucleic acid at the end of the molecule
    D. proteins at a specific amino acid sequence
    E. DNA at the 3' terminal end *only*

12. All chemosynthetic autotrophic prokaryotes belong to the

    A. bacteria
    B. fungi
    C. protozoa
    D. viruses
    E. tracheophytes

13. The carbon dioxide carried in the blood from the tissues to the lungs is MOST commonly found in the form of

    A. carbaminohemoglobin
    B. free carbon dioxide
    C. carbonic acid
    D. bicarbonate ions
    E. membrane-bound carbon dioxide

14. The regulation of body temperature, water balance, and appetite are a function of the

    A. thalamus
    B. hypothalamus
    C. medulla oblongata
    D. anterior lobe of pituitary
    E. cerebrum

15. In sex-linkage

    A. the recessive autosomal characters of the father are expressed in the sons
    B. X-linked characters of the mother must be expressed in the daughters
    C. the X-linked characters of the mother are never expressed in the daughters
    D. the primary sexual characteristics are determined by the sex hormones
    E. normal male fruitflies and humans always have a Y-chromosome

16. Assuming Hardy-Weinberg conditions, when 16 percent of a population is homozygous recessive for a trait, the percent that is heterozygous is

    A. 30 B. 25 C. 48 D. 24 E. 36

17. One of the evolutionary adaptations of reptiles for a terrestrial environment was

    A. a thin, pliable skin
    B. a four-chambered heart
    C. air breathing lung
    D. a shelled egg with extraembryonic membranes
    E. legs for rapid locomotion

18. According to the theory of natural selection, the environment *selects* ONLY those characteristics which

    A. fit the organism to future environmental change
    B. *increase* the life span of the individual
    C. *increase* the number of offspring which reach reproductive age
    D. result in stronger individuals
    E. affect social behavior

19. If acetylcholine were released at a synapse and acetyl-cholinesterase was inhibited, the

    A. postsynaptic neuron would not respond to the acetylcholine
    B. postsynaptic neuron would produce a single nerve impulse
    C. postsynaptic neuron would produce an abnormally long series of nerve impulses
    D. acetylcholine would not diffuse across the synapse
    E. acetylcholine would spontaneously decompose

20. Cystic fibrosis is inherited as a simple autosomal recessive. Suppose a woman who is heterozygous for this trait marries a man who is also heterozygous for it. What is the probability that they will have a child who is heterozygous for the trait?

    A. 0 B. 1/4 C. 1/2 D. 2/3 E. 3/4

4 (#1)

KEY (CORRECT ANSWERS)

1. C
2. B
3. B
4. A
5. E

6. D
7. E
8. A
9. C
10. B

11. A
12. A
13. D
14. B
15. E

16. C
17. D
18. C
19. C
20. C

TEST 2

DIRECTIONS: Each question or incomplete statement is followed by several suggested answers or completions. Select the one that BEST answers the question or completes the statement. *PRINT THE LETTER OF THE CORRECT ANSWER IN THE SPACE AT THE RIGHT.*

1. Which of the following statements is TRUE of the archenteron?　　1.____

   A. The cavity of the archenteron is called the blastocoel.
   B. The cavity of the archenteron represents the beginning of the primitive gut.
   C. The archenteron is formed during blastula formation.
   D. The cavity of the archenteron represents the first cavity of the developing heart.
   E. The archenteron is formed by a closing of the neural tube.

2. Which part of the cell is involved MOST directly with the synthesis of ribosomal subunits?　　2.____

   A. Nucleolus　　　　　　　　　B. Microtubules
   C. Endoplasmic reticulum　　　D. Golgi apparatus
   E. Nuclear envelope

3. Which of the following substances is a nucleotide?　　3.____

   A. Estrogen
   B. Growth hormone (somatotropin)
   C. Insulin
   D. Adenosine triphosphate (ATP)
   E. Amylose

4. Which of the following is NOT a function of microtubules?　　4.____

   A. Maintaining or controlling the shape of the cell
   B. Movement of chromosomes during anaphase
   C. Temporary storage of proteins prior to secretion
   D. Forming the structural elements of the centrioles
   E. Activity of cells and flagella

5. The thymus gland is involved in　　5.____

   A. the regulation of calcium metabolism
   B. the development of the immune response
   C. regulation of the activity of the thyroid gland
   D. endocrine and exocrine functions
   E. reproductive physiology

6. At different stages during the normal sequence of events in the menstrual cycle, there is an increase in progesterone, FSH, and estrogen.　　6.____
   Which one of the following is the CORRECT sequence of *initial* increases in each substance, beginning with menstruation?

   A. Estrogen, FSH, progesterone
   B. FSH, estrogen, progesterone
   C. Estrogen, progesterone, FSH
   D. FSH, progesterone, estrogen
   E. Progesterone, estrogen, FSH

7. Suppose an individual is heterozygous for ten different independently assorting genes. How many genetically different gametes will be possible from this individual?

   A. 10   B. 20   C. 10^2 D. 200   E. 210

8. Viruses may not be considered true living organisms because they

   A. are too small
   B. can only reproduce in the cells of another living organism
   C. are not eukaryotes
   D. are extremely primitive organisms
   E. can only replicate in an anaerobic environment

9. One of the MAJOR advantages in using scanning electron microscopy as opposed to transmission electron microscopy is that

   A. greater magnification can be obtained
   B. greater resolving power can be obtained
   C. the specimen does not have to be treated with chemicals
   D. a three-dimensional image can be obtained
   E. there is no advantage

10. The following gland is both endocrine and exocrine in function.

    A. Thyroid   B. Liver   C. Adrenal
    D. Pancreas   E. Pituitary

11. Sucrose is

    A. a disaccharide of glucose and fructose
    B. a trisaccharide of galactose, glucose, and fructose
    C. the technical term for blood sugar
    D. the major subunit of cellulose
    E. the major subunit of starch

12. The intracellular ion that is PRIMARILY responsible for triggering muscle contraction is

    A. sodium   B. potassium   C. phosphorus
    D. calcium   E. magnesium

13. In which two of the following phyla do most biologists place the MOST primitive bilaterally symmetrical animals?

    A. Chordata and Hemichordata
    B. Coelenterata (Cnidaria) and Ctenophora
    C. Onycophora and Arthropoda
    D. Echinodermata and Chaetognatha
    E. Platyhelminthes and Nemertina

14. A classic example of primary embryonic induction is the induction by the vertebrate chordamesoderm of the

    A. vertebrae   B. axial musculature
    C. neural tube   D. heart
    E. liver primordium

15. In which of the following organelles is water synthesized from oxygen and hydrogen?

    A. Nucleus
    B. Mitochrondria
    C. Ribosomes
    D. Lysosomes
    E. Golgi apparatus

16. The biological significance of the evolution of fleshy fruits such as the apple and the peach is that such fruits are

    A. necessary for seed transpiration
    B. to protect the seeds from being eaten by animals
    C. exposed to rigorous natural selection because the matured ovary wall is triploid
    D. important sources of vitamin C for the plant
    E. adaptations to securing seed dispersal by animals

17. In a simple food chain, animals with the SMALLEST population *probably*

    A. are least likely to be an endangered species
    B. have a very high biotic potential
    C. are physically smaller than the others in the food chain
    D. are herbivorous
    E. are carnivorous

18. Which of the following enzymes acts on carbohydrates?

    A. Carboxypeptidase
    B. Trypsin
    C. Chymotrypsin
    D. Lipase
    E. Amylase

19. All of the following processes require energy input EXCEPT

    A. active transport
    B. muscle contraction
    C. DNA synthesis
    D. maintenance of the resting potential of neurons
    E. osmosis

20. The movement of fluid from the arteriole end of a mammalian capillary bed into the interstitial spaces is PRIMARILY due to

    A. hydrostatic pressure
    B. osmotic pressure
    C. active transport by the capillary walls
    D. contraction of skeletal muscles
    E. contraction of smooth muscle of the capillary walls

KEY (CORRECT ANSWERS)

1.	B	11.	A
2.	A	12.	D
3.	D	13.	E
4.	C	14.	C
5.	B	15.	B
6.	B	16.	E
7.	E	17.	E
8.	B	18.	E
9.	D	19.	E
10.	D	20.	A

EXAMINATION SECTION
TEST 1

DIRECTIONS: Each question or incomplete statement is followed by several suggested answers or completions. Select the one that BEST answers the question or completes the statement. *PRINT THE LETTER OF THE CORRECT ANSWER IN THE SPACE AT THE RIGHT.*

1. According to the Second Law of Thermodynamics,

    A. energy can neither be created nor destroyed
    B. energy can be created or destroyed
    C. any system isolated from an energy source tends to decrease in entropy
    D. organisms could not evolve
    E. any system isolated from an energy source tends toward its least ordered state

2. The distinction between the anaerobic metabolism of glucose in muscle cells and in yeast cells is the

    A. formation of lactic acid (lactate) in muscle cells and the formation of ethanol in yeast cells
    B. formation of acetate in yeast cells and lactate in muscle cells
    C. synthesis of more ATP per glucose molecule in muscle than in yeast cells
    D. formation of carbon dioxide in muscle but not in yeast cells
    E. synthesis of less ATP per glucose molecule in muscle cells

3. Organisms that obtain their energy from light can be termed

    A. autotrophic   B. holotrophic   C. chemotrophic
    D. heterotrophic   E. heliotrophic

4. An investigator isolated small particles from cancer cells which hydrolyzed protein and concluded that these were

    A. ribosomes   B. lipid vacuoles
    C. lysosomes   D. food vacuoles
    E. mitochondria

5. The first enzyme-catalyzed reaction in the glycolysis of glucose is

    A. deamination   B. lipolysis   C. phosphorylation
    D. hydrolysis   E. carboxylation

6. The generation of ATP (adenosine triphosphate) by the electron transport system (respiratory chain) occurs

    A. on the inner membrane of mitochondria
    B. on the outer surface of the nuclear envelope
    C. in the cytoplasm
    D. in the Golgi apparatus
    E. on the endoplasmic reticulum

7. Messenger ribonucleic acid (mRNA) differs from deoxyribonucleic acid (DNA) in that RNA

   I. contains thymine instead of uracil
   II. contains a ribose sugar
   III. is single-stranded

   The CORRECT answer is:

   A. I only
   B. II only
   C. III only
   D. I and III
   E. II and III

8. The so-called dark reactions (light-independent reactions) of photosynthesis

   A. do not occur during the daytime
   B. use the direct energy of light quanta
   C. occur in all plants cells
   D. do not require the products of the light reactions
   E. result in the assimilation (fixation) of carbon dioxide

9. If animal muscle cells are deprived of oxygen, anaerobic glycolysis will result and pyruvic acid will then be converted to

   A. alcohol
   B. glucose
   C. lactic acid
   D. phosphoric acid
   E. acetyl CoA

10. A sample of blood is added to a test tube containing a 1.6% salt solution. A short while later, the red blood cells are observed to be smaller and wrinkled in shape due to water loss.
    This indicates that

    A. red blood cells are isotonic to the 1.6% salt solution
    B. red blood cells are hypertonic to the 1.6% salt solution
    C. red blood cells are hypotonic to the 1.6% salt solution
    D. the 1.6% salt solution is hypotonic to the red blood cells
    E. the 1.6% salt solution is isotonic to the red blood cells

11. Which of the following is the key intermediate compound linking glycolysis to the Krebs cycle?

    A. NADH
    B. ATP
    C. Cytochrome b
    D. Succinic acid
    E. Acetyl Co A

12. A plant kept in the dark will not be able to produce glucose because light is necessary

    A. for the oxidation of glucose
    B. to excite electrons in the CO_2 molecules
    C. for activating enzymes necessary for converting CO_2 to glucose
    D. for sufficient ATP and reduced NADP to be available to synthesize glucose from CO_2
    E. for glucose phosphorylation

13. The First Law of Thermodynamics implies that living organisms cannot create their own energy but can only convert one form of energy into another.
    What, then, is the ULTIMATE source of energy for most living organisms?

A. Chemical energy from the glucose molecule made by plants during photosynthesis
B. The chemical energy released by the numerous hydro-lytic reactions in a cell
C. Heat energy from the sun
D. Light energy from the sun
E. ATP made in the mitochondria of both plants and animals

14. Which of the following is NOT a function of any hormone?

    A. Affects membrane transport of substances
    B. Regulates water balance in the body
    C. Changes the amount of activity of enzymes
    D. Promotes transcription of messenger RNA
    E. Acts as a source of energy

15. Which of the following pairs of structures have similarity of function? _____ nervous system.

    A. Thyroid gland and sympathetic
    B. Adrenal cortex and sympathetic
    C. Adrenal cortex and parasympathetic
    D. Adrenal medulla and parasympathetic
    E. Adrenal medulla and sympathetic

16. In the nephron of the kidney, filtration occurs between

    A. Bowman's capsule and Henle's loop
    B. the glomerulus and Bowman's capsule
    C. the proximal tubule and Henle's loop
    D. Henle's loop and the vasa recta
    E. the peritubular network and the convoluted tubules

17. The stimulation of parasympathetic nerves would produce a(n)

    A. increase in peristaltic activity
    B. increase in perspiration
    C. decrease in salivary gland activity
    D. increase in blood pressure
    E. none of the above

18. Clotting of human blood

    A. requires that hemoglobin be present
    B. results from fibrin joining globulin
    C. is a result of platelets releasing fibrinogen
    D. depends on the formation of fibrin from fibrinogen
    E. is accelerated when Ca^{++} is removed

19. The muscle cells of the human heart are PRIMARILY nourished by

    A. blood within the four chambers of the heart
    B. fluid in the pericardial cavity
    C. the lymphatic system
    D. blood delivered by the coronary arteries
    E. blood delivered by the ductus arteriosus

20. Carbon dioxide passes from tissues to blood to lungs by

    A. diffusing from a region of high concentration to an area of lesser concentration
    B. diffusing from a region of lower to one of higher concentration
    C. active transport
    D. irreversibly binding to hemoglobin
    E. chemiosmosis

21. Products of digestion absorbed in the mammalian small intestine

    A. are carried directly to the heart by the posterior vena cava
    B. are carried to the spleen for processing
    C. must be further digested in the blood before they can be absorbed by the cells
    D. are processed by the cells of the small intestine, which then secrete ATP into the blood
    E. are carried to the liver by the hepatic portal vein

22. Which of the following are typically autotrophic?

    A. Protozoa   B. Plants   C. Animals
    D. Fungi   E. Bacteria

23. Of the following phyla, the one that contains more species than the others combined is

    A. Annelida   B. Arthropoda   C. Mollusca
    D. Echinodermata   E. Chordata

24. All chordates

    A. possess backbones
    B. possess a dorsal, tubular nerve cord at some stage of life
    C. lack larval forms
    D. have endoskeletons composed of cartilage
    E. have a water vascular system

25. In which of these kingdoms are the organisms entirely heterotrophic?

    A. Protista and Fungi   B. Plantae and Fungi
    C. Animalia and Fungi   D. Protista and Animalia
    E. Monera and Protista

26. Mendel's law of segregation reflects the fact that

    A. linkage never occurs in peas
    B. alleles segregate differently in males and females
    C. each member of an allelic pair of genes enters a separate cell during meiosis
    D. during the course of development, DNA becomes segregated in the nucleus, RNA in the cytoplasm
    E. increasing specialization in the course of evolution is characterized by a segregation of tissue types

27. A diploid cell (2N = 20) has how many tetrads at metaphase I?

    A. 0   B. 10   C. 20   D. 40   E. 80

28. For the human ABO blood typing system, which of the following is ALWAYS determined by a homozygous genotype?
Type

   A. A
   B. B
   C. AB
   D. O
   E. all of the above

29. During the synthesis of a polypeptide at the ribosome site, the completed polypeptide is released when the

   A. ribosome reaches a termination codon
   B. ribosome reaches a termination anticodon
   C. tRNAs are depleted
   D. amino acids are depleted
   E. ribosome reaches the 5' end of the mRNA

30. A particular double-stranded DNA molecule was found to have 24% of its bases consist of adenine (A).
What percentage of its bases would be expected to consist of guanine (G)?

   A. 24   B. 26   C. 48   D. 52   E. 76

31. In humans, a phenotype resulting from a homozygous auto-somal recessive pair of genes would be expected to appear

   A. in unequal numbers in the two sexes
   B. phenotypically in every generation as long as one of the original parents manifested the trait
   C. only in those individuals who had at least one parent with the gene
   D. in approximately one-fourth of the children produced by two heterozygotes
   E. none of the above

32. One form of colorblindness is caused by a gene c carried on the X chromosome in humans. The gene is recessive to its normal allele C. Far more men are colorblind than women.
Geneticists explain this by pointing out that

   A. women possess no X chromosomes in their cells
   B. men carry no genes for color vision on their Y chromosomes
   C. men carry more genes for colorblindness than women do
   D. colorblindness is inhibited by female sex hormones
   E. colorblindness is promoted by male sex hormones

33. Sexual reproduction as compared with asexual reproduction ordinarily results in

   A. more offspring
   B. a greater inducement to reproduce
   C. greater genetic diversity in the offspring
   D. a higher frequency of well-adapted individual off-spring
   E. fewer individuals carrying recessive alleles

34. Gastrulation involves the

    A. formation of the blastocoel
    B. formation of germ layers
    C. loss of the blastopore
    D. formation of the blastula
    E. final differentiation of the stomach

35. Of the germ layers comprising the early human embryo, which one forms MOST of the central nervous system?

    A. Ectoderm   B. Mesoderm   C. Endoderm
    D. Notochord   E. Dermis

36. Embryonic induction is a process in which

    A. embryonic tissues influence adjacent tissues to differentiate
    B. an unfertilized egg is induced to develop
    C. genes are transferred from one developing tissue to another
    D. resting potentials are induced in neurons of embryos
    E. the maternal parent induces expression of recessive genes in embryos

37. One of the loveliest sounds in nature is bird song. Such song is commonly associated with

    A. hunger   B. pugnacity   C. territorially
    D. orientation   E. happiness

38. A deciduous forest biome differs from that of the grassland biome in that the forest biome receives more

    A. sunlight
    B. CO_2 for photosynthesis
    C. fixed nitrogen from the soil
    D. moisture
    E. ultraviolet light

39. Which of the following situations is MOST likely to result in genetic drift?

    A. An increase in population size
    B. A lack of gene mutation
    C. A prevention of emigration
    D. Random mating
    E. Isolation of a small population from a larger one

40. Under Hardy-Weinberg conditions,

    A. dominant alleles eventually replace recessive alleles
    B. evolution occurs at a rapid rate
    C. the frequency of dominant alleles slowly increases
    D. gene frequencies remain constant
    E. a 50%-50% equilibrium is reached between dominant and recessive alleles

KEY (CORRECT ANSWERS)

1.	E	11.	E	21.	E	31.	D
2.	A	12.	D	22.	B	32.	B
3.	A	13.	D	23.	B	33.	C
4.	C	14.	E	24.	B	34.	B
5.	C	15.	E	25.	C	35.	A
6.	A	16.	B	26.	C	36.	A
7.	E	17.	A	27.	B	37.	C
8.	E	18.	D	28.	D	38.	D
9.	C	19.	D	29.	A	39.	E
10.	C	20.	A	30.	B	40.	D

300 BASIC PRINCIPLES OF THE BIOLOGICAL SCIENCES

CONTENTS

		Page
I.	GEOGRAPHIC DISTRIBUTION	1
II.	ECOLOGICAL RELATIONSHIPS	1
III.	TAXONOMY	3
IV.	MODIFICATION OF SPECIES	3
V.	GENETICS AND HEREDITY	6
VI.	EMBRYONIC DEVELOPMENT	8
VII.	MORPHOLOGY AND PHYSIOLOGY	8
VIII.	ORGANIZATION	11
IX.	PROTOPLASM AND CELLS	11
X.	ENERGY, MATTER AND LIFE	14
XI.	PALEONTOLOGY	15
XII.	APPLIED BIOLOGY	16

300 Basic Principles of the Biological Sciences

I. GEOGRAPHIC DISTRIBUTION
   1. Living things are not distributed uniformly or at random over the surfaces of the earth, but are found in definite zones and local regions where conditions are favorable to their survival.
   2. Stretches of water act as barriers to purely terrestrial animals, and stretches of land bar the migrations of the inhabitants of water.
   3. Life exists from the depths of the ocean to the mountain heights.
   4. Each species of animal or plant tends to extend its range until some impossible barrier is encountered.
   5. The distribution of any group of land animals will depend upon three factors—first, upon the region where the group happened to originate; second, upon the connections which this region then and later happened to have with other land masses; and third, upon the fate of the group in the different regions to which it obtained access.
   6. Discontinuous widespread distribution is characteristic of old groups of animals and means that they formerly occupied also much of the intervening space.
   7. Most regions that are surrounded by barriers are devoid of a very great variety of species of animals or plants. However, the larger the area isolated, the greater the variety of forms.
   8. For most species of organism, periods of great scarcity of individuals' alternate with waves of great abundance, and the peaks of the waves succeed each other in a regular cycle.
   9. When new species are introduced into a country, few individuals or species will find themselves in the same balance as in their old home. For the majority, conditions will be unfavorable; they will fail to gain a footing and some will disappear. If the introduced species chances to be better suited, especially if it is removed from its old enemies and parasites, its numbers will increase often far beyond anything possible to it in its native country; not infrequently its abundance will force it into changed habits.
   10. In general, the natural flora and fauna of a region is the most luxuriant that it can support.
   11. New species of plants and animals appear at some definite point on the earth and then spread out from that location as a center.

II. ECOLOGICAL RELATIONSHIPS
   A. <u>Environment and Living Things</u>
      1. The environment acts upon living things, and living things act upon their environment.
      2. The environment of living things changes continually.
      3. All living things are continually engaged in an exacting struggle with their environments.
   B. <u>Life Necessities</u>
      1. Food, oxygen, certain optimal conditions of temperature, moisture, and light are essential to the life of most living things.
      2. Life, as we know it, is dependent upon complex chemical compounds of carbon, nitrogen, hydrogen, oxygen, and other elements.
      3. Water is essential to all living things because protoplasmic activity is dependent upon an adequate water supply.

4. Life may exist under conditions of light from bright sunlight to the complete darkness of caves or of depths of soil or water.
5. The range of temperature for life activities is very narrow as compared with the range of possible temperatures. There is a minimum temperature below which, and a maximum temperature above which, no life processes are carried on. The temperature range for life processes is from many degrees below 0°C. to nearly the boiling point of water.

C. Limiting Factors
1. Life is wholly confined to the surface of the planet earth and to a few miles above and below its surface (as far as our certain knowledge goes) and no one single form of life is able to span even these limits.
2. Living organisms cannot live in the upper levels of the atmosphere because of deficiency of oxygen for respiration, deficiency of pressure upon the exterior of the body, and intense cold.
3. The numbers of any species depend, on the one hand, upon its rate of reproduction and growth, and on the other, upon its death rate from accident, enemies, and disease.

D. Interdependence
1. All plants and animals are engaged in a constant struggle for energy.
2. Every living species is continually producing a multitude of individuals, many more than can survive, varying more or less among themselves, and all competing against each other for the available energy.
3. Change in the numbers of organisms in communities may be rapid even though the environmental conditions apparently alter slowly and gradually.
4. The existence of organisms depends upon their interrelations with the environment which includes both the inorganic world and other organisms.
5. A balance in nature is maintained through interrelations of plants and animals with each other and with their physical environment.
6. When the balance of nature is disturbed, disastrous results often follow.
7. The first forms of life were altogether independent, but evolution has resulted in the general interdependence of organisms,
8. Certain associations of plants and animals are the result of a struggle for survival; for example, community or social life, parasitism and symbiosis.
9. All gradations of association occur in intimate associations between organisms, from those which are mutually beneficial to the individuals concerned (symbiosis) to those in which one member secures all the advantage at the expense of the other (parasitism).
10. Commensalism usually evolves, not in the direction of mutualism, but toward parasitism.
11. The parasite-host relationship is usually specific and requires not only marked adaptation on the part of the parasite but often also an adjustment on the part of the host.
12. It is indispensable to successful parasitic existence that the relationship be so adjusted that means are provided for the escape of the parasites or their offspring in order that new generations in new hosts may obtain.
13. True parasites secure their nourishment from the host plant or animal without exerting an injurious effect; pathogens damage the host by invading the tissues, multiplying there and producing infection.
14. A characteristic of many parasites is that they have alternate hosts.

15. Saprophytic organisms are responsible for decay by which process the necessary raw materials for growth of new organisms are released from dead matter.
16. The continuance of higher forms of life in anything like the present kinds and numbers would be impossible without bacteria and molds. They break down the complex carbohydrate and protein substances of dead plants and animals into simpler substances which may then be used again by living plants.
17. All the higher forms of terrestrial life are dependent either directly or indirectly on the soil bacteria for their nitrogen supply.
18. Life depends for its primal food supply upon chlorophyll-bearing plants and, for its sustained supply, upon bacteria. The whole of life, considered chemically, is one cyclic process from chlorophyll-bearing plant to bacteria and so again to chlorophyll-bearing plant.
19. The oxygen of the atmosphere is removed by animals and returned by chlorophyll-bearing plants.
20. The nutritional processes of different classes of organisms supplement each other in such a manner that they result in a nutritional balance among living things.

E. Soil and Soil Minerals
1. Plants and animals are directly or indirectly dependent on the soil.
2. All plant and animal life, along with the climate and varying weather, play an active part in helping to form and to change the soil.
3. Parent material for the development of soils is formed through the physical disintegration and chemical decomposition of rock particles and organic matter.
4. Only the topsoil, with its rich organic matter, its porous structure, and its living organisms, can hold the water and provide the minerals necessary to the life of most plants.

III. TAXONOMY
1. The present variety in living forms has resulted from the modifications through long periods of time of simpler and less varied ancestral types, and by degeneration in many groups of organisms from more complex organisms.
2. Similar organisms are grouped together because they are believed to be related through common descent.
3. Evolutionary relationships in organisms are formulated on the basis of structural similarity.
4. In all organisms, increasing complexity of structure is accomplished by an increasing division of labor.
5. In general, living things give evidence of a definite progression from simple to complex forms.
6. The greater the similarity in structure between organisms the closer is their kinship; the less the similarity in structure, the more remote is their common ancestry.

IV. MODIFICATION OF SPECIES
A. General
1. All life comes from preceding life.
2. One of the most "constant" features of natural phenomena is variability, but variability is always within definite limits.
3. Living things, even of the same kind, are never exactly alike, not even with regard to single traits (characteristics) such as color or shape.
4. Organisms which have no means of reproduction other than asexual show very little variation.
5. The evolution of the earth and the living things inhabiting it has resulted from the operation of natural forces.

6. Living things alter their types; present species have not always existed, but have originated by descent from others which in turn were derived from still earlier ones, and so down to the first living forms.
7. The forms of living things have changed slowly but steadily in the past except for those resulting from mutations,
8. Evolution has needed enormous lapses of time for its operations.
9. The existing forms of life on the earth are not all the forms of life which have existed; there has been a great variety of animals and plants which have passed away.
10. The crises of evolution when they occur are not crises of variation but of selection and elimination; not strange births but selective massacres. The germ plasm has gone on throwing up mutations at about the same rate age after age.
11. Most of the species of modern animals are of relatively recent origin; having evolved from others in the past and probably continuing to evolve into other species of animals.
12. As nature progressed in the production of new forms, new potentialities also were added.
13. Variation and heredity together are responsible for the appearance and the continuation of the processes of evolution.
14. In organisms, the more similar the body structures and their mode of origin, and the greater the number of such structures, the closer the relationship of the organisms.
15. If two or more groups of organisms have similar homologous structures they have descended from similar ancestors or from the same common ancestor.
16. Analogous structures in plants and animals serve to carry on similar functions but they are not similar in basic plan or mode of origin.
17. Adult organisms that differ greatly from one another but which show fundamental similarities in embryological development have originated from similar ancestors.
18. Similarity between organisms suggests common ancestry; the nature of the differences between them indicates which is the more primitive type.
19. The embryos of different animals, in addition to being more like each other as development is traced backward, show also a widening contrast with their parents and their adult destiny.
20. The greater the period that has elapsed since two stocks diverged, the greater the difference in the terminal products.
21. In organisms inhabiting similar environments evolution has often produced convergence - the molding of unrelated stocks into similar forms by the needs of their way of life.
22. Animals of diverse origin living among similar surroundings tend to become, at least superficially, alike and they often develop parts that have the same function.
23. Isolation of a piece of land or a body of water from the rest of the world always permits its animal and plant inhabitants to evolve along their own peculiar lines and each race involved tends to become more uniform.
24. New types of living things arise through variations in previously existing kinds.
25. Plants and animals in the course of their generations are changed and molded to meet the requirements of their existence, and the individuals and types best adapted to their life situations are the ones that survive.
26. During the main evolution of any stock, for each type of organism that lives on to be ancestral to the next evolutionary phase, there are considerable numbers thrown off to live a few tens of thousands of years and die without descendants.

27. Every species of organism is subject to certain checks or controls in the form of enemies and only those members that are most capable of avoiding their enemies survive to reproduce new offspring and thereby transmit many of their characters to their offspring.

B. <u>Mutations</u>
1. The genes of all organisms are subject to change, such changes producing heritable modifications in organisms called mutations.
2. The history of organisms shows that evolution and race divergence has been the result of mutations.
3. All heritable variations which are not the result of recombinations of genes are mutations, which are changes in genes, in some cases induced by environmental agents.
4. New kinds of living things have arisen through mutation.
5. Any hereditary change that follows the laws of Mendelian heredity is due to a gene mutation.
6. Mutations occur independently of the activities of individuals as more or less haphazard hereditary variations.

C. <u>Adaptations</u>
1. All living things are slowly changing, both structurally and functionally, in response to changes in their physical environments.
2. The surface of the earth and the atmosphere surrounding the earth are undergoing constant changes; therefore in order to survive, organisms must migrate, hibernate, aestivate, build artificial shelters, or otherwise become adapted to these changes.
3. Species not fitted to the conditions about them do not thrive and finally become extinct.
4. The organisms most likely to survive and reproduce are those that are structurally and physiologically best fitted to their environments.
5. Some of the differences between related groups of organisms separated by a geographical barrier are due to adaptive responses to slightly different environmental factors.
6. In higher plants and in the higher air-breathing vertebrates, a progressive emancipation from life in water and an adaptation to life on dry land is traceable.
7. The chief difference in the structure of organisms from the lowest to the highest are resultant of the means adopted to perform certain functions under different exigencies imposed by the environment and mode of life.
8. Protective adaptations aid survival.
9. The biological functions of color are to conceal, to disguise, or to advertise.
10. Chlorophyll-bearing plants are adapted for food making.
11. In a living organism, adaptation of action and adaptation of structure are necessary for survival.
12. Every living organism possesses some body parts which are adapted for the life it leads.
13. Each species of living organism is adapted, or is in the process of becoming adapted, to live where it is found.
14. The power of living things to change is definitely restricted; specialization reaches the limit of efficiency prescribed by mechanical or chemical laws.
15. The more highly specialized an organism is, the more likely it is to become extinct if its environment changes.

16. An adaptive character may give its possessors a definite advantage over other members of the species, and so in the course of generations, due to the elimination of the non-possessors of this character, and of the conferring of this character upon others by heredity, becoming a character of all the members of the species.
17. Animals and plants lacking some means of mechanical support are debarred from terrestrial life.
18. In the water, free swimming organisms are very light becuase their specific gravity is only slightly greater than that of the medium in which they live.
19. Water-living organisms do not merely dilute their weight but counteract it by accumulating lighter substances inside themselves.
20. Those organisms which cannot adjust themselves to their environment lose out in the struggle for existence.

V. GENETICS AND HEREDITY
   A. General
      1. Living things come only from living things.
      2. The germ plasm of animals and plants passes on from generation to generation and there has been a continuous stream from the first organism to the present living organisms.
      3. The fundamental function of the germ plasm is the perpetuation of the species; the body or somoplasm serves as the vehicle for the germ plasm.
      4. Every cell originated from a cell and every chromosome from a chromosome.
      5. The genes in the chromosomes of eggs and sperms are the physical basis of heredity.
   B. Chromosomes
      1. All cells within one multi-cellular individual, except the gametes in animals and the spores in plants, are characterized by the same chromosomal content, as they all originated by cell division from a common cell.
      2. All individuals of a unicellular species, except asexual species, contain the same set or "similar sets" of chromosomes.
      3. Each kind of living thing has its characteristic chromosome complement, and the constancy of that complement is preserved at each cell division. Different species show the utmost diversity in number, size, and form of chromosomes.
      4. The number of chromosomes in the somatic cells of all the individuals of a species is a constant, except in chimeras, gynandromorphs, etc.
      5. In the maturation of the sex cells at the pairing of the chromosomes, except for the single sex chromosomes in some organisms, the two members of each pair come originally, one from the paternal line and one from the maternal line.
      6. In fertilization in most bi-sexual organisms, the egg contributes half (+ 1 or -1) the specific number of chromosomes to the zygote as does also the sperm.
      7. The separation of homologous chromosomes at reduction division in the germ cell is a matter of chance, the separation in any one pair occurs absolutely without reference to what had occurred in any other pair in the cell.
   C. Genes
      1. The hereditary characteristics possessed by any organism depend wholly upon the genes that were transmitted to it in the reproductive cells received from its parents.
      2. The hereditary characters in all organisms are determined by the genes which are carried in the chromosomes.
      3. Living things reproduce offspring which possess the genes of their ancestors though these offspring do not necessarily resemble any one of these ancestors.

4. In most cases, a character is not determined by a single gene, but by the interplay of two or more genes; in this interaction the genes may interfere with, modify, counteract, or reinforce each other.
5. Genes that lie in the same chromosome tend to remain together in reduction division so that the characters which they determine are linked in inheritance.
6. The greater the distance two genes lie apart in the chromosome the more often will they separate and cross over when a chromosome fragments and part of it adheres to another chromosome.
7. The sex chromosome may carry the genes for a number of characters other than sex. Such characters are sex linked.

D. Meiosis
1. Meiosis or "chromosome reduction" from the diploid to the haploid number occurs at some stage in all organisms in which sexual processes take place; and when followed by the return to the diploid number of chromosomes at fertilization, it keeps the number of chromosomes constant for the species.
2. In plants and animals subject to parthenogenetic development (development from unfertilized germinal cells), reduction of the number of chromosomes does not occur.
3. During the process of maturation in an egg or a sperm, corresponding maternal and paternal chromosomes, with their genes, go to different cells in the reduction division so that each secondary oocyte or spermatocyte receives one, but not both, of these chromosomes with its genes.
4. No relation exists between the common origin of chromosomes from the same gamete and their later distribution during chromosome reduction. Chance alone seems to determine how the chromosomes are distributed.
5. The heredity of an individual organism produced by sexual means is determined by what occurs to the chromosomes in the reduction division in maturation and in fertilization.
6. In plants the gamete-bearing phase of the life cycle is haploid; the spore-bearing phase is diploid. The reduction division occurs during spore formation.

E. Mendel's Laws
1. Since the genes of the two parents combine at random in the germ cells and since the germ cells meet at random in fertilization, the individuals of any generation occur in certain predictable ratios.
2. In the second and later generations of a hybrid, every possible combination of the parent character occurs, and each combination appears in a definite proportion of the individuals.
3. Every individual organism is composed of distinct hereditary characters which are transmitted by distinct hereditary factors (genes). In a hybrid the different parental genes are combined. When the sex cells of the hybrid are formed the two parental genes separate again, remaining quite unchanged and pure, each sex cell containing only one of the two genes of one pair.
4. All individuals of the first generation of hybrids, the F_1 generation, are uniform in appearance in alternative inheritance. Only one of the two parental characters, the stronger or the dominant one, is shown; in intermediate inheritance a mixture of the parental characteristics is shown.
5. In a cross of the F_2 generation of hybrids the genes which determine the characters are segregated in the gametes so that a certain percent of the offspring possess the dominant character alone, a certain percent the recessive character alone, while a certain percent are again hybrid in nature.

6. In polyhybrid crossings (F individuals with two or more pairs of hereditary characters) all possible combinations of the parental characters are shown in characteristic ratios.
7. Sex is inherited; it follows a given distribution of the chromosomes according to definite Mendelian ratios.
8. Animals resemble each other more and more closely the farther back we pursue them in embryological development.
9. The life history of the individual tends in a very general way to recapitulate the history of the race.
10. Acquired characters are not inherited.
11. Fluctuating variations found within a pure line are not inherited and cannot change the character of the offspring permanently.
12. Heredity supplies the native capacities of an organism; environment determines to a large extent how fully these capacities will be developed.
13. Cells within an organism are dependent upon their immediate cellular environment as well as their genes, in the process of becoming what they finally become.
14. Many hereditary characters are subject to non-genetic or environmental variation in expression.
15. Inbreeding in animals or plants results in a uniform strain.
16. Reversion occurs only when different varieties of plants or animals are crossed, or in subsequent generations following a cross, never in genetically pure stocks.
17. Hybridization gives variation, isolation gives fixation, and fixation gives speciation.
18. New types of organisms, different enough to be regarded as new species, may result from a cross.

VI. EMBRYONIC DEVELOPMENT
1. All embryos start from a single fertilized egg cell and grow through division and redivision into the form of the organism which produces the egg cell.
2. Similarities in the embryological development of organisms show hereditary relationships between these organisms and the closer two species are related the longer they parallel one another in development.
3. The action of "organizers" (probably chemical in character) produced in the developing embryo causes the developing egg, which at first acts as a whole, to produce specialized parts which develop independently.

VII. MORPHOLOGY AND PHYSIOLOGY
 A. Physical Support and Movement
  1. In many multicellular organisms body form is secured and maintained either by the consistency of the tissues and the internal pressure of body fluids, or by the secretion of special substances which are formed into supporting structures.
  2. A characteristic of living organisms is the power of independent motion, either of protoplasm within the cell or of the body as a whole.
  3. The power of contraction which results in movement is possessed by all protoplasm to a greater or lesser degree.
  4. The difference in motion and locomotion between animals and plants is one of degree.
 B. Material for Growth and Replacement
  1. Growth and repair are fundamental activities for all protoplasm.
  2. Plants and animals utilize similar food substances but they are obtained in different ways.

3. The carbohydrate foods made by the chloroplasts of chlorophyll-bearing plants are the original source of all energy used by plants themselves (except by the autotrophic bacteria) as well as that used by animals.
4. Starches, fats and proteins are produced by plants and it is upon these that all animals depend primarily for food.
5. The food requirements of every living thing are: fuels capable of yielding, when oxidized, the supply of energy without which life cannot continue; materials for growth and for replacement for the slight wearing away of the living tissue involved in any activity; minerals, the necessary constituents of cell structures, of cell products, and of the bathing fluid of cells; the vitamins or "accessory" fo.od factors.
6. An animal cannot live without proteins. They are necessary in cell growth and maintenance; so are necessities in the diets of animals. Plants are able to use carbohydrates and nitrates to build up the proteins necessary for growth and maintenance of their cells.
7. Digestion in plants and animals is carried on by enzymes, or organic catalysts, which are made by the organisms themselves and which take part in and speed up the chemical reactions but do not undergo any permanent chemical change themselves.
8. Digestion accomplishes two things: it makes food soluble in water, thus enabling the nutrients to pass through membranes and thereby reach and enter the cells; it reduces complex nutrients (fats, proteins, and carbohydrates) to simple building materials which in turn can be rebuilt into whatever living material or structural feature is necessary at the place of use.
9. All cells contain autolytic enzymes that at death are capable of producing digestive changes which result in the final disintegration of the body,

C. <u>Respiration and Release of Energy</u>
1. Cellular respiration (aerobic decomposition) occurs in all living cells and all organisms possess structures by means of which it can be carried on. Its first step is intake of oxygen either directly from the air or dissolved in water, its final product is carbon dioxide, and free energy is released. In the cells it is accomplished at ordinary temperatures by the intervention of special enzymes.
2. Anaerobic decomposition (fermentation) is accomplished at ordinary temperatures by the intervention of special enzymes, dissimilation occurs in the absence of oxygen, its final products are carbon dioxide and alcohol, and free energy is released.
3. The respiratory process of both plants and animals involves exactly the same gaseous exchange and accomplishes the same function the release of energy.
4. Oxygen free in the atmosphere or dissolved in water supplies the respiratory needs of practically all living organisms, except for a few parasitic and anaerobic animals, and a number of bacteria and fungi which can extract the oxygen needed for their energy production from the organic substances on which they feed.
5. Carbon dioxide set free during the respiration of both plants and animals is absorbed by plants and used as a raw material of photosynthesis.

D. <u>Internal Transportation</u>
1. Circulation is carried on in all living organisms. With increase in size and complexity of the body of an organism there goes a corresponding elaboration of the transportation (circulatory) system.

E. Disposal of Wastes
1. In organisms the end products of metabolism, water, carbon dioxide, and nitrogenous compounds are either stored in the cells as insoluble crystals; are eliminated in solution by diffusion, or osmosis (excretion); are incorporated into useful cell products (secretion); or are recombined into food substances within the organism.

F. Integration of Activities
1. All living things respond to stimuli in their environment.
2. The nature of the response made by a cell to a stimulus is determined by the nature of the responding protoplasm, as well as by the kind of stimulus.
3. In general, the extent of a response is rather definitely fixed for any given nerve cell. If a cell responds at all, it does so to its full capacity.
4. From the simple to the complex organisms there is an increasingly elaborate coordination of receptivity of stimuli and response to stimuli.
5. The multitude of interrelated neurons of the nervous system of higher animals forms a complex system through which every organ of the body is in connection with every other organ.
6. Every animal comes into the world with a certain inherited endowment of congenital behavior.
7. All animals can modify to some extent their inherent modes of reaction.
8. Inherent reactions in animals are unlearned, independent of intelligence, and more or less inflexible in their operation; under natural conditions they are usually beneficial to the individual or the race.
9. The intelligence shown by the members of a phylum of higher animals usually bears a direct relation to the stage of development of the special sense organs and to the proportionate size of the brain.
10. Much of the behavior of living animals depends on their nervous organization, and they exhibit a great variety of behavior because the nervous organization varies in complexity.
11. The secretions of the endocrine glands are absorbed directly into the blood stream from the gland tissue that produces them and are absorbed from the blood by the tissues of the organs whose activities are regulated by these substances.
12. In animals certain waste products as well as vitamin and endocrine substances exert regulatory effects on the activities of various organs in the body.

G. Reproduction
1. Reproduction is a fundamental biological process that provides for the continuance of life on the earth by providing new individuals.
2. The ability and necessity of members of a species to produce other individuals like themselves is essential for the welfare and maintenance of the species, since no living thing can maintain itself for an unlimited period of time.
3. Reproduction in all organisms is a process of growth in which a single cell or a group of cells is separated from the parent body and develops into a new individual.
4. All the modes of reproduction of organic life are alike in their nature, varying only in complexity of development; they fall into two general categories, asexual and sexual reproduction.
5. The most primitive method of reproduction employed by organisms is the splitting of the whole body into two halves, each of which grows into a complete new individual.

6. Asexual reproduction in organisms may be brought about by fission (simple division, by external or internal budding, or by sporulation.
7. Offspring produced asexually are almost always like the parent; they will have exactly the same or similar chromosomes and the same gene complex.
8. Alternation of generations or a somewhat parallel process is characteristic of all higher plants, but is comparatively uncommon with animals.
9. Sexual reproduction is an almost universal method of reproduction and occurs in representatives of every phylum of plants and animals.
10. All sexually reproduced individuals begin their careers as single fertilized cells.
11. The reproductive elements and their union in fertilization are fundamentally the same in plants and animals.
12. In sexual reproduction a male cell from one parent unites with a female cell from the other parent to produce the young (except in the few cases of self-fertilization).
13. Throughout the plant and animal kingdoms there is a general preference for cross-fertilization; an avoidance of the union of eggs with male elements from the same individual. In those animals and in the great majority of plants which are hermaphrodite, there are usually precautions to restrain self-fertilization.
14. In organisms which reproduce by sexual means fertilization serves two functions: stimulating the egg to develop, and introducing the hereditary properties of the male parent.
15. Sexual union in plants and animals affords a method of variation due to the combining of the egg and sperm, with their chromosomes and genes, at the time of fertilization.
16. The genes in the chromosomes of the egg and the sperm are the carriers of the structural characters of the parents to the next generation.
17. In the vast majority of organisms it is the male which has the unsymmetrical chromosome complement, and the sperms therefore are the determiners of sex.
18. Regeneration is almost universal among living things; from the simple to the more complex animals the abilities to regenerate lost parts and to reproduce asexually fall off, gradually and independently, as the body becomes more specialized.
19. In many organisms the number of young which are produced bears a definite relation to the chance of survival; the smaller the chance the more numerous the offspring.
20. The less the amount of parental care given to the offspring the greater is the need for the animal to be prolific.

VIII. ORGANIZATION
1. The smallest unit of living material capable of existing independently and of maintaining itself is the unit called the cell.
2. The cell is the unit of structure and function in all organisms.
3. Cells are organized into tissues, tissues into organs and organs into systems, the better to carry on the functions of complex organisms.
4. From the lower to the higher forms of life, there is an increasing complexity of structure, and this is accompanied by a progressive increase in division of labor.
5. In all organisms, the higher the organization the greater the degree of differentiation and division of labor and of the dependency of one part upon another.
6. In plants and animals, organs of the same structural plan are often applied to the most diverse functions.

IX. PROTOPLASM AND CELLS
  A. General
    1. Protoplasm is the physical basis of all life.

2. The distinctive properties of organisms depend upon the complexity of the molecular organization of protoplasm, the one essential constituent of every living thing.
3. The physical and chemical properties of plant and animal protoplasm are similar.
4. Many of the rhythmic changes of protoplasm, such as ciliary action, heartbeat, and rhythmic processes in cell division, are based upon reversible changes in the colloidal state.
5. Protoplasm is built only by protoplasm and every cell comes from a cell.
6. None of the materials present in living protoplasm leaves it when death ensues, for a given bit of protoplasm weighs exactly the same after death as when alive.
7. Life and protoplasm in a cell will remain indissolubly associated for an indefinite period of time unless the cell suffers an accident, or becomes diseased, or is unable to throw off the toxic waste substances that accumulate with age as a result of normal metabolism.
8. Carbon and nitrogen are the basic elements in the protoplasmic compounds.
9. Every cell consists essentially of a mass of protoplasm which is usually differentiated into a central portion, the nucleus, and an outer portion, the cytoplasm.
10. In cells the fundamental processes of food intake, digestion, regeneration of lost structures, and survival are controlled by the nucleus.
11. The nucleus of a cell always contains a complex of protein materials, chromatin, the specialized vehicle which transmits hereditary characters in organisms.
12. The size of cells bears no constant relation to the size of the animals or plants in which they are found.

B. Mitosis
1. The fundamental process of reproduction in all organisms whose cells possess nuclei is cell division which results in the precise distribution of the chromatin of the nucleus.
2. Cell division is the essential mechanism of reproduction, of heredity, and to a large extent, of organic evolution.
3. All cells arise through the division of previous cells (or protoplasm), back to the primitive ancestral cell (or protoplasm).
4. Growth and development in organisms is essentially a cellular phenomenon, a direct result of mitotic cell division, and it is always controlled and guided by the axiate organization of the cell.

C. Life Processes
1. The orderliness of the life processes of an organism is not an isolated orderliness, but one aspect of the orderliness of the universe.
2. Many of the processes of change in the universe are rhythmic, or periodic, and life processes constitute no exception to the rule.
3. The fundamental life processes are the same in all organisms.
4. All chemical processes that belong to life itself are processes that occur in solution.
5. The colloidal nature of the cell material as a whole furnishes the basis of some of the fundamental life processes.
6. Throughout the life of every organism there is a building up and a tearing down of protoplasm with constant transformations of energy.
7. An organism must have certain materials for its life processes and each organism must secure the required materials that it cannot build for itself.

8. All cells produce certain chemical compounds, secretions, which may be used in the processes going on within the cell, in cavities adjoining the cells, or at considerable distances from the cells where they are produced.
9. Enzymes, vitamins, and hormones are chemical regulators (stimulators and suppressors) of the reactions that occur in living organisms.

D. Photosynthesis
1. The work of the chlorophyll of all chlorophyll-bearing plants is essential to all living things.
2. All living things, except chemosynthetic bacteria, depend directly or indirectly on photosynthesis for food.
3. The forms of all chlorophyll-bearing plants are adapted for carrying on photosynthesis.
4. In the presence of sunlight the chloroplasts of chlorophyll-bearing plants convert carbon dioxide and water into intermediate substances, and these into sugar, and sugar into starch, and liberate oxygen; thus directly or indirectly producing practically all the food in the world.
5. In photosynthesis, the energy of sunlight is used to lift the carbon to an energy level from which, as it descends, it furnishes the energy for the building of many compounds and for the carrying on of life processes.
6. All the energy used by chlorophyll-bearing plants in their secondary building processes comes from compounds formed in photosynthesis.

E. Metabolism
1. The protoplasm of a cell carries on continuously all the general processes of any living body: the processes concerned in the growth and repair or upbuilding of protoplasm (anabolism) and the processes concerned with the breaking down of protoplasm and elimination of wastes from the cell (catabolism). The sum of all these chemical and physical processes is metabolism.
2. In cells a quantitative gradient in metabolic rate runs from the apical to the basal pole of the cell, and the various formed components of the cell are arranged in definite relation to the gradient.
3. When anabolism exceeds catabolism, as it does in all young animals, growth is inevitable.
4. Living organisms, during the growth period, increase the mass of the cell from within through the ingestion and utilization of food substances. When the cell reaches a maximum size, mitosis usually results.
5. All living things grow by intussusception or assimilation, making over the materials which are taken into the body into the kind of material of which the body is composed.
6. All living cells require oxygen to provide energy or to build new protoplasm.
7. All living things, except a few anaerobes and autotrophic bacteria, secure their energy by oxidizing food.
8. Oxidation (combustion) furnishes the essential source of heat in the animal body; and other factors remaining constant, the more heat so produced the warmer the animal body.
9. The amount of oxygen taken into the body of an organism and absorbed by the cells is directly proportional to the amount of energy released in the body.
10. Decomposition of the carbon compounds of organisms provides a replenishment of carbon in the atmosphere in the form of carbon dioxide. Thus carbon is continually subjected to a series of cyclic changes from living to non-living substances.

11. All plants, and a few simple animals, are able to recombine nitrogenous byproducts of respiration into proteins by re-synthesizing them anew with carbohydrate molecules.
12. Diffusion, the spread of fluids and their dissolved substances, throughout the protoplasm of a cell or the tissues of an organism is an important method of conveying oxygen from the surface of a cell to the interior, or digested foods from the place of digestion to the protoplasm that will use them, or substances that stimulate any activity to the organ that responds to them, or the waste materials from the place where they are formed to the place where they are stored or excreted.
13. Osmosis, the diffusion of molecules of a solvent (usually water) through a semi-permeable membrane (a layer of cells or the membrane of a single cell) from the point of higher concentration of the solvent to a point of lower concentration, with a stoppage of the flow of molecules of the solute, is a basic process in plant and animal physiology.
14. Turgor in cells is maintained by osmotic pressure; cell membranes are semi-permeable with respect to water and the substances dissolved in it and where the concentration of the solute is higher within the cell than outside, the entrance of water into the cell is accomplished mainly by osmosis.
15. Throughout the organic world there is a cyclic relation between death and the continuance of organic life.
16. Species can and do become extinct, but they usually live on for ages in spite of the death of individuals.

F. Characteristics of Living Things
1. Most living things differ from non-living things by being able to perform the control functions of irritability and spontaneous movement.
2. All living organisms (except viruses and bacteriophage) carry on the common life processes: reproduction, growth, nutrition, excretion, respiration, and irritability.
3. There is a definite size limit for each species of plant and animal.
4. The smaller an organism, the greater is the proportion of its surface to its weight, since surface increases as the square of its length, weight as its cube.
5. In most organisms, large size is accompanied by tissue differentiation and special organs for different kinds of work.
6. The bodies of most animals exhibit some degree of symmetry, either spherical, radial, or bilateral.
7. The bodies of most animals exhibit bilateral symmetry which is an adaptation for forward motion.
8. At every stage of development the individual is an integrated organism; all of its cells, tissues, and organs are correlated and act together as a unit
9. Individuality in an organism is maintained throughout Life in spite of the fact that the actual chemical constitution of the living substances composing it is constantly changing.
10. Except for those organisms which exhibit metagenesis, all living things are able in one way or another to produce new living things like, or nearly like, themselves.
11. All living things die, but life continues from age to age.

X. ENERGY, MATTER AND LIFE
1. The earth's position in relation to the sun is a determining factor of life on the earth.
2. The energy of solar radiation is continually working changes in the surface of the earth and the atmosphere surrounding the earth; all life on the earth is affected directly or indirectly by these changes.

3. Energy can be transformed into mass and mass into energy, but the sum total, mass plus energy, remains constant.
4. Energy and matter are not created or destroyed in the reactions associated with the life processes, but are passed on from organism to organism in endless succession.
5. The energy which makes possible the activity of most living things comes at first from the sun and is secured by the organism through the oxidation of food within its body.
6. Energy changes accompany all chemical changes in living organisms and every chemical change has physical concomitants.
7. Physically all animals are fundamentally mechanisms, driven by the energy liberated in the oxidation of food.
8. As long as life continues in any organism, energy is being released.
9. There are no elements in living matter which are not found in its lifeless environment; the energy by which life is operated is the same energy by which the simplest physical and chemical transformations are brought about.
10. There is a cycle, from inorganic substances in the air and soil to plant tissue, thence to animal tissue, from either of the last two stages via excretion or death and decay back to the air and soil. The energy for this everlasting rotation of life is furnished by the radiant energy of the sun.
11. The phenomena of life involve chemical change, so that wherever life processes are being carried on, chemical changes are taking place. However, chemical change may proceed without involving life.
12. All living organisms have other living things which compete with them for the available energy.
13. There are no living chemical compounds; life is a property of the coordinated association of the different organic and inorganic substances which make up protoplasm.

XI. PALEONTOLOGY
   A. Fossils
      1. Fossils, dated by the rocks in which they are found, reveal portions of the actual story of life's past changes by a progression of forms from simple to complex.
      2. Organisms whose fossils are found in any quantity lived and died in the period when the strata in which their remains are found were laid down.
      3. In fossilization, it is usually the hard parts of organisms that are preserved. Succession of Fossils
   B. Succession of Fossils
      1. The present is the key to the past; the succession of fossils in the rock shows a progressive series from simple to complex.
      2. When a large thickness of rocks shows every evidence of having been laid down steadily and continuously, year after year, it may well change its character. If it changes its character, the character of the animals and plants which live on and in it will change too.
      3. The fact of primary importance in the history of life displayed by the geological periods is the orderly succession of living forms.
      4. The older layers of rocks contain forms which are extremely unlike the now living animals and plants, while the more recent layers contain types more similar to our contemporary ones.

16

5. Each formation of sedimentary rock has its peculiar assemblage of fossils and there is a definite relation between the fossils found in rocks and the position of these rocks in the geologic timetable.
6. The most primitive and simplest forms of life exist in the oldest rocks, and organisms found in younger and younger rocks represent higher and higher forms.
7. Fossilization is the fate of very few animals and plants. The great majority of dead things simply decay and disappear and their material is returned to the general circulation of nature to be built up into the bodies of new organisms.

XII. APPLIED BIOLOGY
  A. Diseases
    1. All communicable diseases are caused by micro-organisms.
    2. For each disease caused by an organism a specific microbe exists.
    3. Viruses require living cells for their growth and they multiply only within living cells.
    4. Infection by micro-organisms is possible only under the following conditions:
        (a) The infecting organism must enter the host in sufficient numbers;
        (b) It must enter by an appropriate avenue;
        (c) It must be virulent;
        (d) The host must be receptive.
    5. For most species of organisms the great checks on increase in numbers are enemies, disease, and competition between individuals of the same species and of one species with another for food and other necessities of life.
    6. A parasitic organism harms its host in various ways and to various degrees, by actively attacking the tissues, by shedding poisons (toxins) which are distributed throughout the body of the host, by competing with the host for food, or even by making reproduction of the host impossible.
    7. Every influence exercised by micro-organisms upon man and his environment, whether beneficial or detrimental, is the result of a chemical change in the substances from which they secure their nutrition or of a chemical product synthesized from their nutrients.
    8. The antitoxins produced by the body of an organism are specific.
    9. Most cases of fermentation, souring, and putrefaction are brought about by living micro-organisms.
    10. Certain one-celled organisms escape adverse conditions by forming highly resistant spores which often survive until conditions are again favorable.

GLOSSARY OF BIOLOGICAL TERMS

CONTENTS

	Page
Abdomen...... Allergen	1
Allergy ...... Antibiotics	2
Antibodies ...... Axon	3
Bacillus ...... Blood Count	4
Blood Platelets ...... Capillaries	5
Carbohydrates ...... Chlorophyll	6
Chlorophyll Bodies ...... Colon	7
Colony ...... Cro-magnon Man	8
Crop...... Diastase	9
Diatoms ...... Embryo	10
Embryology ...... Fatty Acids	11
Female Parent ...... Fruit	12
Fungus ...... Gizzard	13
Gland - Hexapods	14
Hilum ...... Inorganic	15
Insects ...... Linkage	16
Lipase .... Milt	17
Mitosis ...... Nodules	18
Notochord ...... Pepsin	19
Peripheral Nervous System .... Primates	20
Prolactin .... Retina	21
Rh Factor ..... Spawning	22
Spermatophytes .... Thallophytes	23
Thiamin .... Villus	24
White Blood Count .... Zoospore	25

GLOSSARY OF BIOLOGICAL TERMS

A

ABDOMEN - The posterior section of the body; that section behind the thorax; the stomach region in vertebrates.

ABSORPTION - The passage of dissolved substances into the villi for distribution through the body.

ACETYLCHOLINE - A neurohumor.

ACNE - An infection of the fat glands in the skin. Causes a skin eruption of the face.

ACQUIRED CHARACTERISTICS - Traits of organisms developed during their lifetime because of environmental influences.

ADAPTATION - The character of any organism or its parts which especially suits it to live in its particular environment. If an organism is not adapted to its environment, it dies.

ADDICT - A person who cannot get along without a constant supply of narcotics

ADENOIDS - Large masses of tissue in the back of the throat. May interfere with breathing, especially in children.

ADRENAL GLANDS - Two spongy masses, one above each kidney. Manufacture the hormone, adrenin, useful in emergencies.

ADRENALIN - One of the hormones secreted by the adrenals; also a neurohumor.

AGAR - A clear, jelly-like substance; used to make cultures of bacteria.

AGE OF REPTILES - The fourth geologic era, when giant reptiles dominated the earth.

AGGULTININ - Any organic substance which causes red blood cells or bacteria to clump together.

AIR SACS - The microscopic ends of the air tubes in the lungs. Oxygen and carbon dioxide are exchanged in the air sacs.

ALBINO - A plant or animal which lacks the genes for the development of color. It is usually white.

ALCOHOL - The liquid obtained by the fermentation of sugar by yeasts. Intoxicating in drinks. Used by industry and to preserve specimens.

ALGAE - Simple, green plants with roots, stems or leaves. May be one-celled or many-celled.

ALIMENTARY CANAL - The food canal. Includes the gullet, stomach, small and large intestines.

ALLERGEN - A foreign substance which causes an allergic reaction in a person sensitive to it, such as ragweed pollen.

ALLERGY - A condition in which a person is very sensitive to certain pollens, foods, dust, feathers, or other substances.

ALPINES - A race of Caucasoid stock, supposed to have inhabited originally a strip of Europe between the northern and southern regions.

ALTERNATION OF GENERATIONS - Reproduction in which the offspring are not like their parents, but like their grandparents, as in mosses and ferns; specifically, the alternation of gametophyte and sporophyte in the life cycles of some plants.

ALTITUDE SICKNESS - Bodily changes caused by the scarcity of oxygen at higher altitudes.

AMBER - A fossilized material from trees, yellow-brown in color. Found on the shores of the Baltic Sea. May contain fossil insects.

AMEBA - One of the simplest single-celled animals.

AMEBIC DYSENTERY - Disease in human beings caused by a species of ameba in the intestine.

AMINO ACIDS - The end results of protein digestion. The "building blocks" of protoplasm.

AMPHIBIA - A group of cold-blooded vertebrates, such as frogs, toads, and salamanders. Born in water and have gills which are later replaced by lungs.

ANAPHASE - Third stage in mitosis when chromosomes are pulled to opposite sides of the cell.

ANEMIA - A physical condition caused by a lack of iron (hemoglobin) or by a lack of sufficient red blood cells.

ANESTHETIC - An agent that causes a partial or complete loss of sensation or feeling.

ANGIOSPERMS - Flowering plants, one of the two subdivisions of the spermato-phytes.

ANNELIDS - Segmented worms.

ANNUAL - A plant that lives through only one growing season.

ANNUAL RING - Growth ring in woody tissue of trees and shrubs.

ANOPHELES - Mosquito that carries malaria

ANTENNA - A projecting sense organ, such as the "feeler" of insects.

ANTERIOR - Toward the front or head end of an animal that has a right and a left side.

ANTHER - The pollen-forming structure at the top of the stamen.

ANTHRAX - A disease of cattle and sheep caused by the anthrax bacillus which lives in the blood stream.

ANTHROPOLOGY - The science of man.

ANTIBIOTICS - Organic compounds made by living things and effective in stopping the growth of certain germs; penicillin is an antibiotic.

ANTIBODIES - The chemical substances produced by the blood in response to the presence of bacteria or viruses. Important in immunity.

ANTIGEN - Any substance which, when introduced into an animal's body, stimulates the production of antibodies.

ANTISEPTIC - A chemical such as iodine, that helps destroy disease germs.

ANTITOXIN - A substance produced by animal bodies that overcomes the harmful effects of the toxins of disease germs; as diphtheria antitoxin.

ANUS - Opening at the posterior end of an animal's food tube.

AORTA - The large artery through which blood is pumped from the ventricle to the general body circulation.

AORTIC ARCHES - The ten pulsating blood vessels that join the dorsal and ventral blood vessels near the anterior end of the earthworm; sometimes called "hearts" of the earthworm.

APPENDIX - Blind tube attached to the end of the caecum of the large intestine in some mammals, including man.

ARACHNIDS - The class of arthropods to which spiders, mites, and ticks belong.

ARALEN - New antimalarial drug.

ARCHEOPTERYX - Oldest known bird fossil, having some reptilian characters.

ARTERIOLES - The very smallest branches of the arteries; they lead into the capillaries.

ARTERIES - Strong, elastic blood vessels that carry blood away from the heart.

ARTHROPODS - Phylum of segmented animals with many jointed legs and an exo-skeleton; includes several classes.

ASCORBIC ACID - Vitamin C; prevents and cures scurvy.

ASEXUAL REPRODUCTION - Reproduction without sex; reproduction without the uniting of two cells; reproduction by only one parent.

ATABRINE - A synthetic drug used as a substitute for quinine in treating malaria.

ATOM - A minute particle of matter.

AURICLES - The two thin-walled upper chambers of the heart. Receive blood from large veins.

AUTONOMIC - Pertaining to that part of the nervous system which is nearly, but not quite, independent of the central nervous system.

AUXINS - Plant hormones.

AXON - The branch of a neuron which carries impulses away from the cell body.

B

BACILLUS - A rod-shaped bacterium.

BACTERIA - Single-celled, microscopic plants, lacking in chlorophyll. Causes decay, disease and fermentation.

BALANCE OF NATURE - The condition in nature in which the plant and animal populations are in normal balance with each other, so that no one species becomes overabundant; well illustrated in a balanced aquarium; also called NATURAL EQUILIBRIUM.

BANDING - The process of attaching a numbered metal band or tag to an animal in order to find out where it travels.

BEHAVIOR - The responses of an organism to stimuli.

BENIGN - A new growth of cells of comparatively harmless nature, such as warts

BERIBERI - A disease resulting from a lack of vitamin Bi (thiamin). Causes paralysis of the nervous system and loss of appetite.

BICUSPIDS - Two-pointed teeth of mammals, immediately in front of the molars.

BIENNIAL - A plant that lives through two growing seasons, and bears flowers and fruits only in the second season.

BILE - A greenish-yellow, bitter liquid made by the liver and poured in the small intestine. Changes oils and fats into a milky fluid.

BINOMIAL SYSTEM - The system of naming plant and animal species; the two-name system.

BIOLOGICAL CONTROL - Control which uses natural enemies of insects or other pests in the fight against them.

BIOME - Any community of plants and animals.

BIOPSY - The removal and examination of a bit of tissue from a living body.

BIRDS - Class of vertebrates that have feathers and breathe by lungs throughout life.

BLADDER - The organ which receives urine from the kidneys and stores it for a time.

BLASTODERM - The first layer of cells formed by the early divisions of the ovum of the chick and many other animals.

BLASTULA - The hollow ball of cells constituting an early stage of the embryonic development of many animals.

BLOOD - A liquid tissue consisting of water, minerals, and red and white blood cells. An adult has about six quarts of blood.

BLOOD COUNT - A count of the number of red or white blood cells in a cubic millimeter of blood.

BLOOD PLATELETS - Small bodies in the blood which, under suitable conditions, break down, releasing a clot-starting substance.

BOLL WEEVIL - A beetle whose grub destroys the cotton plant.

BRAIN - A large mass of nerve cells and their fibers that fills the skull. Consists of the cerebrum, cerebellum and medulla.

BREATHING - The taking in of oxygen and giving off of carbon dioxide by living things. Some biologists limit the term of this process in animals.

BRONCHIAL TUBES - Tubes branching from the lower end of the windpipe and leading into the lung tissue.

BRONZE - A hard metal made of copper and tin. Used by men in the Bronze Age before iron was discovered.

BRYOPHYTES - The phylum which includes the mosses and liverworts.

BUDDING - A form of asexual reproduction in which a small bud of the parent produces a new individual, as in some yeasts, sponges, and hydras; also the grafting of a bud from one tree to another, as in peaches.

BULB - An underground part of a plant, such as the onion. Rich in food value and capable of producing a new plant the next season.

C

CAECUM - A pouch or tube closed at one end, as the end of the large intestine in man, to which the appendix is attached; pyloric caeca of fishes open into the intestine just below the stomach.

CALCIUM - A chemical found in many vegetables and in milk. Important in building healthy bones and teeth.

CALORIE - A unit of measure of the energy obtainable from food.

CALORIE, GREAT - The amount of heat required to raise 1,000 grams of water from 3.5°C. to 4.5°C.; used in reference to foods; the calorie used in physics is the amount of heat required to raise one gram of water from 3.5°C. to 4.5°C.

CAMBIUM - A layer of living cells from which new xylem and phloem cells are formed in the stems and some roots of dicots and gymnosperms.

CAMBRIAN - First period of the third geologic era.

CANDLING - The examination of a hen's egg by placing it in front of a bright light in a darkened room. Used to detect undesirable eggs.

CANINES - The tearing teeth of mammals; very prominent in carnivores.

CAPILLARIES - The smallest blood vessels, with walls one-cell thick. Connect arteries to veins.

CARBOHYDRATES - A class of foods (starches and sugars) composed of carbon, hydrogen, and oxygen. The number of hydrogen atoms in a molecule and graphite; a component part of protoplasm.

CARBON DIOXIDE - A compound of carbon and oxygen, each molecule of which contains one atom of carbon and two atoms of oxygen.

CARNIVORES - Order of the flesh-eating mammals, such as lions, tigers, cats, and dogs.

CARTILAGE - A smooth, shiny type of connective tissue on the ends of bones. Also called gristle.

CATTALO - The offspring obtained by crossing a cow with a bison (buffalo).

CAUCASOIDS - One of the three main stems or stocks of living man.

CAUDAL - Pertaining to the tail.

CELL - A unified mass of protoplasm, usually composed of a nucleus and cytoplasm surrounded by a cell membrane and by a cell wall in plants; the unit of structure of living things.

CELL DIFFERENTIATION - The changing of embryonic cells into specialized cells, as muscle, wood, nerve.

CELL MEMBRANE - Thin bounding layer that covers animal and young plant cells; also the thin layer of cytoplasm that lines the cell wall of mature plant cells; also called the CYTOPLASMIC MEMBRANE.

CELL THEORY - The theory that all living things are made of cells and cell products; first advanced by Schleiden and Schwann in 1838-1839.

CELLULOSE - Organic compound found in the cell wall of nearly all plant cells, but not commonly found in animal cells.

CELL WALL - The hard, woody coating around plant cells. Helps to protect and support the cell. Dried lumber consists of cell walls.

CENTRAL CYLINDER - Woody tissue in the center of roots.

CENTRAL NERVOUS SYSTEM - The brain and spinal cord of a vertebrate.

CEREBELLUM - The part of the brain lying behind and below the cerebrum. Controls muscular coordination.

CEREBRAL HEMORRHAGE - A hemorrhage in the brain, usually followed by paralysis.

CEREBRUM - The upper part of the brain, consisting of two halves, each with deep grooves. Controls thought, speech, memory, and voluntary acts.

CHEMICAL CHANGE - A change in matter that involves a change in the kinds of atoms in the molecules.

CHLOROPHYLL - The green material found in the cells of green plants. Important in making starch and sugar.

CHLOROPHYLL BODIES - Small bodies found inside the cells of green plants. Contain the green chlorophyll which helps carry on photosynthesis.

CHLORPOPLAST - Small definite body of cytoplasm containing chlorophyll, found in some cells of green plants.

CHORDATES - Phylum of animals having a dorsal supporting rod of gristle, either in the embryo, as in vertebrates, or throughout life, as in the lancelet, and having a dorsal hollow nerve cord.

CHOROID COAT - The dark coat of the vertebrate eye.

CHROMATIN - Material in the cell nucleus which takes a dye readily. Forms the chromosomes.

CHROMOSOMES - Threads of chromatin seen in dividing cells. Contain the genes.

CILIA - Hair-like threads that beat back and forth. Enable paramecia to swim. Are present on cells that line the breathing passages, and help remove dust.

CITRUS FRUITS - Acid fruits, such as oranges and lemons. Rich in vitamin C.

CLEANED-TILLED CROPS - Crops which are cultivated in rows, such as potatoes and corn.

CLIMAX - Final stage in a plant succession, tending to persist indefinitely; examples: beech-maple forest, wheat-grass grassland.

CLOSED SEASON - A time of year when the hunting of certain animals is forbidden by law.

CLOSE-GROWING CROPS - Crops like clover, hay, and wheat which grow close together and cover the soil.

CLOT - A jelly-like mass which forms when blood leaves a blood vessel. Consists of a mass of fibers and blood cells. Prevents further bleeding.

COCCI - Bacteria that are round in shape. Include bacteria that cause pneumonia and scarlet fever.

COCHLEA - The portion of the inner ear in which sound vibrations reach the endings of the auditory nerve.

CODLING MOTH - Chief insect enemy of apples; the larva is the so-called apple worm.

COELENTERATES - The phylum which includes the corals, hydras, jellyfish, and sea anemones.

COLCHICINE - A chemical which is applied to plants in order to double the number of chromsomes. May result in new varieties.

COLD-BLOODED - Pertaining to a vertebrate whose temperature changes with that of its surroundings.

COLLAR CELLS - Flagellated cells in the lining of the cavities in sponges, whose flagella keep a current of water flowing through the body.

COLON - The large intestine.

COLONY - Group of individuals organically joined together, with each individual more or less independent, as in some of the protozoa.

COMMON ANCESTOR - An organism that was an ancester of two or more species or varieties of organisms.

COMPOSITES - A family of flowering plants having a compound head of flowers, such as dandelions or daisies.

COMPOST - Mixed fertilizing materials, such as heaps of decaying crop residue,

COMPOUND - A substance whose molecule is composed of two or more kinds of atoms in chemical combination.

CONDITIONED REFLEX OR REACTION - Behavior in response to a stimulus other than the usual or normal one; an acquired response.

CONE - Seed-bearing organ of evergreens and other naked-seeded plants.

CONJUGATION - The uniting of two cells, often of similar size and appearance, as in spirogyra and paramecium.

CONTACT SPRAYS - Sprays that kill insects upon touching them.

CONTOUR PLOWING - A method of plowing a hillside so that the furrows go around the hill instead of up and down.

CONTROL - A part of an experiment which tests or checks the result. Provides a basis for comparison.

CORNEA - Transparent layer covering the front of the vertebrate eye.

CORONARY ARTERIES - The arteries which supply the tissues of the heart.

CORONARY HEART DISEASE - Heart condition in which coronary arteries decrease in diameter.

CORONARY THROMBOSIS - The formation of a blood clot in a coronary artery.

CORPUSCLE - Blood cell; a red blood corpuscle is a blood cell that carries oxygen; a white blood corpuscle is a blood cell that aids in the defense against germ attack.

CORTEX - The tissue in a root or stem that lies between the fibrovascular tissue and the epidermis; the outer layers of an organ such as the brain.

COTYLEDON - Seed leaf; single in mbnocots, double in dicots; numerous in naked-seeded spermatophytes.

CRANIAL NERVES - Nerves from the brain; 12 pairs in man.

CRETIN - One born with an abnormally deficient thyroid or none at all. Usually idiocy results unless thyroxin is given regularly in childhood.

CRO-MAGNON MAN - A type of prehistoric man very much like men of today. Lived in caves and decorated them with animal paintings.

CROP - An enlarged portion of the food tube of earthworms and birds in which food is stored when first swallowed; also plants for harvest, as a crop of corn.

CROP RESIDUES — Remains of crops, after harvesting, such as straw and stubble.

CROP ROTATION - A plan which prevents the loss of important soil minerals over a period of time. Different crops are planted in an area each year.

CROSSBREEDING - A breeding process for combining the traits of plants or animals of two different kinds.

CROSSING OVER - The breaking of two adjacent chromosomes, during separation, with the subsequent union of a fragment (or fragments) of one with a fragment (or fragments) of the other.

CRUSTACEA - Class of arthropods to which the crayfish and barnacle belong.

CULTURE - The growth of bacteria or other organisms in suitable surroundings, as a culture of staphylococci on agar. A pure culture is a culture containing only one kind of organism, as a pure culture of diphtheria bacilli;. a culture medium is a particular material, such as agar or beef broth, in or on which bacteria are grown; also man's learned way of life.

CUTTING - A piece of a root, stem or leaf which can be planted to produce a complete new plant.

CYCAD - A seed plant of the naked-seeded class.

CYST - A sac, or an encased resting stage such as that of the trichina.

CYTOLOGY - The study of cells.

CYTOPLASM - That part of the cell that lies outside the nucleus. Carries on all life activities except reproduction.

D

DAPHNIA - A tiny water flea found in ponds. Invertebrate, related to the lobster.

DEFICIENCY DISEASE - Disease caused by lack of vitamins, minerals, amino acids or other necessary elements in the diet.

DENDRITES - The branches of a neuron which carry impulses toward the cell body.

DEOXYGENATED BLOOD - Blood that has lost its oxygen to the cells.

DEPRESSANT - A drug or other agent that slows down such vital body functions as breathing rate and heartbeat.

DIABETES - A disease in which sugar is incompletely burned in the body. Caused by failure of the pancreas island cells to make the hormone, insulin.

DIAPHRAGM - The large muscle which separates the chest cavity from the abdomen. Makes breathing possible by contracting and relaxing.

DIASTASE - The enzyme which digests starch in a sprouting grain of corn.

DIATOMS - One-celled algae that have glassy shells.

DICOTYLEDONS - Subclass of flowering plants having two cotyledons in the seed, netted-veined leaves, and one or more rings of wood in the stem; they include most of our common flowering plants, such as beans, geraniums, hardwood trees; commonly called dicots.

DIFFUSION - Spreading of molecules from areas of their greatest density toward areas of less density; sometimes applied loosely to any intermingling of molecules.

DIGESTION - A process of chemical change that prepares food for absorption. Goes on in the mouth, stomach, and small intestine with the aid of enzymes.

DINOSAURS - Extinct reptiles, many of enormous size. Died out sixty million years ago.

DIPLOID NUMBER - Twice the number of chromosomes found in a gamete; 48 is the diploid number in man.

DOMINANT - The trait in a contrasting pair (such as tallness and dwarfness) that shows in a hybrid; tallness is dominant in peas.

DORSAL - Pertaining to the back or upper side of an animal.

DUCKBILL - A rare Australian mammal that lays eggs.

DUCTLESS GLAND - A gland that secretes a hormone directly into the blood stream and does not deliver its secretion through a duct.

DUODENUM - The first part of the small intestine leading from the stomach.

E

ECHINODERMS - The phylum of the spiny-skinned animals, such as the starfish, sea urchins, and their relatives.

ECOLOGY - Biology that deals with the relations of organisms to each other and to their nonliving environment.

ECTODERM - The outer layer of cells of a gastrula, an embryological term; has also been applied to the outer body layer of cells in hydra and other adult coelenterates.

EGG - The sex cell produced in the ovary of the female. Develops into an embryo if fertilized by a sperm cell.

ELECTRON - One of the constituents of all atoms; a single charge of negative electricity.

ELEMENT - A substance whose molecules contain only one kind of atom; 96 elements are known.

ELODEA - A water plant belonging to the dicots.

EMBOLISM - A blood clot that has been carried away from its original site and lodged in a blood vessel too small to let it pass.

EMBRYO - The form of a plant or animal in the beginning stage of life.

EMBRYOLOGY - The study of the growth and development of embryos.

ENDODERM - The inside layer of cells of a gastrula, an embryological term; has also been applied to the inner layer of hydra and other adult coelenterates.

END ORGANS - Sensitive outer endings of sensory neurons; better called receptors.

ENDOSPERM - The storage tissue in monocot seeds and in a few dicot seeds, such as the castor bean.

ENERGY - The capacity to do work.

ENTOMOLOGY - Study of insects.

ENZYMES - Substances made in gland cells, that can cause chemical changes. Example: pepsin, which digests proteins.

EPIDERMIS - The outer layer of cells on an organ or organism; skin.

EPIGLOTTIS - The flap of tissue that covers the top of the windpipe during swallowing.

EPITHELIAL TISSUE - Covering tissue, including epithelium (skin) and endo-thelium (lining tissue).

EPOCH - A subdivision of a geological period.

ERA - One of the five main divisions of geologic time.

EROSION - The wearing away of the earth's surface by water, ice, and winds.

ESOPHAGUS - That portion of the food tube which connects mouth region or pharynx and crop or stomach.

EUGENICS - That branch of genetics which aims at improving mankind by breeding; the science of being well born.

EUGLENA - A one-celled plant-animal.

EUSTACHIAN TUBE - Tube connecting the middle ear with the throat.

EVOLUTION - The process of change by which plants and animals develop from simpler to more complex forms.

EXOSKELETON - External skeleton.

EYESPOT - Spot of pigment, usually red, sensitive to light.

F

F_1 GENERATION - First generation of offspring from a cross.

F_2 GENERATION - Offspring of the F_1 generation.

FATTY ACIDS - The end-products of fat digestion. Can pass into the villi.

FEMALE PARENT - The parent that produces the ovum or egg.

FERMENTATION - A chemical change brought about by enzymes produced by microbes. In the making of beer or wine, yeasts ferment sugars into alcohol and carbon dioxide.

FERTILIZATION - The uniting of a sperm nucleus with an egg nucleus. Results in the development of an embryo.

FERTILIZED EGG - The cell formed by the union of the egg and the sperm; an egg after a sperm has united with it; also called a zygote.

FERTILIZER - Chemical substance added to the soil to feed plants. Also used to replace the minerals removed by former crops.

FIBRINOGEN - A chemical in the blood which helps the blood to clot. Forms fibers that entangle blood cells.

FIBROVASCULAR BUNDLE - A group of xylem and phloem cells, as the stringy fibers in celery.

FILAMENT - Thread-shaped alga or fungus composed of cells end to end; the stalk of a stamen; the projections on a fish's gill that are filled with blood.

FISHES - Vertebrates that breathe by gills throughout life, and usually possess scales and fins.

FLAGELLATE - A one-celled animal bearing one or more flagella.

FLAGELLUM - A long hairlike or whiplike projection from a cell.

FLATWORMS - Phylum which includes the tapeworms, planaria, and their relatives.

FLUORINE - A chemical used to help prevent tooth decay. Small amounts may be placed in a city's water supply.

FLYWAYS - The pathways in the sky which are used by migrating birds each season.

FOCAL INFECTION - A localized pocket of infection, as at the rooth of a tooth or in a tonsil; always a threat to the health.

FOLIC ACID - A B vitamin which prevents severe anemias.

FOOD CHAIN - A series of organisms, each of which depends for its food on the one following it in the series.

FORTIFIED - Given added value (in nutrition). A food is fortified when an important food substance is added to it. Margarine is fortified with Vitamin A. Milk may be fortified with Vitamin D.

FOSSIL - The remains of ancient plants and animals sometimes found in rock layers.

FRATERNAL TWINS - Twins developed from two separate fertilized ova.

FRUCTOSE - Fruit sugar; a simple sugar, $C_6H_{12}O_6$.

FRUIT - A ripened ovary, together with any intimately connected parts.

FUNGUS (plural - fungi) - Simple plant, of the thallophyte phylum, lacking chlorophyll. Includes bacteria, yeasts, molds, mushrooms, rusts, and smuts. Lives on dead or living plants and animals.

G

GALL BLADDER - A round sac on the liver which stores bile and releases it into the small intestine.

GAMETES - Reproductive cells which fuse; the female gamete is called an ovum or egg, and the male gamete a sperm.

GAMETOPHYTE - In an alternation of generations, the plant that produces the gametes.

GANGLION - A group or mass of cell bodies of neurons.

GASTRIC JUICE - The digestive juice made by the stomach. Digests protein. Made of water, weak-acid, and pepsin.

GASTRULA - The two-layered folded-in stage or jellyfishlike stage of many animal embryos; it consists of ectoderm and endoderm.

GEIGER COUNTER - An instrument that ticks when near any radioactive substance.

GEL - A substance consisting of a network of fibers in which are suspended particles of a liquid; cooked egg white is a gel.

GENES - The invisible particles in the cell nucleus which control the inheritance of traits.

GENUS - The group (between family and species) named first in the scientific name of a plant or animal; a genus is a group of related species.

GERM - Any one-celled plant or animal which causes disease.

GERMINATION - The sprouting of a spore or seed.

GESTATION PERIOD - Time required for a mammal embryo to develop from fertilization to birth.

GILL - An animal organ in which the blood absorbs oxygen out of the air that is dissolved in water.

GILL ARCH - The bony arch supporting a fish's gill.

GILL FILAMENTS - The fingerlike projections of a fish's gill; these filaments are filled with blood.

GILL RAKERS - The projections from the side of the gill arch; these fit together and form a strainer in the back of the fish's mouth.

GILL SLIT - The opening on the side of a fish's throat where the water current used in breathing leaves the mouth and flows out over the gill filaments

GIZZARD - The muscular stomach of earthworms and birds and other animals, in which the food is crushed and partly digested.

GLAND - An organized group of cells which make and pour out juices such as enzymes and hormones.

GLOTTIS - The opening from the mouth into the windpipe in air-breathing vertebrates.

GLUCOSE - A simple sugar that can pass through cell membranes. Turns Benedict's solution brick red.

GLYCERINE - A clear liquid obtained after the digestion of fats.

GLYCOGEN - A carbohydrate stored in the liver and present in muscles; often called animal starch.

GOITER - A swelling of the thyroid gland in the neck. Often caused by a lack of iodine in the diet.

GONORRHEA - An infection of the reproductive system, caused by bacteria.

GRAFTING - The act of inserting a bud or a twig into a slit in the bark of a rooted tree. When the tissues join, the new bud or twig is nourished by the tree.

GRANTIA - A genus of sponges.

GREEN-MANURE CROPS - Crops that are planted to be plowed under, as rye and many legumes often are.

GROWTH HORMONE - Hormone produced by the pituitary gland. Promotes normal growth. Too much in childhood may result in giantism.

GUARD CELLS - The two cells on either side of a leaf's stomate which regulati the size of the opening.

GULLET - The food tube which connects the mouth to the stomach.

GYMNOSPERMS - Plants of the spermatophyte phylum that have naked seeds, as pines, cycads, and their allies.

H

HAPLOID NUMBER - The number of chromosomes in a gamete; 24 is the haploid number in man.

HEMOGLOBIN - An iron-rich chemical found in the red blood cells. Combines with oxygen in the lungs and gives it up to tissue cells.

HEMOPHILIA - A serious physical condition in which blood fails to clot properly. Inherited by sons from mothers who are carriers.

HERB - Any seed plant that does not develop annual rings of persistent woody tissue.

HERMAPHRODITE - An animal having both male and female reproductive organs, as an earthworm.

HEXAPODS - The class of true insects in the arthropod phylum, also called the INSECTA.

HILUM - The scar showing where a seed was attached in a pod, as on a lima bean.

HORMONE - A chemical made by certain glands and poured into the blood stream Includes insulin, adrenin, thyroxin and growth hormones.

HOST - An organism within or upon which a parasite lives.

HUMORS-AQUEOUS AND VITREOUS - The liquids that fill the two chambers in the vertebrate eye.

HUMUS - Organic matter in the soil.

HYBRID - A plant or animal which has two different genes for a trait, as the offspring of pure tall and dwarf peas. Also, the offspring of two different kinds of plants or animals.

HYBRID VIGOR - Increased size or strength of a hybrid, as in the cattalo.

HYDRA - Fresh-water relative of the jellyfish.

HYDROPHYTES - Plants that grow in wet places, such as water lillies.

HYPOCOTYL - Root region of an embryo plant within the seed.

I

ICHNEUMONS - A family of insects useful to man because they parasitize many harmful insects.

IDIOT - A person with the mental ability of a three-year-old child. I.Q. between 0 and 25.

IMBECILE - A person who is mentally deficient. I.Q. between 25 and 50.

INBORN REFLEX - A pathway in the nervous system of an animal that functions without training or practice.

INCISORS - The cutting teeth on the front of mammal jaws.

INCOMPLETE DOMINANCE - A situation in which neither gene of a pair is dominant. Result is a blending of traits. A red snapdragon crossed with a white results in a pink flower.

INCOMPLETE RESPIRATION - Type of respiration in which oxidation of food is not completed, but stops when alcohol and carbon dioxide (or other substances) are produced; fermentation is an example of incomplete respiration carried on by yeasts and some bacteria.

INCUBATION - The period of time it takes to hatch a bird out of the egg. Also the time it takes for a disease to appear after the first contact with the germ.

INFRARED - Those lights rays just beyond the red end of the visible spectrum.

INOCULATION - The introduction of bacteria or a virus into surroundings suited to their growth, as the inoculation of clover seeds with nitrogen-fixing bacteria or the inoculation of persons with cowpox virus to produce immunity against smallpox.

INORGANIC - Term applied to anything that is not alive and not produced by living things.

INSECTS - Class of arthropods that have three body regions and six legs, and usually wings.

INSULIN - The hormone made by the pancreas island cells. Helps the body burn and store sugar, and prevents diabetes.

INVERTEBRATES - Animals which do not have a backbone. Includes worms, jelly-fishes, clams, insects, lobsters.

INVOLUNTARY MUSCLE - A group of cells which contract when stimulated by nerve fibers. Not controlled by the mind.

IODINE - A chemical used by the thyroid gland in making thyroxin. Prevents some types of goiter.

ION - An electrified particle of matter formed when a neutral atom or other particle loses or gains one or more electrons.

IRIS - The colored tissue surrounding the pupil of the eye. Controls the amount of light entering the eye.

IRRITABILITY - The capacity of protoplasm to receive impulses from and to respond to stimuli.

IRON - A chemical which is needed in making hemoglobin. Prevents anemia.

ISLETS - Clusters of insulin-producing cells in the pancreas.

ISONIAZID - A recently-discovered drug which may prove useful in fighting tuberculosis.

ISOTOPE - Any of two or more forms of the same element which differ only in the number of neutrons their atoms contain; a radioisotope is a radio-active isotope.

L

LACTEAL - End of a lymph vessel in the center of a villus; it absorbs digested fats out of the intestine.

LARVA - The wormlike stage of an insect having complete metamorphosis, as a caterpillar; the young form of various animals where markedly different from the adult.

LEGUME - Any plant that has a blossom shaped like a pea and a pod of the pea or bean type; also used to refer to the podlike fruit of such plants.

LENS - The focusing portion of the eye.

LENTICEL - Breathing pore in the young bark of trees.

LICHENS - Compound plants consisting of algae and fungi which live intimately together; common on barren rock surfaces.

LIMESTONE - A type of sedimentary rock that is rich in lime.

LINKAGE - A term used to refer to the fact that the genes in a given chromosome are linked together and hence transmitted together to the offspring.

LIPASE - An enzyme in the pancreatic and intestinal juices which aids in digesting fats, but only when bile is present.

LIVER - The largest gland in the body. Makes and pours out bile and stores extra sugar as animal starch.

LIVERWORTS - Relatives of mosses, belong to the same phylum.

LYMPH - That part of the blood serum which is outside the blood vessels; it surrounds each living cell; it circulates slowly back toward the heart through lymph vessels and re-enters the blood stream near the heart.

LYMPH NODE - One of the masses of tissue through which the lymph passes on its way back toward the heart; a lymph gland.

M

MAGGOT - Larval stage of a fly.

MALE PARENT - The parent that produces the male gametes or sperms.

MALTOSE - A sugar formed from starch by the action of ptyalin; $C_{12}H_{22}O_{11}$.

MARSUPIALS - Pouched mammals.

MEDULLA - The bulb-like part at the bottom of the brain. Connects the brain to the spinal cord. Controls breathing and circulation.

MESODERM - The middle layer of cells of an embryonic stage developed from the gastrula or from a similar stage.

MESOPHYTES - Plants that grow in soil with medium amounts of water.

METABOLISM - The sum total of the chemical changes going on in a living organism; BASAL

METABOLISM TEST - measures the rate at which oxygen is used in the human body; useful in diagnosis of thyroid diseases.

METAMORPHOSIS - Marked and more or less sudden changes in the development of young animals, as the change of an insect larva into a pupa or pupa into an adult or a tadpole into a frog; in insects INCOMPLETE METAMORPHOSIS is that in which the young resemble the adult in general form; COMPLETE METAMORPHOSIS is that in which the young do not resemble the adult.

METAPHASE - Second stage in mitosis during which the double chromosomes grouj along a middle plane.

MICRON - 1/1000 of a millimeter or 1/25,000 of an inch; the unit used in measuring microscopic objects.

MICROPYLE - The little opening near the hilum of a seed; the pollen tube usually enters the ovule through it.

MILT - The material produced by the testes of male fish. Contains the sperm cells.

MITOSIS - Cell division in which the chromosomes duplicate themselves.

MOLLUSK - A soft-bodied invertebrate. Usually has a shell outside the body. Includes the snail, the octopus, and the clam.

MORON - A person with an I.Q. between 50 and 70.

MORPHOLOGY - Study of the form and structure of plants and animals.

MULE - The hybrid resulting from crossing a male donkey with a female horse.

MUTATION - A sudden change in a gene. The new trait which results is inheritable.

MUTATION THEORY - De Vries's theory of evolution.

MYCELIUM - Fine white threads that make up the main plant body of many fungi, such as molds and mushrooms.

MYRIAPODS - A class of arthropods, including the centipedes and millipedes.

MYXEDEMA - A disease caused by lack of thyroxin, characterized by puffy fatness.

N

NATURAL SELECTION - A theory which states that nature weeds out the unfit, allowing only the superior to reproduce, and pass on their good traits. In time better types of plants and animals develop.

NEUROHUMORS - Substances produced by neurons, such as acetylcholine or adrenalin.

NEURON - A nerve cell; ASSOCIATIVE - a central transferring neuron in a reflex arc; SENSORY - a neuron along which impulses travel in toward the central nervous system; MOTOR - a neuron along which impulses travel outward from the central nervous system.

NEUTRON - One of the constituents of the nucleus of nearly all atoms; an uncharged particle in the nucleus.

NIACIN - The recently accepted name of the antipellagra vitamin, formerly called nicotinic acid.

NITRATE - A compound in which nitrogen is combined with oxygen and at least one other element, such as potassium; example, KNO_3.

NITROGEN - An element which makes up 80 per cent of the air. Important in protein manufacture in plants.

NITROGEN CYCLE - The course of the element nitrogen from the air into organic compounds in living things and back into the air again.

NITROGEN-FIXING BACTERIA - Bacteria usually found in the roots of peas, clover, and alfalfa. Take in nitrogen and change it to a form useful to green plants.

NODULES - Little lumps on the roots of clover and other legumes, in which nitrogen-fixing bacteria live.

NOTOCHORD - A lengthwise elastic rod of cartilage lying just below the nerve cord in all chordates, at least in the embryo.

NUCLEOPROTEIN - Any protein composed of a protein plus a nucleic acid molecule; germs and viruses are believed to be nucleoproteins.

NUCLEUS - A thick, round structure in the cell, containing the chromatin. Takes part in the reproduction of the cell and controls heredity.

NYMPH - The young of certain insects, such as grasshoppers and termites, that have incomplete metamorphosis.

O

ORGAN - A group of tissues organized to do one job. Example: the heart, stomach, skin, eyes, or kidney.

ORGANIC COMPOUND - Any compound that contains carbon is usually called an organic compound, although there are exceptions, such as carbon dioxide.

OSMOSIS - A special kind of diffusion, in which water molecules diffuse through a semipermeable membrane.

OVIDUCT - The duct from the ovary through which eggs are passed; in some animals the fertilized eggs develop in the oviduct.

OVULE - The part containing the egg nucleus in flowering plants. After fertilization, each ovule develops into a seed.

OVUM - An egg cell.

P

PALISADE LAYER - A layer of green cells just under the upper epidermis of a leaf.

PANCREAS - A gland below the stomach. Makes digestive enzymes which are poured into the small intestines, and contains island cells which make insulin.

PARAMECIUM - A common protozoan found in ponds. Moves by means of cilia on its surface.

PARASITE - An animal or plant that obtains its food by living inside or on another living thing. Includes the tapeworm, hookworm, louse, ringworm, and many bacteria.

PARATHYROIDS - Glands located near the thyroid; the parathyroids secrete a hormone which regulates the body's assimilation of calcium.

PASTEURIZATION - A process in which a substance (such as milk) is heated to 150°F. and quickly chilled in order to kill disease germs.

PELLAGRA - A severe skin rash and nerve illness caused by a lack of niacin (a B vitamin).

PEPSIN - The enzyme produced by the gastric glands that line the walls of the stomach. Starts the digestion of protein.

PERIPHERAL NERVOUS SYSTEM - All parts of the nervous system except the brain and spinal cord.

PERISTALSIS - The progressive contraction of circular muscles in the food tube of higher animals which forces the food onward.

PETALS - The colored parts of a flower which help to attract insects.

PHARYNX - The anterior end of the food tube of many animals.

PHLOEM - Food-conducting cells in the roots, stems, and leaves of ferns and seed plants.

PHOTOSYNTHESIS - The process by which a green plant combines water and carbon dioxide to make sugar or starch. Sunlight is necessary to do this. Oxygen is the by-product.

PHYLUM - One of the main groups of the plant or animal kingdom.

PINEAL GLAND - Ductless gland situated at the base of the brain.

PISTIL - The female part of the flower which contains the ovary. Grows into a fruit after fertilization.

PISTILLATE FLOWERS - Flowers that contain pistils but no stamens.

PITUITARY GLAND - A gland the size of a pea, lying in the skull just below the brain. Controls growth and other life activities, and makes a number of hormones. The "master gland."

PLACENTA - A membrane attached to the wall of the uterus. Food passes from the blood of the mother to the embryo by way of the placenta.

PLANARIA - A common flatworm.

PLASMA - The liquid part of the blood. Contains antibodies, hormones, and digested foods.

PLATELETS - Tiny particles in the blood which help the blood to clot.

PLEUROCOCCUS - A single-celled green plant, common in the green smears on the shady side of tree trunks.

PLUMULE - That portion of a seed-plant embryo which grows into the shoot.

POLLEN - The powder-like particles made in the stamens of plants. Each pollen grain develops a sperm nucleus when it sprouts on the tip of the pistil.

POLLEN TUBE - The part of a sprouting pollen grain sent down the pistil. The sperm nucleus inside this tube is delivered to the egg nucleus in the ovule.

POLLINATION - The transfer of pollen from a stamen to a pistil either by insects or by wind.

PORIFERA - The phylum of the sponges.

PRIMATES - Order of mammals that walk more or less upright, including monkeys, apes, and man.

PROLACTIN - A hormone secreted by the pituitary body; stimulates mothering behavior and the secretion of milk in mammals.

PROPHASE - First stage of mitosis during which each chromosome duplicates itself, gene by gene, and the chromosomes shorten by contracting into tight spirals.

PROTEIN - A basic food substance containing carbon, hydrogen, oxygen, and nitrogen. Necessary for growth and repair of tissues. Found in meat, milk, beans, and many other foods.

PROTHALLIUM - The gametophyte of the ferns and their relatives.

PROTHROMBIN - The substance in blood plasma from which thrombin is made; necessary if blood is to clot.

PROTON - One of the constituents of the nucleus of all atoms; a single charge of positive electricity.

PROTOPLASM - The living material found in the cells of all living things. Carries on all the life activities.

PROTOZOA - One-celled animals, such as the ameba and paramecium.

PSEUDOPODIUM - Projected lobe of cytoplasm by which an ameba moves.

PTERIDOPHYTES - Phylum of the ferns, club mosses, and horsetails.

PTOSIS - The falling down of an organ or part of the body, as the stomach or an eyelid.

PTYALIN - A digestive enzyme in saliva which aids in changing starch to maltose.

PUPA - The more or less quiescent stage between larva and adult in the complete metamorphosis of insects.

PURE - A term used in genetics to refer to a plant or animal carrying both genes alike in a given pair; as a pure tall or a pure dwarf pea; pure tails produce only tall descendants when self-pollinated.

R

RECEPTORS - The endings of nerves. Sensitive to touch, chemicals, taste, sound, temperature, and other stimuli.

RECESSIVE TRAIT - A trait that does not show up in a hybrid. Hidden by the dominant trait.

REDUCTION DIVISION - Cell division in which the number of chromosomes is reduced to half; it usually occurs in animals when sperms and eggs are being formed.

RENNIN - An anzyme in the gastric juice which curds milk.

RESPIRATION - The oxidation of food within a living cell; external evidences may be the entrance of oxygen and release of carbon dioxide; sometimes used to include breathing in higher animals.

RETINA - A layer of light-sensitive cells in the vertebrate eye.

RH FACTOR - A bloodtype found in most people which sometimes causes damage to the blood of babies.

RIBOFLAVIN - Vitamin 62. Found in milk, lean meat, eggs, and many vegetables Necessary for normal growth.

RICKETTSIA - A type of minute disease-producing agents that may be intermediate between bacteria and viruses, causing typhus fever and a few other diseases.

ROTIFER - A small many-celled animal often found among protozoa.

S

SANDSTONE - A type of sedimentary rock formed from sand under great pressure.

SCHICK TEST - A test to determine if a person is immune to diphtheria. A small quantity of diphtheria toxin is placed under the skin. If a red spot appears, the person lacks immunity.

SCION - The bud or twig that is attached to the stock in grafting.

SCURVY - A condition caused by lack of vitamin C. The teeth loosen, joints ache, and blood vessels break under the skin.

SEDIMENTARY ROCK - Rock made from sediment that has been under pressure; rock characterized by layers; stratified rock.

SEED - A developed ovule consisting of a protective coat, stored food, and an embryo plant.

SEED DISPERSAL - The scattering of seeds to places more or less distant from the parent plant.

SEED FERNS - Extinct plants of fern type, but bearing seeds instead of spores

SEED LEAVES - The two halves of a seed (as in the bean) containing stored food. Help feed the sprouting baby plant.

SEMICIRCULAR CANALS - The portion of the inner ear in which the sense of balance is located.

SEMIPERMEABLE MEMBRANE - A membrane through which some kinds of molecules diffuse readily while others diffuse with difficulty or not at all.

SEPALS - The tiny, green, leaf-like parts found below the petals. Protect the closed flower buds.

SETA - One of the bristles used by an earthworm in locomotion.

SEX-LINKED GENES - Genes found in the X chromosome. Examples are the genes for hemophilia and color blindness, which affect males chiefly.

SOL - A substance that consists chiefly of a liquid such as water in which are dispersed many particles of limited size (1/1000 micron to 1/10 micron); protoplasm may be a sol.

SPAWNING - The shedding of eggs and milt into the water during the reproductive process of fish.

SPERMATOPHYTES - Phylum of seed plants.

SPHINCTER - A ringlike muscle like the one at the opening of the stomach into the small intestine.

SPIRACLES - Breathing pores of insects.

SPIRILLAE - Cork-screw shaped bacteria.

SPIROGYRA - A filamentous alga common in pond scum.

SPORE - A single-celled (occasionally two-celled) reproductive body, formed sexually or nonsexually, with or without a resistant wall, produced by plants and some protozoa.

SPOROPHYTE - In an alternation of generations, the plant that produces asexual spores.

STAMEN - The male organ of the flower, in which the pollen is made.

STAMINATE FLOWERS - Flowers that contain stamens but no pistils.

STAPHYLOCOCCUS - Certain round bacteria that often form clusters like bunches of grapes; called staph, for short.

STIGMA - The top of a pistil; here the pollen germinates.

STOMATE - Opening in the epidermis of a plant leaf through which there is an exchange of gases between the air spaces and the outside atmosphere.

STYLE - The stem of a pistil.

SUCCESSION - A series of changing plant (or animal) population at a given location; example: lichens, mosses, ferns, herbs, shrubs, poplars, pines, oaks, beech-maple climax.

SYMBIONTS - Different organisms living intimately together to the advantage of both.

SYMBIOSIS - A partnership between two dissimilar organisms in which they live intimately together and help each other, as the alga and fungus partnership in a lichen.

SYMPATHIN - A neurohumor, now usually called ADRENALIN.

SYNAPSE - The point at which a nerve impulse passes from one person into another.

SYSTEM - A group of organs cooperating to do one big job. For example, the digestive, breathing, nervous, and circulatory systems.

T

TELOPHASE - Last stage in mitosis during which two new nuclei are formed and two new cells formed from one.

TERRACING - A method of farming used on steep hillsides. Reduces erosion by catching water in ditches.

THALLOPHYTES - Lowest phylum of the plant kingdom, including algae and fungi.

THIAMIN - The chemical which is called vitamin Bi. Prevents beriberi.

THROMBOKINASE - Substances released from injured cells and brokendown blood platelets which change prothrombin to thrombin if calcium ions are present.

THYROXIN - The hormone made by the thyroid gland. Rich in iodine. Helps the body burn food.

TISSUE - A group of similar cells doing the same work, such as nerve, bone, blood, or muscle tissue.

TRANSPIRATION - The loss of water by evaporation, mostly through the stomates of the leaves of a plant.

TRILOBITE - A fossilized primitive arthropod found in abundance in Paleozoic rocks; extinct by the end of the Paleozoic Era.

TROPISM - The turning of an organism away from or toward a stimulus; a positive tropism is toward; a negative tropism is away from.

TRYPTOPHAN - An amino acid that is essential in man and other animals.

TUBER - A short underground stem used as a storage organ, as the Irish potato.

U

ULOTHRIX - A genus of algae.

USE-AND-DISUSE THEORY - Lammarck's theory of evolution, now discarded.

V

VACCINE - A substance consisting of dead or weakened bacteria or viruses. Used to produce immunity in people and animals.

VACUOLE - A tiny cavity inside a plant or animal cell. Filled with liquid.

VAGUS NERVES - The pair of cranial nerves which supply the heart, stomach, and other organs.

VEINS - Blood vessels which carry blood back toward the heart.

VENTRAL - The lower or front side of an animal.

VENTRICLES - The two thick-walled chambers of the heart.

VERTEBRATES - Animals which have a backbone. Include fish, frogs, snakes, birds, deer, and man.

VESTIGIAL ORGAN - A remnant of a once useful organ, as toe bones in a bird's wing.

VILLUS - Tiny, finger-like projections on the walls of the small intestine. Absorb digested foods.

W

WHITE BLOOD COUNT - A count of the white blood cells in a cubic millimeter of blood; a procedure much used in diagnosing appendicitis and other acute infections.

WIDE CROSSING - The practice of crossing two very different animals. For example: a lion with a tigress, or a horse with a zebra.

X-Y-Z

X-CHROMOSOME - One of a pair of chromosomes that controls the sex of the individual. Females have two X-chromosomes.

XEROPHYTES - Plants that grow in very dry conditions, such as the cactus.

XYLEM - Wood cells which serve as passageways for water in the roots, stems, and leaves of ferns and seed plants.

Y-CHROMOSOME - Chromosome found in males only. Males have one X-chromosome and one Y-chromosome.

ZOOSPORE - A spore that can swim, as in ulothrix